Errata

Page 25: In the chapter heading Protsetantism should read Protestantism.

Page 65: In the chapter heading Christans of Evangelcal Fath should read Christians of Evangelical Faith.

Page 175: In the part heading Evangelical's should read Evangelicals'.

Page 209: In footnote 12 "More Atheist..." should read "Atheist..."

THE RUSSIAN PROTESTANTS

THE RUSSIAN PROTESTANTS

Evangelicals in the Soviet Union:
1944-1964

Steve Durasoff

Rutherford . Madison . Teaneck
FAIRLEIGH DICKINSON UNIVERSITY PRESS

© 1969 by Associated University Presses, Inc.
Library of Congress Catalogue Card Number: 72–76843

Associated University Presses, Inc.
Cranbury, New Jersey 08512

SBN: 8386 07465 8
Printed in the United States of America

Dedicated to the Russian evangelical
who has recently completed a century of survival
and faces the second with faith for revival

Acknowledgments

With gratitude the following are listed for granting permission to quote from copyright sources:

Abingdon Press, New York (1938), *The War Against God* by Sidney Dark and R. S. Essex.

American Friends Service Committee, Philadelphia (1956), *Meeting the Russians: American Quakers Visit the Soviet Union 1956* by Quaker Report.

Serge Bolshakoff, Oxford, London, *Russian Nonconformity: the Story of "Unofficial" Religion in Russia* by Serge Bolshakoff.

Broadman Press, Nashville (1958), *Encyclopedia of Southern Baptists* edited by Norman Wade Cox.

Broadman Press, Nashville (1955), *Baptist World Fellowship: A Short History of the Baptist World Alliance* by F. Townley Lord.

Broadman Press, Nashville (1966), *The Truth That Makes Men Free: Official Report of the Eleventh Congress* edited by Josef Nordenhaug.

Broadman Press, Nashville (1960), *Tenth Baptist World Conference* edited by Arnold T. Ohrn.

Broadman Press, Nashville (1943), *Baptists in the U.S.S.R.* edited by J. H. Rushbrooke.

Columbia University Press, New York (1959), *Pattern for Soviet Youth: A Study of the Congresses of the Komsomol, 1918-1954* by Ralph Talcott Fisher Jr.

Columbia University Press, New York (1957), *Soviet Education* edited by George L. Kline.

Columbia University Press, New York, "The Russian Bible Society," American Slavic and East European Review, No. 7 by S. R. Tomkins.

The Current Digest of the Soviet Press, New York (1963), I. Vorobyev article, Vol. XV, No. 40.

John S. Curtiss of Duke University, Durham, North Carolina, *Church and State in Russia: The Last Years of the Empire* by J. S. Curtiss.

Doubleday & Company, Inc., New York, *Tongue Speaking: An Experiment in Spiritual Experience* by Morton T. Kelsey. *The Penkovskiy Papers* translated by Peter Deriabin. *The Kremlin vs. the People* by Robert Magidoff.

Faith and Life Press, Newton, Kansas (formerly Mennonite Book Concern) (1931), *The Development of the Missionary Interest and Philanthropic Interest Among the Mennonites of North America* by Edmund George Kaufman.

The Story of the Mennonites by G. Henry Smith.

From the Steppes to the Prairies by Cornelius Krahn.

William C. Fletcher, the author of *A Study in Survival: The Church in Russia, 1927–1943* published by Macmillan, New York (1965). Quotes are from the University of Southern California (1964) dissertation "The Russian Orthodox Church in the USSR, 1927–1943: A Study in Survival."

George A. Foster, the author of "The Attitudes of Russian Communism to Religion," a B.D. thesis, Duke Divinity School, 1933.

Casimir C. Gecys, the author of "The Soviet Bill of Rights," Ph.D. dissertation, Fordham University, 1952.

Mrs. Donald Gee, *Pentecost,* London, edited by the late Donald Gee.

The Gospel Publishing House, Springfield, Mo. (1947), *What Meaneth This?* by Carl Brumback.

The Gospel Publishing House, Springfield, Mo. (1961), *The*

Promise Fulfilled: A History of the Modern Pentecostal Movement by Klaude Kendrick.

The Gospel Publishing House, Springfield, Mo. (1937), *Knowing the Doctrines of the Bible* by Myer Pearlman.

The Gospel Publishing House, Springfield, Mo. (1954), *We Believe: A Comprehensive Statement of Christian Faith* by Ralph M. Riggs.

The Gospel Publishing House, Springfield, Mo. (1947), *Upon All Flesh* by Donald Gee.

The Gospel Publishing House, Springfield, Mo. (1953), *Systematic Theology* by Ernest S. Williams.

The Gospel Publishing House, Springfield, Mo. *The Pentecostal Evangel.*

Harper & Row, Publishers, Incorporated, New York (1911), *The Baptist World Alliance: Second Congress* edited by Philip L. Jones.

Harper & Row, Publishers, Incorporated, New York (1946), *Religion in Russia* by Robert Pierce Casey.

The Hartford Seminary Foundation, Hartford (1954), *Church in Communist Society* by Matthew Spinka.

Harvard University Press, Cambridge (1921), *Russian Dissenters* by Frederick C. Conybeare.

Harvard University Press, Cambridge (1959), *The Soviet Citizen: Daily Life in a Totalitarian Society* by Alex Inkeles and Raymond A. Bauer.

Harvard University Press, Cambridge (1965), *The Soviet Youth Program* by Allen Kassof.

Houghton Mifflin Company, Boston (1961), *Societ Society* edited by Alex Inkeles and Kent Geiger.

Hutchinson Publishing Group Ltd., London (1920), *Modern Saints & Seers* by Jean Finot. Published by Rider & Co.

The Judson Press, Valley Forge, Pa. (1950), *Eighth Baptist World Congress* edited by Arnold T. Ohrn.

The Judson Press, Valley Forge, Pa. (1964), *The Christian Religion In Its Doctrinal Expression* by E. Y. Mullins.

The Judson Press, Valley Forge, Pa. (1950), *A History of the Baptists* by Robert G. Torbet.

Carey Kingsgate Press, now under The Baptist Union, London (1923), *Third Baptist World Congress* edited by W. T. Whitley.

Carey Kingsgate Press, now under The Baptist Union, London (1947), *Seventh Baptist World Congress* edited by Walter O. Lewis.

Carey Kingsgate Press, now under The Baptist Union, London (1955), *Golden Jubilee Congress* edited by Arnold T. Ohrn.

Little, Brown and Company, Boston (1953), *The Russian Church and the Soviet State 1917–1950* by John Shelton Curtiss.

The Lutheran World Federation, Geneva (1962), Lutheran World, Vol. IX No 2 "Prague in Retrospect" by Darril Hudson.

McGraw-Hill Book Company, New York (1951), *Soviet Attitudes Toward Authority: An Interdisciplinary Approach to Problems of Soviet Character* by Margaret Mead.

McGraw-Hill Book Company, New York (1964), *The Faith of the Russian Evangelicals* by J. C. Pollock.

McGraw-Hill Book Company, New York (1964), *They Speak With Other Tongues* by John L. Sherrill.

Mennonite Brethren Publishing House, Hillsboro, Kansas (1955–1959), *The Mennonite Encyclopedia,* Four Volumes.

Mennonite Publishing House, Scottsdale, Penn. (1929), *Feeding the Hungry: Russia Famine 1919–1925* by P. C. Hiebert.

National Council of American-Soviet Friendship, Inc., New York, permission for the American Russian Institute (1945), *Religion Today in the U.S.S.R.* by W. H. Melish.

National Council of American-Soviet Friendship, Inc., New

York, permission for the American Russian Institute (1946), *An American Churchman in the Soviet Union* by Louie D. Newton.

National Council of American-Soviet Friendship, Inc., New York (1959), *The Story of American-Soviet Relations, 1917–1959* by Harry F. Ward.

Oxford University Press, London (1961), *The Ecumenical Movement* by Norman Goodall.

Oxford University Press, London (1963), *The Churches and Christian Unity* by R. H. W. Bevan.

Frederick A. Praeger, Inc., New York (1964), *Communist Propaganda Techniques* by John C. Clews.

Frederick A. Praeger, Inc., New York (1955), *Church and State Behind the Iron Curtain* edited by Vladimir Gsovski.

Frederick A. Praeger, Inc., New York (1967), *Religion and the Search for New Ideals in the USSR* edited by William C. Fletcher and Anthony J. Strover.

Prentice-Hall, Inc., Englewood Cliffs, N. J. (1963), *The Baptist Way of Life* by Brooks Hays and John E. Steely.

Rand McNally & Company, Chicago (1964), *20th Century Russia* by Donald W. Treadgold.

Religion in Communist Dominated Areas, New York, edited by Paul B. Anderson.

Charles Scribner's Sons, New York (1965), *USSR: A Concise History* by Basil Dmytryshyn.

Sheed & Ward Inc., New York (1942), *Religion in Soviet Russia, 1917–1942* by N. S. Timasheff.

The Richard R. Smith Co., Inc., Peterborough, N. H. (1966), *The World Council of Churches: A Study of Its Background and History* by David P. Gaines.

St. Anthony's Guild, Paterson, N. J. (1959), *Religion in Russia from Lenin to Khrushchev* by L. L. Braun, A. A.

St. Martin's Press, Incorporated, New York, N. Y. (Macmillan & Co., Ltd), *Religion in the Soviet Union* by Walter Kolarz.

Stanford University Press, Stanford (1949), *The Socialized Agriculture of the USSR: Plans and Performances* by Naum Jasny.

University of Notre Dame Press, Notre Dame, Indiana, for *The Russian Revolution and Religion: A Collection of Documents Concerning the Suppression of Religion by the Communists, 1917–1925* edited by Boleslaw Szezesniak.

Vanguard Press, Inc., New York (1927), *Religion Under the Soviets* by Julius F. Hecker.

Contents

13

PART II
The 1944 Merger of the Evangelical
Christians and the Baptists

PART III
The Addition of the Pentecostalists

Introduction

An outstanding example of the current accelerated ecumenical movement in the United States is the Consultation on Church Union, a proposed merger that would unite a number of Protestant denominations involving twenty-five million members. This book explores the interaction of several Protestant bodies in Russia that emerged a century ago and uncovers interesting episodes involved in the official mergers of four Protestant denominations in the USSR.

Included in the mergers was the unexpected union of the Russian Baptists and the Russian Pentecostalists, a surprising alliance quite unexpected in the contemporary evangelical world. They have labored together as on an island of Christian fellowship surrounded by a sea of agnosticism and militant atheism. Although other Russian Baptists and Pentecostalists refused to join the united evangelicals whose headquarters address is Box 520, Moscow, the majority of believers have registered and are worshipping together despite recurring problems and misunderstandings about glossolalia, or speaking in tongues. These findings should provide evangelicals and students of religion in the Soviet Union as well as the world's thirty million Baptists and ten million Pentecostalists with new insights into the struggles, defeats and triumphs of these Russian Protestants.

Among the relatively few doctoral studies written on religion in Russia, the first on Russian Protestants was completed by Andrew Q. Blane in 1964,[1] four years before my thesis was accepted at New York University. The second such dissertation is the basis of this book, slightly modified for general readership. It introduces the earliest ecumenical efforts of the Russian evangelicals in their near successful merger initiated in 1884 by Colonel Pashkov in a climate of persecution zealously administered by the rulers of autocracy and Orthodoxy. In 1920, this time amidst the confusion of the new Soviet regime and the Civil War, the Protestant merger was but a hair's breadth short of consummation. Not until 1944, when Soviet-pressure for ecclesiastical centralization was the order of the day, were the former blunders of the intransigent evangelical leaders overcome by enthusiastic cooperative ventures of believers during the war years.

Recent books and periodicals have focused attention upon the importance of the Russian evangelicals, notably *Religion in the Soviet Union* by Walter Kolarz, *The Faith of the Russian Evangelicals* by J. C. Pollock, and *Religion in Communist Dominated Countries,* edited by Paul B. Anderson. In this book I have attempted to present a systematic, comparative study of the Baptists, Evangelical Christians, Christians of Evangelical Faith (Pentecostalists), and the Mennonites—the four denominations responsible to the All-Union Council of Evangelical Christians-Baptists (AUCECB) which is headquartered in Moscow's only Protestant church. They have simplified their correspondence abroad by using an abbreviated mailing address: The Baptist Union of the USSR, P. O. Box 520, Moscow. Many members from all four denominations have consistently refused all overtures to join the union and during the sixties more than 25,000 members within the union have staged a mass exodus, boldly demanding

---

[1] "The Relations Between the Russian Protestant Sects and the State, 1900–1921," unpublished Ph.D. dissertation, Duke University, 1964.

the Soviet's permission to organize their own independent evangelical union. They were flatly refused.

Carefully selected sources in both the Russian and English languages have been utilized. Every issue of *Bratskii vestnik* (The Fraternal Messenger), the official organ of the AUCECB was analyzed, as were many Soviet antireligious publications. The interest manifested by both scholars and religious leaders during my years of research was most encouraging.

Additional related material was provided by the recorded interviews of ministers and educators with Russian religious leaders and antireligious propagandists during their sojourns in the USSR. These findings were compared with my own visits to the Soviet Union in 1959 and 1963.

Although my grandfather was a Russian priest in Saratov who ministered among the dissenting Old Believers (originally within the Russian Orthodox Church before the schism of 1666), my interest in Russia's spiritual awakening was not aroused until the closing months of World War II. At that time a detachment of young Soviet soldiers was billeted in an American compound near my post of duty with the 130th General Hospital in Ciney, Belgium. Following the hasty acquisition of some two hundred gospels from the United States I visited the Red Army soldiers and quickly distributed the Scripture portions into their eager, outstretched hands. After briefly examining the gospels a number of them queried, "What is this?" causing me to feel that I was confronting a generation quite unfamiliar with the Bible, a microcosm of Soviet youth in the USSR.

The desire to undertake this work lay dormant until 1959 when, as pastor of the Hempstead Assembly of God, I visited Soviet Russia and Poland for two months. Ideological exchanges were experienced with Soviet officials while faith was shared with Russian pastors and priests. For five consecutive evenings spontaneous, unhindered dialogues took place in the Russian language with literally hundreds of Soviet citizens in the shadow of the famed Isaac Cathedral in Leningrad. The friendliness and spiritual hunger of these people shall never be forgotten. Further knowledge and intuitive understanding came from Russian pastors serving in Eastern Europe and the United States who were kind enough and found it easier to share with me, providing invaluable insights and interpretive information.

Cooperative librarians in New York University, Columbia University, Union Theological Seminary, St. Vladimir's Seminary, Research Library of Radio Liberty, Oral Roberts University, and the Library of Congress facilitated the research. Evangelist Oral Roberts, president of the university bearing his name, provided the impetus I needed to launch into a doctoral program and New York University professors Lee A. Belford, Jesse J. Dossick, and Robert Magidoff provided indispensable guidance and constructive criticism in the development of the thesis. Never fully appreciated and usually thanked less is my wife Nadja, whose encouragement was there when needed.

THE RUSSIAN PROTESTANTS

PART I

THE ORIGIN OF THE MENNONITES, BAPTISTS, EVANGELICAL CHRISTIANS AND PENTECOSTALS IN RUSSIA

PART 1

1

Russian Protsetantism Foreshadowed

i. Christianity in Russia

Millions of Protestants in Russia? Indeed, following World War II the Russian evangelicals maintained that their membership and adherents approximated four million Soviet citizens. The predominant religious group in the USSR is the Russian Orthodox Church, of course, one that claimed fifty million members when it joined the World Council of Churches at New Delhi in 1961.

Not an ancient nation, Russia was founded as a state when the Viking chief Rurik was invited to rule in Novgorod in 862 A.D. More than a century passed before Christianity in the form of Byzantine Orthodoxy was embraced as the religion of Russia in 988 A.D. Prince Vladimir of Kiev was so enthused with the religion from Constantinople that he ordered his subjects to follow him in a mass baptism in the Dnieper River.

Protestantism, interpreted broadly as a protest against the beliefs and emphases of the established religion, is traced back to the fourteenth century in Russia, preceding Martin Luther's reformation movement which was spearheaded in 1517. Five centuries had passed during which time Eastern Orthodoxy spread slowly among the heathen and many converts were obtained by the sword rather than by persuasion. The gradual substitution of the Greek Orthodox clergy by the Russians lowered the educational standards at the same time that elaborate ritual formalism obscured the essentials of the faith. Poor semi-literate

25

village priests stood in sharp contrast to the wealthy higher
clergy who increased their vast holdings, power and pres-
tige.

Before the close of the fourteenth century the *Strigol'-
niks,* named after their leader who was once a barber,
exhibited the first signs of protest and challenge against
the authoritarian position of the church. They spurned
the hierarchy, repudiated most of the rites, and opposed
the higher clergy for its wealth and political power. The
Strigol'niks attempted to return to a primitive apostolic
Christianity and were the likely forerunners of the Russian
evangelicals. As a result of the energetic measures administered by the offended clergy, the *Strigol'niks* leaders were
executed and the "heresy" was suppressed early in the
fifteenth century.[1]

The *Zhidovstvuiushchie,* or Judaizers, appeared in Novgorod in the late fifteenth century, and from there spread
to Moscow. They did not originate within the fold of the
church but had an independent origin, descending from
Jewish proselytes who later were influenced by Christian
ideas. As did the *Strigol'niks,* they too rejected the church
hierarchy, monasticism, fasts, and refused to bow to icons.
They further denied the doctrine of the trinity and the
divinity of Christ. The Church Councils of 1490 and 1504
condemned the sects and anathemized them.[2]

The polemists rendered a service in the cause of reform
by providing copied collections of their popular works
against the "heretics" of the fifteenth and sixteenth centuries. The Russian Orthodox Church made no distinction
between Protestant and Catholic beliefs until 1639, for
their teachings were all regarded as "Latin heresy."[3]

---

[1] G. M. Livshits, *Religiia i tserkov' v proshlom i nastoiashchem*
(Minsk: Izdatel'stvo ministerstva vysshego srednogo spetsial'nogo i
professional'nogo obrazovaniia BSSR, 1961), p. 115.

[2] *Ibid.,* p. 116.

[3] Paul Miliukov, *Outlines of Russian Culture—Part I: Religion
and the Church* Perpetua ed. (New York: A. S. Barnes and Company, 1960), p. 81.

Russian Orthodoxy itself experienced the great schism of 1666, introduced by the ultra-Orthodox dissidents who were called Old Believers. The schismatics refused to accept minor church reforms, yet disagreement among themselves soon divided them into two camps, the Priestists and the Priestless.[4]

The Lutherans and the Reformed Calvinists were among the first foreigners to follow the earlier Protestant dissenters. Before the October revolution the Lutherans had spread over eight consistorial districts. The two largest, Moscow and St. Petersburg, contained 1,136,000 Lutherans, 70 per cent of whom were Germans. The remainder were Finns, Estonians, Latvians, Swedes, Armenians, and some Russians. The last General Synod of Lutherans convened in 1928 and the once flourishing Lutheran churches in Russia's two largest cities have disappeared.[5]

The Reformed Calvinist Church opened its first house of worship in Moscow in 1629, whereas Ivan the Terrible had granted the Lutherans permission to build within a mile of the Kremlin as early as 1575. The Reformed Church would be nonexistent today were it not for the Soviet territorial annexations in Transcarpathian Ukraine, where 95,000 Hungarian members resided, and in Galicia, where thirty Ukrainian Reformed Churches had active congregations. In Lithuania only two Reformed pastors remained when the Red Army occupied the tiny Baltic republic.[6]

This book is limited to the origins and the development of the All-Russian evangelical believers, save for the German Mennonites who joined the evangelical union in 1963. These believers present a constant thorn in the flesh of the Communist Party and its vast network of antireligious activities.

---

[4] Paul Milyoukov, *Russia and Its Crisis* (Chicago: University of Chicago Press, 1905), pp. 90–96.

[5] Walter Kolarz, *Religion in the Soviet Union* (New York: St. Martin's Press, Inc.), pp. 249, 252.

[6] *Ibid.*, pp. 245, 271, 273.

The development of Russian sectarianism favored the paths of mysticism and rationalism, each revealing itself to be a natural enemy of ritualistic piety. They endeavored to eliminate all externals and intermediaries between God and man. This movement against religious formalism appeared in two diverse manners. One repudiated church tradition, maintaining that it was possible to base one's faith on the direct instructions as expressed in the gospel. The other regarded even the gospel as a superfluous intermediary between the Lord and His people since direct communication with God could be arranged by worshipping "in the Spirit." At this point all bonds of tradition and Scriptures were broken, resulting in a mystical form of Christianity.[7] The Biblicists produced the evangelicals in Russia, while the latter brought forth such sects as the *Khlysti, Skoptsy,* and *Dukhobors.*

ii. The *Khlysti, Skoptsy, Dukhobors,* and *Molokans*

The earliest of the contemporary dissenters, the *Khlysti,* appeared at the close of the seventeenth century. An extreme mystical movement led by the Old Believer Daniil Filippovich, the *Khlysti* revered but one book, the book of the Dove, the Holy Spirit. Filippovich was believed to be the incarnate "God of Sabaoth" and the peasant Ivan Suslov, "Christ," his adopted son.[8] During their services this sect of flagellants, who preferred to be called "God's People," whipped themselves, cried, jumped, sang, shrieked and were reported to have received the gift of prophecy and to have spoken in other tongues. They declined in the beginning of the second half of the nineteenth century.[9] Divisions in the *Khlysti* introduced splits

---

[7] Miliukov, *Outlines* . . . , I, pp. 77, 78.
[8] *Ibid.,* pp. 90, 91.
[9] Livshits, *op. cit.,* p. 120.

called *Old Khlysti, New Khlysti, Old Israel, New Israel, Durmanobtsy, Shaloputy,* etc.[10]

The *Skoptsy* (Castrators) or "White Doves," their preferred name, also separated from the *Khlysti* in about 1770. Kondratii Selivanov, their illiterate peasant leader, not only claimed deity but called himself Peter the Third, and promised his followers the kingdom at St. Petersburg.[11] In order to ensure victory over the temptation of fleshly sins castration was introduced, the rite of emasculation which became the baptism with fire.[12] Never a large sect their decline began at the close of the nineteenth century.[13]

Simultaneously with the *Skoptsy* the *Dukhobors,* or Spirit-Wrestlers, appeared among the *Khlysty* in Ekaterinoslav district.[14] Under the teacher Siliian Kolesnikov, the *Dukhobors* were stigmatized by local bishop Ambrose as a sect of *Pneumatomachi* that "fought against the Holy Spirit."[15] The sectarians interpreted the title in a positive manner—to mean that the Spirit fought in them. Their rationalist interpretation of the mysteries of Christianity enabled them to see Jesus Christ as the Son of God in the sense in which every man is God's son. They rejected all ritualism and found their Bible in the book of life.[16] The *Dukhobors* denied any responsibility for military service and large waves of them emigrated to Canada at the close of the nineteenth century as a result of persistent persecution in Russia. The sect found a strong friend in Lev Tolstoi, who used the proceeds from his book *The Resurrection* to enable many *Dukhobors* to reach Canada.

In Tambov, a *Dukhobor* preacher named Pobirokhin,

---

10 *Ibid.,* p. 119.

11 Miliukov, *Outlines* . . . , I, p. 93.

12 Frederick C. Conybeare, *Russian Dissenters* (Cambridge: Harvard University Press, 1921) , p. 367.

13 Livshits, *op. cit.,* p. 121.

14 *Ibid.*

15 Conybeare, *op. cit.,* p. 264.

16 Livshits, *op. cit.,* p. 122.

represented himself as the Christ, declared his intention of pronouncing judgment on the universe. His son-in-law, Simon Uklein, already a doubter of the validity of the *Dukhobor* doctrines, lost faith entirely and severed all relations with the sect.[17] Uklein then founded the *Molokans,* a sect that became the connecting link between the mystical, Bible-rejecting sects and the emerging Bible-centered evangelicals, many of whom were former leaders among the "Milk Drinkers." The Orthodox Church had named Uklein's sect the *Molokans* because its members drank milk on fast days.[18]

Although the *Molokans* rejected all sacraments, including baptism and communion, they knew their Bible so well that the village priests seldom risked controversies with them, expecting defeat and humiliation by means of their incessant use of the citation of chapter and verse from the gospel during discussions.[19]

iii. *The Mennonites*—The Last Shall Be First

During the rise of the *Molokans* at the end of the eighteenth century, the Mennonites were beginning to spread in colonies across south Russia. Although the most recent to join the All-Union Council of Evangelical Christians-Baptists, the Mennonites were the first of the four AUCECB members to arise in Russia. In 1788 the first contingent of Mennonites, composed of 228 poor families, left Danzig for Khortitsa, located on the shores of the Dnieper in New Russia (later known as the Ukraine).[20] It was 800 years earlier that Prince Vladimir had decided to adopt the Greek Orthodox religion and enforce a general baptism upon the people of Kiev in the Dnieper River.

---

[17] Miliukov, *Outlines* . . . , I, p. 100.
[18] *Ibid.,* p. 102.
[19] Conybeare, *op. cit.,* p. 316.
[20] S. D. Bondar, *Sekta mennonitov v Rossii* (Petrograd: Tipografiia V. D. Smirnov, 1916), p. 17.

The Mennonites derived their name from Menno Simons in the sixteenth century. A former priest who accepted the Anabaptist position, Menno Simons not only renounced Roman Catholicism, but also rejected the views of Luther on the baptism of infants as he accepted the position of leadership among a quiet group of anti-paedo-baptists.[21] He preferred the name "Brethren" in order to disassociate his followers from the stigma of the volatile Muensterites, but in time his adherents came to be known as Mennonites. Menno allowed no place for military service and it became a dogma, forbidden to all its members.[22]

Empress Catherine II initiated colonization in Russia by inviting all foreigners, except Jews, to settle in Russia. She issued two manifestoes, namely those of December 4, 1762, and July 22, 1763. Foreign colonization began with the arrival of many Germans, the majority of whom were Mennonites. According to the edict of September 7, 1787, Catherine promised the Mennonite colonists freedom of religion, exemption from military service, 175 acres and a $250 loan for each family, and ten years of tax exemption.[23]

For almost a century the Mennonites enjoyed privileges that enabled them to form a democratic island within a sea of autocracy. They erected model schoolhouses wherein compulsory attendance was practiced for their children, ages six to fourteen. Competent teachers were licensed, and unified textbooks in study courses were offered in the German language.[24] A *Bezbozhnik* (Godless) publication maintained that the Mennonites possessed a "form of false democracy," that nowhere had a religion given itself so

---

21 V. E. Ziuriukin, *Mennonity* (Pokrovsk: "Unzere Virtshaft," 1923), p. 10.

22 Livshits, *op. cit.*, p. 126.

23 Bondar, *op. cit.*, pp. 2, 16.

24 C. H. Smith, *The Story of the Mennonites* (Newton, Kansas: Mennonite Publication Office, 1957), pp. 413, 414.

easily to serve the bourgeois interests and the land owners, that schools were designed in order to teach Bible reading and to prevent their youth from attending Russian schools.[25] *Bezbozhnik* rendered no praise for the industriousness and productivity of the Mennonites who manufactured farm and milling machinery, resulting in large-scale farming. The colonists enjoyed a well-developed mutual aid system as they spread over three million acres of land by World War I, helping to make the Ukraine the granary of Russia. Instead of praise, charges were made that the Mennonite landowners had introduced the exploitation of labor and the rise of wealthy capitalists.[26] So productive were the Mennonites that a Minnesota senator urged Congress to offer them opportunities to settle in the Middle West in order to increase American wheat production, which was then finding competition on the London wheat market from Russian shipments.[27]

In 1870 the colonists were shaken by the news that they had but ten years in which to prepare for Russian citizenship, a status that would bar them from any special privileges, including military exemption. The negative reaction to military conscription and the government enforcement of a general progressive Russianization spurred one-third of all the Mennonites in Russia to emigrate to Canada and the United States. A general exodus was halted by a compromise measure which permitted young Mennonites to fulfill their state obligation in forestry service. All expenses for the forestry workers were underwritten by the Mennonites. The average sum was 200,000 rubles a year.[28]

---

[25] A. Reinmarus and G. Friezen, *Mennonity* (Moskva: Akts-izd-o-vo "Bezbozhnik," 1930), pp. 19, 21.

[26] *Ibid.*, pp. 17, 18.

[27] Cornelius Krahn (ed.), *From the Steppes to the Prairies* (Newton, Kansas: Mennonite Publication Office, 1949), p. 10.

[28] *Novyi entsiklopedicheskii slovar'* (St. Petersburg: Brok-gayz-Efron, c. 1911), p. 281.

In the course of time a number of Mennonites who settled in Russia maintained little more than the outward form of religion in order to retain all of the material benefits to be derived by virtue of membership in the colonies. This led to a protest movement against the deadening formalism of the Old Mennonites and resulted in the emergence of the Mennonite Brethren Church. In all, seven additional Mennonite sects appeared in Russia,[29] the two largest, noted above, both erred in exhibiting more zeal than brotherly love.[30] It was in 1845 that the dissatisfied Mennonites invited the pietist Eduard Wüst, a Lutheran pastor from Württemberg, Germany, to minister to them. Trained in the University of Tuebingen, Wüst promoted evangelism, mission festivals, and prayer meetings. This "apostle of revival" labored for fourteen years in south Russia and "left a great harvest of saved Lutherans and Mennonites."[31] It was not until eighteen families in Gnadenfeld drew up a document on January 6, 1860, to start a new church that the Mennonite Brethren Church was officially founded.[32]

iv. Early Baptist Influence Upon the Mennonites

German Baptist leaders such as Johann Gerhard Oncken, who founded the European Continental Baptist movement in 1834, influenced the Mennonite Brethren from the very beginning. Their emphasis on revival methods, cataclysmic conversions, and immersion as the only correct form of baptism aided in the futher separation of the Mennonite Brethren from the Old Mennonites. Abraham

---

[29] Reinmarus and Friezen, *op. cit.,* pp. 22, 23.

[30] *The Mennonite Encyclopedia: A Comprehensive Reference Work on the Anabaptist-Mennonite Movement,* Vol. IV (Hillsboro, Kansas: Mennonite Brethren Publishing House, 1959), p. 389.

[31] A. Karev, "The Russian Evangelical-Baptist Movement," *Bv,* No. 3, 1957, p. 6.

[32] Mennonite Encyclopedia, Vol. IV, *loc. cit.,* p. 389.

Unger, the spiritual leader of the new movement, had already become acquainted with Oncken and prevailed upon him to visit Russia. The German Baptist spent ten days visiting newly established, yet unorganized groups in 1869 and assisted in the ordination of Unger as elder. Further correspondence enabled Oncken to extend his influence upon the Mennonite Brethren.[33] In this manner, a century before they joined the AUCECB in 1963, the Mennonite Brethren churches enjoyed close relationship with the first Russian Baptists who appeared in south Russia. Mennonite and Baptist pastors shared in a reciprocal ministry, conducting baptismal immersions for members of the other denomination when found more convenient, and the two fellowships partook of communion services together, laboring faithfully as sowers of the evangelical seed among the Russians.[34] The significance of such cooperation can be evaluated properly when we realize that the disagreements on baptism and communion were sharp enough to delay the merger of the Baptists and the Evangelical Christians for decades.

---

[33] *Ibid.,* p. 60.
[34] Karev, *Bv,* No. 3, 1957, pp. 8, 15.

2

The Russian Baptists and Evangelical Christians

i. The Eighteen Sixties

The translation of the Bible from the Church Slavonic to the Russian language was completed during the eighteen sixties. This decade was most suitable for the propagation of a multiude of ideas. Freedom, life, and movement were in the air and activity in the field of literature was intense. Turgenev had written *Fathers and Sons,* Dostoevski produced *Crime and Punishment,* and Tolstoi created the epic *War and Peace.*

After the Emancipation of the serfs in 1861 many thousands of peasants wandered across Russia supplied with Scriptures in the vernacular, the distribution of which gave great impetus to the evangelical movement. Obscured for centuries the Scriptures were now placed into the hands of an increasingly literate people.

The Scotsman Melville, known in Russia as Vasilii Ivanovich, was a leader and example to a host of colporteurs as he devoted sixty years of his life to the circulation of Scripture portions during the reign of four tsars. Kasha Iagub, born in Umrii, Persia, continued the work of Melville. A graduate of Moody Bible Institute in Chicago, Iagub evangelized among the poor throughout Russia and Siberia under the name of Iakov Deliakovich Deliakov for almost thirty years with great success. The widow he married was the grandmother of Iakov I. Zhidkov, the first president of the All-Union Council of Evangelical Christians-Baptists.

In 1862, the complete Bible in the Russian language became a reality. Colporteurs of the Bible Society covered the Russian Empire, trying to reach everyone—rich and poor, simple and wise, educated and ignorant. Thus did the Bible become available to all the Russian people. In the Molokan, Stundist, and Evangelical-Baptist homes it became the book of the family, zealously studied and reverently observed.[1]

Within the vastness of Russia, the Evangelical-Baptist movement arose almost simultaneously in three areas. In the Caucasus, the evangelicals received the name of Baptists; participants in the Ukraine were called Stundists; and the believers in St. Petersburg, known first as *Pashkovites,* were later identified as Evangelical Christians.

In reality this was a single movement of a Russian religious reformation, confirmed by their nearly identical doctrine and their subsequent unity in one mighty Evangelical-Baptist movement.[2]

The movement in Russia did not emerge from a religious vacuum. Rather it appealed to dissatisfied, openhearted people among the Orthodox and the *Molokans,* who were seeking a faith that could be translated into joyful, victorious, and practical Christian living. The *Molokans* provided a less favorable soil for the planting of the gospel seed than did the Orthodox.

The religious pride of the Spiritual Christians (Molo-

---

[1] *Ibid.,* p. 34.
[2] "From the History of the Russian Evangelical-Baptist Movement in the USSR," *Bv,* No. 5, 1947, p. 5.

kans) caused them to look down upon others as being in error. But as the Ethiopian eunoch waited for a Philip to come along, even so did the Molokans who searched the Scriptures for further truth, such as Voronin, Ivanov, and Pavlov.[3]

ii. *Nikita I. Voronin*—The First Immersed Russian Evangelical

Nikita Isaevich Voronin, a wealthy merchant and former *Molokan* leader, experienced his conversion by means of personal, prayerful study of the Russian Bible. This caused him to seek out others with similar conversion experiences. Deliakov (Kasha Iagub), upon visiting Tiflis, was instrumental in bringing Voronin and Martin Kal'veit together. Kal'veit, a German Baptist from Lithuania, shared his evangelical beliefs with Voronin, including his understanding on the mode of water baptism. Shortly thereafter, Voronin became the first Russian evangelical believer to be baptized by immersion. Administered by Martin Kal'-veit, Voronin's baptism occurred on August 20, 1867, in the Kur River, Tiflis (now Tbilisi). This is claimed by the AUCECB to be the time and place of its historic origin.[4]

Baptists, however, already existed in the Russian Empire—in Finland (first baptism in 1856), Poland in 1858, and Latvia in 1861. Aleksandr V. Karev, General Secretary of the AUCECB, granted no credit to these Baptists for the rise of the Evangelical-Baptist movement among the Russian people.[5]

At the 1928 Baptist World Congress held in Toronto, Canada, the Russian delegate Ivanov-Klyshnikov described the Baptist movement in Russia as one entirely inde-

[3] Karev, *Bv*, No. 3, 1957, p. 34.
[4] *Ibid.*, p. 8; (Blane, *op. cit.*, pp. 6, 7).
[5] *Ibid.*, p. 17.

pendent of the efforts of any missionary, emerging solely by means of the individual study of the Scriptures in response to a deep inward longing for truth. Before his Baptist brethren from many countries of the world he disclaimed the work of any Baptist missionaries in Russia.[6] However, many years later, AUCECB executive A. I. Mitskevich recorded another version:

> The education of the Russian Baptists, from the very beginning, came under the great influence of the German Baptist fellowship, whose leader, brother Oncken, ordained the outstanding pioneer of the Russian Baptist fellowship, brother Vasilii Gur'evich Pavlov, known to all . . .[7]

V. G. Pavlov, a gifted *Molokan*, was baptized by Voronin and sent by the brethren to the Hamburg Baptist Seminary, although he was but twenty-one years of age. He returned to Russia in 1876 and studied briefly at a Hebrew religious school. His aptitude for learning foreign languages was phenomenal. Besides the family of Slavonic languages, he was able to communicate the gospel in Osetin, Georgian, Armenian, Persian, Tartar, Turkish, Rumanian, Greek, Arabic, Swedish, French, German, English, and other languages.[8]

Another outstanding pioneer worker in the Caucasus was V. V. Ivanov, who, during forty-eight years of faithful ministry was arrested over thirty times. Close to 1500 converts were baptized by him.[9]

From *Molokan* backgrounds, among the outstanding pioneers of the Evangelical-Baptist movement, were I. A.

---

6 W. T. Whitley (ed.), *Fourth Baptist World Congress* (Toronto: Stewart Printing Service, 1928), p. 75.

7 A. I. Mitskevich, "The Question of Unity," *Bv.* No. 6, 1963, p. 50.

8 *Bv*, No. 5, 1947, p. 39.

9 *Ibid.*, p. 49. (Ivanov, V. V. was the assumed name of this son of *Molokan* E. T. Klyshnikov, due to persecution).

Goliaev, D. I. and G. I. Mazaiev, S. P. and V. P. Stepanov, I. S. Prokhanov, I. I. Zhidkov, and others. The majority of the *Molokans* ultimately fused with the Baptists, who,

> . . . energetic and well organized, were able to take over the running of the religious affairs of the *Molokans* . . .[10]

In his extensive travels through the Soviet Union, J. F. Hecker rarely noticed a *Molokan* meeting house without a Baptist chapel next to it.

Although they were foreigners, it was evident that the ministries of Melville the Scot, Kasha Iagub the Syrian, and Martin Kal'veit the German, were instrumental in the free flow of the evangelistic stream as it covered the vast Caucasus.

iii. Tsimbol, Riaboshapka, and Ratushnyi— Aggressive Stundists

Independent of the Caucasian movement, the second stream issued from the Ukraine. The numerous Protestant colonies in the south Ukraine provided the source of a new religious movement among the Russian peasants. Drawn by the good working conditions and the better way of life of the German colonists, many Russian peasants and workers arrived annually to the colonies from all ends of Russia. Despite the government restrictions against the proselytizing of any Russians by the colonists, the laborers were invited to the "Stunde," or "Bible hours." In the homes of evangelistic Germans they heard preaching in the Russian language and learned to read in order to study the Bible. Many were called *Stundists* in jest by the Orthodox as they visited the "Stunde." German pastors, such as Jacob Spener and the Bonekempers, both father

---

[10] Julius F. Hecker, *Religion Under the Soviets* (New York: Vanguard Press, 1927), p. 152.

and son, encouraged the pious to devote certain hours, especially on holidays, to the reading of the Scriptures. At a time when less than 5 per cent of the peasants could read and write, not one *Stundist* in a hundred was illiterate.[11]

Conversions followed and the *Stundist* circles multiplied. The "Bible hours" continued in peasant homes for six years before Efim Tsimbal was baptized in the Sugakle River by Abraham Unger in 1869, to become the first *Stundist* to be immersed in water.[12] In that same year Tsimbal baptized Ivan G. Riaboshapka, who, in 1871, baptized Mikhail T. Ratushnyi. The three *Stundists* spearheaded the new movement and were successful in gaining many converts among the Orthodox, the dissatisfied *Molokans,* and the *Khlysti.*[13]

So effective were they that Bishop Dmitrii summoned Ratushnyi and invited him to become a member of the Orthodox clergy if he would return to the Russian Orthodox Church. He refused, despite Reformed pastor Bonekemper's exhortation to the *Stundists* not to desert Orthodoxy, but simply to adapt their lives to the precepts of the gospel.[14] The Stundist movement had

. . . become the religion par excellence of the Russian moujik, assuming in time a proportion disquieting to the authorities.[15]

The examples of daily Christian living of many Mennonites and other colonists harmonized with the newly discovered truths found in the available Russian Bibles.

---

11 John Brown, *The Stundists* (New York: Methodist Episcopal Church, 1893), p. 9.

12 Vladimir Bonch-Bruevich, *Iz mira sektantov* (Moskva: Gosudarstvennoe izdatel'stvo, 1922), p. 167.

13 *Bv,* No. 5, 1947, pp. 33–35.

14 Conybeare, *op. cit.,* p. 332.

15 Jean Finot, *Modern Saints and Seers* (London: William Rider and Son, 1920), p. 43.

The serious teaching of this Book opened the way for a miracle: people quit drinking vodka, smoking, and swearing—they were born again, becoming entirely different people. . . . Seekers of truth gathered in their homes where the gospel was read by these people. . . .[16]

The majority of the *Stundists* accepted infant baptism and were satisfied to steer diplomatically between the new and old faiths. Outward conformity to Orthodoxy was mixed with inward contempt. At this point of spiritual conflict the influx of Baptist preachers encouraged many *Stundists* to take a definite stand. The transference to the Baptist ranks was so common that they were called *Stundobaptists* by the Orthodox.[17] By 1877, in over ten provinces between the Austrian border and the Volga River, the *Stundists* had grown to a phenomenal 250,000, with the province of Kiev in the lead, numbering 80,000.[18]

iv. Priest Gossner, Countess Chertkova, and Lord
Radstock in St. Petersburg

The Evangelical movement was short-lived in St. Petersburg fifty years before England's Lord Radstock arrived in the city to conduct what proved to be a highly successful preaching mission. The abortive attempt to evangelize the capital city was made by Herman Gossner in 1824. A former Roman Catholic priest turned Protestant, Gossner carried the evangelical message into the palaces of the aristocrats and his audiences included some ministers of Tsar Alexander I. Among Gossner's opponents were Do-

[16] *Bv*, No. 5, 1947, p. 6.
[17] *Novyi entsiklopedicheskii slovar'* (St. Petersburg: Brokgayz-Efron, 1911), p. 143.
[18] Brown, *loc cit.*, p. 20. (Miliukov, *Outlines* . . . . I, p. 116 cites Iuzov's 1880 estimate of 14 million non-orthodox, including 1,000,-000 Molokans and 1,145,000 unassigned—which probably included the Stundists).

minican monks, then permitted in Russia, and some envious Protestant pastors of near empty churches. Although befriended by Metropolitan Mikhail, who personally translated some of his religious tracts into the Russian language, Gossner was convincingly pictured by Count Arakcheev as an enemy of Orthodoxy. In 1824 he suffered banishment from the city and from the country.[19]

Not until a half-century later did the Evangelical Christian movement come to life by means of the death of little Misha, the son of Countess Chertkova. His tutor, an unnamed believer of evangelical persuasion, led the lad to a conversion experience. Misha thereafter repeatedly asked his socialite mother such questions as "Do you know Christ?" and "Do you love Christ?" She paid no attention until the boy became seriously ill, and only at his death were his continued appeals heeded. The bereaved mother, stricken by the words of her departed son, accepted Christ as her personal Savior and turned her back upon high-society living. Seeking to introduce the gospel message to her generation by means of evangelical preachers, Countess Chertkova made long trips across Europe and finally succeeded in initiating the arrival of Lord Radstock to the capital of Russia.[20]

As a young English officer, Granville Waldegrade, best known as Lord Radstock, served in the troubled Crimean area, fighting with the Russian soldiers. Converted during the hostilities when near loss of life, Radstock returned to Russia in the spring of 1874 as a soldier of Jesus Christ to preach on the shores of the Neva as did Gossner. Russian authors Dostoievski and Leskov wrote about this Oxford University man who was winning the hearts of many Russians in a most unassuming manner. N. S. Leskov attributed the success of Lord Radstock among the aristocrats of Petersburg to Countess Chertkova,

---

[19] "Spiritual Awakening in Petersburg," *Bv,* No. 3, 1957, pp. 36–38.
[20] *Ibid.*

. . . a fanatical woman who discovered him in London and invited him to Russia, personally supporting him. Other than his name, his success must rest upon the efforts of an energetic woman.[21]

Everyone spoke of the "Lord Apostle," some with delight, others in derision and laughter. But in that same year, as Radstock preached a positive gospel in the French language, there was a spiritual awakening. Leskov, writing about the followers of Lord Radstock, admitted that they did not show the slightest hostility toward the Russian Orthodox Church. On the contrary, with few exceptions, he felt that the friends of Radstock were standing more fervently for the Orthodox faith.[22] The few—but influential—exceptions, made up of converted aristocrats, were later presented to the *Bratskii vestnik* proletarian readers in this manner:

The first workers of our movement in Petersburg belonged to the aristocracy. . . . The Decembrists, the first who raised their voices in Russia against the tsarist despotism were also people of aristocratic background. By analogy, we can count our brothers and sisters from the aristocracy—Pashkov, Korf, Bobrinski, Chertkova, Lieven, Gagarin, and others—the "Decembrists of the spiritual liberation."[23]

v. Colonel Pashkov—Evangelical Fervor and Social Action

The conversions of the aristocrats were sincere and lasting. Colonel V. A. Pashkov, brother-in-law of Countess Chertkova, had not been at all religiously inclined before his conversion—he had even left St. Petersburg for Moscow in order to avoid hearing Radstock. From his observation

---

[21] N. S. Leskov, *Velikosvetskii raskol'* (Moskva: 1877), p. 59.
[22] *Ibid.*, p. 106.
[23] *Bv*, No. 5, 1947, p. 10.

he concluded that becoming an evangelical meant complete dedication to a person—Jesus Christ. Every member then became a spark that set a flame in the lives of others.

Following his conversion, Colonel Pashkov terminated his service in the army and became an active preacher, uniting social action with spiritual vitality. He took the movement to the poor, visited jails, opened inexpensive lodging houses, workshops, and homes for orphans. He donated great sums of money to publish over a million pieces of literature and to dispatch many colporteurs across Russia. He arranged and paid for the first edition of the Russian canonical Bible, printed by the British and Foreign Bible Society. Pashkov engaged translator Zasedskaia and published John Bunyan's *Pilgrim's Progress* and *Spiritual Warfare* in the Russian language. All of these publications were the out-reaches of his organization, the "Society for the Advancement of Spiritual-Ethical Reading," established in 1876.[24] Pashkov often was aided by his co-worker Count M. M. Korf, who disputed with the religious censors, convincing them that the literature printed by the "Society" did not support Luther, but was based on the Russian Bible, devoid of any statements against Orthodoxy.

Pashkov's mansion in St. Petersburg, formerly a center of social life of the Russian nobility, now had its doors open for democratic gatherings. As many as 700 would come to hear the gospel. Even the Over-Procurator of the Holy Synod, K. P. Pobedonostsev, was present at an overflow service in the main hall.[25]

vi. *The Conference of 1884* and the Tsarist Police

We have noted the three streams of evangelicals emerging in Russia between 1867 and 1874—in the Caucasus, the

---

Ukraine, and St. Petersburg—each independent and with little knowledge of the others. Blane suggested that the knowledge of a preliminary Baptist conference in south Russia in 1882 "prompted the St. Petersburg group to action."[26] Count Korf, however, credited both idea and initiative for the conference to Pashkov. In March of 1884 he explained,

> . . . the Lord placed the need to call believers to become acquainted with one another and to settle certain questions upon the heart of V. Pashkov. A personal letter was mailed . . . also signed by me. As a result of prayer, the Stundists, Baptists, Mennonites, Molokans, Dukhobors, and Evangelical Christians responded.[27]

Pashkov engaged a spacious hotel in Vyborg and paid the fares of those too poor to defray their own expenses. Over seventy arrived from all corners of Russia. The first session was held in Pashkov's large dining hall, where they discussed key questions on the essence of their faith, including the ordinances of baptism and communion.[28] The mode of baptism became a thorny issue although everyone present acknowledged the sacrament as one ordained of God. The Baptists insisted on the validity of immersion alone, whereas others maintained that the ordinance was to be fulfilled according to one's conscience, consistent with his understanding of the Holy Scriptures.

The following day the discussions continued in the mansion of Princess Lieven with 400 in attendance.[29] The problems of the previous day were compounded when the question of common participation in the Lord's Supper was proposed. The Baptist delegates categorically refused

---

27 I. Motorin, "The First Conference of Russian Believers Concerning the Problem of Unity," *Bv*, No. 2, 1946, pp. 24, 25.

28 *Ibid.*, p. 25.

29 Karev, *Bv*, No. 3, 1957, p. 48. (Possibly the increase comprised local believers.)

to partake in the communion service with the pedobaptists. During a heated exchange of opinions on the debatable issue, Lord Radstock suddenly entered, and with Pashkov as his interpreter said,

> Brethren, on your knees! Our unity is in Christ. He is our peace and life. Let us give him praise and honor.[30]

All the delegates knelt at once, repentant and in fervent prayer. Count Korf penned his impressions:

> Arising from our knees we perceived the unity of the body of Christ and these debates on baptism were terminated. Never can I forget this meeting; for me it was a life-long lesson. Not in the single understanding of a dogma are we to seek unity, but in spirit and in truth. We shall not forget that unity is not uniformity; it can exist in diversity, as in our bodies. It consists of various parts and members which are in unity. So are we united in Christ.[31]

However, despite the moving scene and the response of the delegates, the breaking of bread together was not accomplished.[32]

When the denominational representatives returned to their hotel, they found the police waiting to arrest them. After intense interrogation, they were all placed upon trains destined for their home cities on Easter Sunday.[33] The surprise action abruptly terminated the Conference of 1884, but the failure of a merger of the denominations present was caused by the intransigency of the delegates.

In the meantime the Pashkovite movement spread so

---

[30] Motorin, *loc. cit.*

[31] *Ibid.*

[32] I. I. Motorin, "The Triumph of the Unity of Believers," *Bv,* No. 1, 1964, p. 21.

[33] N. A. Levindanto, *Bv,* No. 1, 1945, pp. 29, 30.

rapidly that repressive measures were proposed to Alexander III in a report by the Over-Procurator of the Holy Synod of the Russian Orthodox Church, Konstantine Petrovich Pobedonostsev. A former professor at Moscow University, Pobedonostsev taught law to Emperors Alexander III and Nicholas II. Tsar Alexander III

. . . followed with tenacity the policies which Pobiedonostsev, his most reactionary tutor, must have inspired him.[34]

The "Society for the Advancement of Spiritual-Ethical Reading" was closed and Pashkov and Korf were required to sign a promissory statement in which they agreed to discontinue preaching, abstain from conducting services, abandon informal prayer, and to terminate their fellowship with the *Stundists* and other religious societies. Upon their refusal to sign, Pashkov and Korf were permanently exiled from Russia by personal command of Alexander III. News of their exile

. . . swiftly spread across Russia. There was great regret. The elder brethren decided to send seventeen brethren to Petersburg to replace the two of us.[35]

Pobedonostsev so persistently persecuted the Baptists, *Stundists*, and Evangelical Christians that they began to call him "The Russian Saul."[36] His twenty-five year rule, from 1880 to 1905, produced some paradoxes. For example, in the same year that the Petersburg Conference was disbanded by the police, another conference was peacefully held in Novovasil'ev, Tavriche, in which the

34 John Maynard, *Russia in Flux* (New York: The Macmillan Company, 1948), p. 143.

35 "Founders of Our Fellowship," *Bv*, No. 5, 1947, p. 44.

36 A. V. Karev, "The Russian Evangelican-Baptist Movement," *Bv*, No. 4, 1957, p. 5.

Union of Russian Baptists were founded (April 30-May 1, 1884). Johann Willer, a Mennonite preacher, was elected its first president![37]

Again, while "The Russian Saul" was using every power available to break the back of the Evangelical-Baptist movement, Dr. Frederick V. Baedeker, a convert of Radstock, was granted official permission to visit all the prisons of Russia. He enjoyed this privilege for eighteen years,[38] personally reaching 40,000 persons in prison and exile with the gospel and Bible distribution. Tolstoi described his prison work in his novel *Resurrection*.[39]

Such events were bright contrasts against the dark periods of police persecution during Pobedonostsev's reign, especially during the years 1894 to 1896. The Over-Procurator recognized the Baptists and *Stundists* as "specially harmful sects."[40] In 1891 he summoned all forty-one episcopate representatives to Moscow for a plenum of the Holy Synod. The burning question of how to cope with the *Stundists*, Baptists, and Evangelical Christians was discussed. Of the forty-one episcopates, twenty-one had been "contaminated" by the evangelicals and the clergymen admitted their inability to stay the rapid growth of these Protestants. As the bishops sought for the answers the Over-Procurator had concrete plans already prepared to initiate further action against the sectarians. He introduced several measures which were later incorporated in the decree of 1893, namely in Articles 187, 189, and 196. This resulted in action against the converts who forsook Orthodoxy and involved anyone aiding in or propagating the "heretical doctrines." The guilty received sentences ranging from eighteen months to four years of imprison-

---

[37] Bondar, *op. cit.*, p. 165.
[38] Robert Sloan Latimer, *Dr. Baedeker and His Apostolic Work in Russia* (London: Morgan & Scott, 1907), p. 44.
[39] *Bv*, No. 3, 1957, pp. 48, 49.
[40] Bonch-Bruevich, *Iz mira . . .* , p. 173.

ment, or exile to Siberia. Further, the law of July 4, 1894, published by the Ministry of Interior Affairs, declared that the evangelicals were dangerous to church and state activities and therefore the right to assemble for services was prohibited.[41] As terrible persecution descended upon the Baptists in the 1890's, Pobedonostsev was determined to decimate the Russian Baptists.[42] It was not until the Edict of 1905 was issued that evangelicals in Russia enjoyed the liberty of faith and conscience, and also the freedom of assembly.[43]

---

[41] Karev, *Bv*, No. 4, 1957, p. 9.

[42] John S. Curtiss, *Church and State in Russia: The Last Years of the Empire (1900–1917)*. (New York: Columbia University Press, 1940), p. 168.

[43] Bonch-Bruevich, *Iz mira . . .*, p. 191.

3

Prokhanov, the Westinghouse Engineer

i. *Ivan S. Prokhanov*, Brilliant and Bold Administrator

During these troublesome times the arrival, in 1888, of nineteen-year-old Ivan Stepanovich Prokhanov in St. Petersburg went unnoticed. Prokhanov was the son of persecuted *Molokans* who had been driven from Saratov to Caucasia in 1862 where, in Vladikavkaz, his father became a wealthy owner of a flour mill. Young Ivan Prokhanov was in the top five of the 1200 who desired to attend the Petersburg Technological Institute. In Russia's capital he found a large but unorganized group of believers. Within a year, by means of a hectograph, he started a religious periodical, "Besseda," despite governmental forbiddance. The writers used Biblical cognomens; his was Zaccheus, quite in contrast to his tall stature. He maintained broad communications with exiled believers and often aided them. In March of 1895 Prokhanov secretly left Russia via Finland to inform the European community of the religious persecution which was in progress. During his three and one-half years abroad he attended the theological colleges in Bristol, London, Berlin, and Paris, where he received a comprehensive view of the Protestant denominations in Western Europe.[1]

Before his return to St. Petersburg, Prokhanov served as an assistant professor at the Riga Polytechnic Institute from 1899 until pressured to leave in 1901, due to his

---

[1] "Ivan Stepanovich Prokhanov," *Bv*, No. 5, 1947, pp. 46–49.

reputation as a leading evangelical. He then accepted
employment at the Westinghouse plant in Petersburg as
an engineer and utilized every free moment for the work
of evangelism.[2]

In 1901 Prokhanov boldly succeeded in printing 20,000
hymnals with censor approval, despite the prohibitory
laws and the ubiquitous Pobedonostsev. As evangelical
meetings were raided and copies of the hymnals, "Gusli,"
were about to be confiscated, to their surprise the police
read the following regulatory inscription on the title
page:

Printed in the Printing Establishment of the Ministry
of Interior, St. Petersburg, . . .[3]

ii. The Manifesto of 1905—Easy Breathing
For the Evangelicals

The Toleration Act of April 17, 1905, was superseded
by the Manifesto of October 17, 1905, which granted freedom of the press, organization of societies and meetings,
and the freedom of political activities. Having published
the new general laws that brought about these reforms, the
government omitted the issuance of special decrees to
liberate religious exiles. On their behalf Prokhanov petitioned Count S. J. Witte, the President of the Council of
Ministers. As a result of the petition, Count Witte liberated those who were imprisoned and exiled for religious
reasons by the means of a special circular.[4]

Accompanying the Manifesto of 1905 was the establishment of the first Duma, which Emperor Nicholas II promised would be an elective body with legislative power.

---

[2] I. S. Prokhanoff, *In the Cauldron of Russia* (New York: John
Felsburg, Inc., 1933) , p. 120.

[3] *Ibid.*, p. 122.

[4] *Bv*, No. 5, 1947, p. 48.

Although greatly limited in power, and far from being the Constituent Assembly for which the strikers and many articulate Russians were asking, the Duma was conceded at least a veto on legislation and it had a right to public discussion on the conduct of officials.[5]

A few isolated evangelicals actually became active in the Dumas. D. I. Mazaev, a Baptist leader with a reputation as a progressive and prosperous farmer, was elected to one of the three North Caucasus seats. However, Mazaev did not occupy the seat and *Bratskii vestnik* suggested that this was due to "someone 'from the top' who interfered."[6] The Komsomols painted Mazaev as an inhuman exploiter of the peasants.[7]

Prokhanov was placed on the ballot for a seat in the St. Petersburg district as a Christian Democrat candidate. Although unsuccessful, he polled more votes than George Plekhanov, the Social Democratic candidate.[8]

Wilhelm Fetler, known in Russia as Vasilii Malov, participated in the 1912-1914 sessions of the Commission on Religious Cults as a consultant on Free Church matters.[9] Fetler, a Baptist from Latvia and an outstanding preacher, established a dozen preaching centers in St. Petersburg, the largest of which was the 2000 seat "Dom evangeliia." His effectiveness drew denunciations in the Moscow press from Orthodox leaders who sought to quench Fetler's "diabolical arrows."[10] In 1914 he was sentenced to exile in Siberia, but by special decision of the cabinet of Ministers this was changed to banishment abroad. Ever active, Fetler organized the Gospel Commission for Work Among Russian War Prisoners in Europe, in 1915.

---

[5] Maynard, *op. cit.*, p. 149.

[6] "Memorial—D. I. Mazaev," *Bv*, Nos. 2–3, 1953, p. 98.

[7] *Komsomol i antireligioznaia propaganda, sbornik statei i ocherkov* (Moskva: Moskovskaia gvardiia, 1937), pp. 78, 79.

[8] Prokhanoff, *op. cit.*, p. 173.

[9] O. Blumit, *Sentenced to Siberia* (Washington, D.C.: Mayflower Publishers, 1947), p. 12.

[10] *Ibid.*, p. 65.

During the years 1916-1920 over two million Russian soldiers were imprisoned in Austria or Germany, among them Protestant sectarians. In addition to Fetler's organization, the Berlin Missionary Society, the Berlin Bible School, the Evangelical Tract Union of Nassau, the Oncken Publishing House of Kassel, and the Christian Tract Society of Stockholm were active among the prisoners. Informal religious services were held in thirty-six camps which continued to hold 250,000 Russian prisoners, "a considerable number of which fell under the evangelical sway of William Fetler and the Christian Tract Society of Stockholm."[11] About 2,000 prisoners were converted to the evangelical cause in these thirty-six camps.[12]

By the end of 1920 more than 500 Russian prisoners had completed a Bible course provided by the Missionary Alliance.[13] The religious awakening was not dissimilar to the rise of *Stundism* and the long-range importance was evident in the missionary spirit of the converted prisoners of war as they returned to the Soviet Union.[14]

During the war the Baptists were accused of being tools of the German Government before the Duma on August 3, 1915. Social Democrat Skobelev condemned this attack upon the sectarians as an attempt to make them scapegoats. He pointed out that before World War I the Baptists had been regarded as largely of English origin, but as the war continued they were branded as a German faith. This resulted in the exile of many noted Baptist leaders. Baptist houses of prayer were closed, and even hospitals organized by the Baptists were not permitted to serve the people.[15]

At the Baptist World Congress of 1911 a Seminary Fund

---

[11] Blane, *op. cit.*, pp. 139, 140.
[12] Blane, *ibid.*, citing Gutsche, *Westliche Quellen des russischen Stundismus* (Kassell: 1957), pp. 105–107.
[13] Blane, *ibid.*, p. 141 citing Gutsche, *ibid.*, p. 107.
[14] *Ibid.*
[15] John S. Curtiss, *op. cit.*, pp. 384, 385 citing *Gosudarstvennaia duma, stenograficheskie otchety*, IV Duma, Session IV Part i, cols. 406, 7.

of over $30,000 was pledged for the training of Baptist preachers in Russia. Dr. R. S. MacArthur and Fetler purchased a site in Petersburg in the name of Mr. J. Urlaub, a businessman residing in the city, because no Baptists were allowed to own property.[16] In 1912 the Ministry of Internal Affairs (MVD) sent a telegram to the President of the Baptist World Alliance politely refusing his request for permission to establish a theological college in St. Petersburg.[17] The War and subsequent revolutions made further progress impossible.[18]

iii. Fetler versus Prokhanov?

Fetler and Prokhanov, the two outstanding leaders in St. Petersburg, appeared to be incompatible. Fetler had nothing positive to say about Prokhanov, who in turn seemed to ignore Fetler, even though the choirs of both men's churches sang together occasionally in the capital. In a lecture to his Bible students in Riga, one of the students present recalled that Fetler spent most of one period downgrading Prokhanov.[19] No doubt personal feelings were involved, for at the 1911 Baptist World Congress Fetler was lauded as the leader and worker in St. Petersburg upon whom, more than any other man in that part of Russia, the future of the Russian Baptists depended.[20] However, when ten vice-presidents were elected, the Congress evidently considered Prokhanov, not Fetler, to be the most outstanding person of the twenty-four delegates present from Russia, as it elected Prokhanov one of the vice-presidents of the Baptist World Alliance.[21]

---

[16] F. Townley Lord, *Baptist World Fellowship* (Nashville: Broadman Press, 1955), p. 130.

[17] Blane, *op. cit.*, p. 83 citing Gutsche, *Westliche, . . .* , p. 85.

[18] Lord, *op. cit.*

[19] Interview with Slavic Minister, November 19, 1964.

[20] Philip L. Jones (ed.), *Second Baptist World Congress* (Philadelphia: Harper & Brother Company, 1911), p. 237.

[21] *Ibid.*, xiii.

J. H. Rushbrooke, one of the presidents of the Baptist
World Alliance, declared that both Russian Unions were
known abroad as Baptists; the difference of names was
attributed to their independent origins. The Evangelical
Christians and the Baptists both became members of the
Baptist World Alliance and both were represented in its
Executive Committee.[22]

iv. The First Russian Evangelical Bible School

Following Pashkov's exile, Ivan V. Kargel' zealously
led the work in St. Petersburg, but when Prokhanov became the aggressive leader, growth was accelerated among
the Evangelical Christians, known first as the Pashkovites.
Prokhanov, master organizer, was elected the first president of the All-Russian Evangelical Christian Union in
1909, when government permission for the creation of the
Union was granted. He was unanimously reelected every
year for twenty years. Although immersed in a Baptist
church in Vladikavkaz, and although he was a student in
a Baptist seminary in Bristol, England, Prokhanov's ecumenical drive for an enlarged fellowship caused him to
attempt to unite all evangelical believers. In 1913 he received permission to found the first school of theology
for Russian evangelicals and served as its principal.[24] Included in the faculty was A. A. Reimer, a Mennonite
preacher from the southern colonies,[25] another instance
of early joint efforts of the future AUCECB members. In
addition, the Mennonites and the Evangelical Christians
also combined efforts to disseminate religious literature

---

[22] J. H. Rushbrooke, *Baptists in the U.S.S.R.* (Nashville: Broadman Press, 1943), p. 4.

[24] No official name appears to have been used. Prokhanov referred
to the institution as the "First Russian Protestant Christian Theological School," p. 167; "Bible College," p. 168; "Bible School," p.
226; Blane, *op. cit.*, called it "Prokhanov's Bible School," p. 92, and
"Prokhanov's Preacher's School," p. 171.

[25] Prokhanoff, *op. cit.*, pp. 167, 168.

by means of a publishing association named "The Rainbow."[26]

A phenomenal growth of the Evangelical Christians from 8,472 members in 1914, to an astronomical membership of 250,000 in 1922 was quoted by Bolshakoff.[27] F. M. Putintsev, editor of the newspaper *Bezbozhnik* and for many years an active antireligionist, conservatively estimated the numerical strength of all the evangelicals during the 1920's at 500,000.[28] In 1909, with the optimism born of faith, Prokhanov predicted that over 500 missionaries would minister across the Russian Empire. By 1928, more than 600 were dispatched over all the Soviet Union, including Siberia.[29]

Russia was divided into seventy provinces, and Prokhanov's Union gradually organized sections in each one of them. The basic unit was the local congregation, entirely autonomous. Wherever five or more local groups were found a sectional association was formed in order to expand missionary work, publications, and religious education in the area. From the school of theology in St. Petersburg the 420 graduates[30] did not begin to meet the constant needs of mushrooming congregations.

v. Prokhanov's Admirers and Despisers

Iakov I. Zhidkov, who worked with Prokhanov in the Westinghouse plant and had labored as his assistant in the thriving St. Petersburg church since 1903—including its vast publishing outreach—may have found it difficult to speak of Prokhanov without bias. He called him

[26] *Ibid.*, p. 149.

[27] Serge Bolshakoff, *Russian Nonconformity* (Philadelphia: The Westminster Press, 1950), p. 119.

[28] F. Putintsev, *Politicheskaia rol' i taktika sekt* (Moskva: Gosudarstvennoe antireligioznoe izdatel'stvo, 1935), p. 449.

[29] Prokhanoff, *op. cit.*, p. 152.

[30] *Ibid.*, p. 229.

... the greatest figure in our Evangelical-Baptist fellowship . . . but very modest. . . . Those who knew Ivan Stepanovich Prokhanov intimately could hardly speak badly of him. Only those who did not, could speak negatively of him.[31]

Evidently many did not know Prokhanov intimately, for derogatory remarks issued from the Orthodox Church, from government sources, and from the Baptists. *Bezbozhnik* ("The Godless"), a Soviet publication, disturbed at the massive amount of literature that Prokhanov had printed, and fully aware of his vast organizational activity, complained that

It is impossible to quiet them down, all the more because the Union of Evangelical Christians has a powerful organization. . . . Behind this success is capitalistic aid. During the first eight months of 1927, they spent 253,712 rubles, of which 218,500, or 85% of their budget came from abroad.[32]

Indeed, the ever-active Prokhanov had raised $100,000 among churches and colleges while in the United States in 1926, and he printed 60,000 Bibles, 15,000 Bible concordances, 60,000 hymnals, etc.[33] Soviet writer A. Dolotov, noting Prokhanov's ambitious plan to build a Christian "City of the Sun," did not doubt the probability of its success. Rather, he struck at its political implications, stating that

Prokhanov even had detailed plans drawn by specially trained engineers. Having received the appropriate

---

[31] I. I. Zhidkov, "Ivan Stepanovich Prokhanov," *Bv*, No. 2, 1945, p. 21.

[32] "Sekta evangelskikh khristian," *Bezbozhnik* (Moskva: 1928), p. 47.

[33] Prokhanov, *op. cit.*, p. 228.

documents, he made several trips to select a site. For us,
the main interest in these plans is in another sphere . . .
in the close ties with the leaders of this "evangelization"
who are from foreign capitals. . . . The bourgeoisie will
never give money solely "for the sake of Christ."[34]

Archimandrite Arsenii, in scoring Prokhanov, gave him a
backhanded compliment by associating him with the German
reformation leader.

> . . . in his homiletics, Prokhanov falls into extreme cor-
> ruption of the truth, and instead of giving bread to his
> hearers, he gives a stone. . . . According to Prokhanov,
> this new religion must replace the old Russian Orthodox
> Church . . . no matter how many new Luthers, Prok-
> hanovs . . . the old . . . the Orthodox, will exist as the
> only saving one.[35]

Unfortunately, the hardest blow came from the Baptists. Even the Soviet writer Dolotov noted the friction
between the Baptists and the Evangelical Christians. He
referred to the December 1925 Conference of the Union
of Baptists in which Prokhanov was charged with mis-
using his post of vice-president of the Baptist World Alliance to the detriment of the Baptist work in the USSR.
Prayer was requested so that the eyes of all sincere believers would be open in order to liberate them from such
leaders who sought not the praise of God.[36] Dolotov wrote:

> For a long time these sects tried to unite, but instead
> there continues to be hostility between them, mainly

---

[34] A. Dolotov, *Tserkov i sektantstvo v Sibiri* (Novosibirsk: Sibkraiizdat, 1930), p. 84; Putintsev, *op. cit.*, p. 449 saw Prokhanov's
attempt as one of the "kulak sectarian elements to create their own
communes . . . and even a city."

[35] Arsenii Rozhdestvensk, *Sektantskii professor' gomiletiki* (Khar'-
kov: 1912), pp. 4, 6.

[36] "About the Relations to I. S. Prokhanov and His Union,"
Baptist, Nos. 1–2 (Moskva: 1926), p. 22.

among the leaders. In 1925, the Baptists wrote a resolution to recommend that all Baptist communities refuse to permit Evangelical Christians to preach in their meetings.[37]

The Baptists were disturbed by Prokhanov's attempts to persuade believers that the name "Baptists" was non Biblical, and he was accused of unethical practices and opportunism among their ranks.

. . . the Evangelical Christians are transmitting terrible corruption to the ranks of Baptist churches . . . they even receive Baptist presbyters who have been excommunicated for vice. . . . Apparently Prokhanov remains persuaded that he will storm toward union only "over the corpse of the Baptist Union."[38]

The Baptist leaders repeated the charge in the presence of Prokhanov and the executive leaders of the Baptist World Alliance, declaring that Prokhanov had said

I will not die, until I step over the corpse of the Baptist Union.[39]

Prokhanov made no comment. The Alliance executives then counseled both groups not to merge into one union for the time being, but to attempt to unify the work rather than to provoke a complete break.

Strangely enough, in 1935, the headquarters of the Baptist Union had to cease its work,[40] the very year that Prokhanov died. In his last days while in the hospital, Prokhanov was asked:

---

[37] Dolotov, *op. cit.*, p. 103.
[38] *Baptist*, No. 8 (Moskva: 1927) , p. 21.
[39] A. Vpechatleniia, "The Third Baptist World Congress in Stockholm," *Baptist*, No. 2 (Moskva: 1925) , p. 10.
[40] *Bv*, No. 3, 1957, p. 63.

"Brother Ivan Stepanovich, do you forgive me and everyone?" He clearly answered, "I already said that I forgive everyone, and the time is coming to declare an evangelical amnesty to all workers of the Gospel. . . ." On his death bed, he urged those present to love everybody.[41]

In a memorial article twenty years after Prokhanov's death, Zhidkov wrote these significant words:

Some tried to cast a shadow on Prokhanov's Union. All were shaken off as dust. His virtue was that he never complained about his accusers and willingly forgave all who were against him.[42]

---

[41] I. I. Zhidkov, "Ivan Stepanovich Prokhanov," *Bv*, No. 2, 1945, pp. 23, 24.
[42] I. I. Zhidkov, "Memorial—Ivan Stepanovich Prokhanov," *Bv*, No. 6, 1955, p. 42.

4

The Conference of 1920—A Hair's Breadth From Unity

i. Preliminary Joint Conferences

The aforementioned incidents cast some light upon the failure of the Evangelical Christians and the Baptists to complete the merger of both unions in 1920, although they were a hair's breadth away from successful unity. No conference since Pashkov's gathering in 1884 was of such importance and promise as the one convened in 1920. Separate conferences had been held by the Baptists in Kiev (1905), Rostov-on-Don (1906), and St. Petersburg (1912). In addition to separate conferences the Evangelical Christians held three joint meetings in which Baptist leaders were invited to the capital to discuss further possibilities of unity.

The first of the three joint conferences was held in St. Petersburg from January 15 to 22, 1907. *Molokan* and Presbyterian representatives also were present and a commission was formed to advance the work of unity.[1] The second, held during the Fourth Conference of Evangelical Christians, attracted five representatives from the Baptist Union. An acceptable decision concerning the excommunication of church members was reached.[2] The third

---

[1] I. I. Zhidkov, "On the Roads of Unity," *Bv*, No. 3, 1957, p. 56–58.

[2] "The Russian Evangelical-Baptist Movement After the October 17, 1905 Manifesto," *Bv*, No. 4, 1957, p. 28.

convened in 1919 at the Sixth Conference of Evangelical Christians and was most profitable, resulting in agreements on a vast project for the uniting of the two unions. The stage was set for the Congress of 1920.

A preliminary conference of five executives from both unions met in Petrograd in January of 1920 and two important advances were gained. Together they agreed to publish a magazine called "The Fraternal Union" and they approved a common seal depicting the image of two staffs in one hand.[3]

ii. The Conference of 1920—Almost Persuaded

In June of 1920, the most important congress to convene on behalf of the work of unity since Pashkov's 1884 convocation assembled in Moscow. After a lengthy discussion agreement was reached on the merger name of "Union of Evangelical Christians and Baptists." The Evangelical Christians were careful to define the unity as one based upon freedom and equality, one in which neither side was to be subjugated to the other, a unity where there was to be no strain upon one another's liberty or the forfeit of spiritual values.

Important decisions such as the selection between St. Petersburg and Moscow as the headquarters of the union, the fair apportionment of executive posts, and church polity were left unresolved, yet these were necessary guides for the practical aspects of the merger. In addition, several questions of dogma needed to be solved in order to avoid future dissension in the churches. Undue attention seemed to be given to insignificant meticulous steps in the performance of rituals such as the laying on of hands, the conducting of baptisms, and the breaking of bread. Years later AUCECB executive I. I. Motorin commented:

[3] "Speech of President I. I. Zhidkov on the Day of Unity," *Bv*, No. 1, 1955, p. 12.

These debates reminded one of the disputes between Patriarch Nikon and the protopope Avvakum on how to cross oneself, whether by two fingers in the name of the two natures of Christ, or with three fingers in the name of the Holy Trinity.[4]

Nevertheless, as a result of the good will emanating from both sides present at the congress, they ceased to major on minors and agreements were reached. The Baptist leader, V. G. Pavlov, and Prokhanov embraced and kissed one another as everyone sang the hymn "For the Gospel Faith of Christ We Stand" and joyfully greeted one another.

But despite the agreement reached in all organizational matters and dogmatic questions, the practical merger of the two unions was not effected.[5]

Zhidkov, reflecting upon this years later, added this illuminating comment:

The unity did not then take place because the administration of the Baptists was in Moscow, but the Evangelical Christians' was in Leningrad [Petrograd] . . . it was difficult to decide where to have the headquarters of the fellowship . . .[6]

iii. Cleavage Instead of Union

Instead of union, cleavage came in 1923, despite the joint efforts of the two groups to alleviate the suffering due to the terrible famine which followed the Civil War of 1918-1921 in the Soviet Union. At the Baptist World

---

[4] I. I. Motorin, "The Triumph of the Unity of Believers," *Bv*, No. 1, 1964, p. 22.

[5] *Ibid.*, p. 23.

[6] Zhidkov, "On the Roads . . . ," *Bv*, No. 3, 1957, p. 63.

Congress, held in Stockholm in 1923, a General Commission of five executive brethren from each Russian union met for further study on unity. Instead of making progress, all efforts toward real unity were discarded for two decades.

After 1923 the question of unity came to a standstill and both rivers flowed on, hardly ever contacting each other. There is no doubt that the reason for this sad picture was the disagreements held by the leaders of both unions.[7]

Dr. J. H. Rushbrooke, one of the presidents of the Baptist World Alliance, called the Union of Baptists the "Southern Baptist Movement" and the Union of Evangelical Christians the "Northern Baptist Movement." He regretted that the older brother, the Southern Baptists, did not always see a true fraternal relation in its younger brother, but was contrary minded. The Baptist World Alliance always considered both as real Baptists, making no distinction between the two.[8]

---

[7] A. V. Karev, "The Russian Evangelical-Baptist Movement," *Bv*, No. 4, 1957, p. 30.
[8] *Ibid.*, p. 12.

5

The Christans of Evangelcal Fath (Pentecostalists)

i. Some Mystical Sects in Russia

The last of the four evangelical groups to appear in the country, the Christians of Evangelical Faith, better known as Pentecostalists, was the third to join the Union. This group came into being and flourished during the nineteen twenties, the decade of spectacular growth among evangelical believers in Soviet Russia.

Long before the appearance of Ivan Efimovich Voronaev, who founded the Christians of Evangelical Faith and guided the Pentecostal believers in their rapid growth in the Ukraine, instances of the "glossolalia" (speaking in unknown tongues) had been noted among various mystical sects in Russia, such as the *Khlysti*, the *Pryguni*, the *Malovantsi*, the *Smorodintsi*, and the *Murashkovtsi*. These sectarian services were of a fanatical nature, and more important, their doctrinal tenets were far removed from those of evangelical believers.[1]

The *Pryguni* (Jumpers) claimed to have their origin in biblical David's dance before the ark of God, and they believed that the Holy Spirit would come upon them when dancing. There were reports similar to those which occurred during the exhaustive dancing of the *Khlysti*,

---

[1] For a description of the origin, history and nature of many sectarians see F. M. Putintsev, *Politicheskaia rol' i taktika sekt.* For contemporary sects see V. A. Mezentsev (ed.), *My porvali s religiei.*

that "the sound of unintelligible words in various tongues" were heard during the rite.[2] A former Baptist led a fanatical sect, the *Molovantsi*, into highly emotional prayers in which the members shouted unintelligible sounds and sometimes imitated various animals and birds. Its leader had a vision of himself as the Firstborn, the Son of God.[3] The *Smorodintsi*, a group from Leningrad, were tongues speakers who rejected the dogma of the Trinity and preached a "Oneness" doctrine in which Jesus was Father, Son, and Holy Spirit.[4] The *Murashkovtsi* were led by Ivan Murashkov, who returned from the United States to Belorussia in 1925 to set himself up as the "Father of Zion," assisted by O. Kiril'chuk, the "Holy Mother of Zion." By the means of prophesying imminent judgment and promoting a safe, distant haven for his followers, Murashkov collected the life's savings from a number of his faithful before absconding to South America.[5]

This strange array of fanatical Russian sectarians, all of whom contained some manifestations resembling the glossolalia, or speaking in tongues, made it difficult for the Baptists and Evangelical Christians to be objective in their relationship to the evangelical Pentecostal followers of Voronaev.

As early as 1908, I. I. Zhidkov (the first President of the AUCECB) recalled a Pentecostal "intrusion" of a union youth conference which he attended in a Moscow apartment where

[2] G. M. Livshits, *Religiia i tserkov' v proshlom i nastoiashchem* (Minsk: 1961), pp. 125, 126. Founded by Lukian Petrov, former *Molokan* preacher. Found mainly in Transcaucasia and Central Asia. Reinmarus and Friezen, *op. cit.*, pp. 14, 23 noted another such group among the Mennonites.

[3] R. S. Latimer, *With Christ in Russia* (London: Hodder and Stoughton, 1910), pp. 156–164.

[4] V. M. Kalugin, *Sovremennoe religioznoe sektantstvo* (Moskva: Gosudarstvennoe iz-vo, 1962), p. 18.

[5] V. A. Mezentsev (ed.), *My porvali s religiei* (Moskva: Voennoe izdatel'stvo ministerstva oborony, 1963), pp. 191–196.

because of the lack of a spiritual awakening a new teaching of the Pentecostals infiltrated the center of believers.[6]

Zhidkov also mentioned a man named Urshan who came to Helsinki from the United States in 1911 and introduced the doctrine of "Jesus Only" (denial of the Trinity) , and maintained that it was obligatory for a Christian to speak in tongues unknown to the speaker. Prokhanov's magazine, *Khristianin,* warned believers in 1912 that this teaching was already doing its damage in Germany.[7]

Inroads were made in Latvia by the "fanatical Pentecostal movement" where at least

> sixteen Baptist churches were influenced by these teachings to stay out of the Latvian Baptist Union, which they regarded as an obstacle to the free working of the Holy Spirit . . .[8]

ii. Voronaev, the Baptist Become Pentecostal

Somewhat like the transference of the *Stundists* to the Baptist ranks in the nineteenth century, the Baptists conversely experienced the exodus of many of their members to the Pentecostalists. Zhidkov did not write kindly of the return of Voronaev to Russia in 1922, but marked him as a former Baptist who brought a new, "harmful" teaching from the United States which caused many Russian Baptists to accept the Pentecostal message.

> Voronaev commanded an intensive work, not only in Odessa, but also in all of the USSR . . . the new teaching entered into the Baptist and Evangelical Christian churches and was divisive. There was a heated struggle

---

[6] Zhidkov, "On the Roads . . ," *Bv,* No. 3, 1957, p. 62.
[7] *Ibid.*
[8] Robert G. Torbet, *A History of the Baptists* (Philadelphia: The Judson Press, 1950) , p 206.

in the ranks of the believers, but Ivan E. Voronaev had accomplished his work, and in 1944, his followers already amounted to almost 20,000 in the Ukraine . . .[9]

The *Concise Scientific-Atheist Dictionary* claimed that the first Pentecostal believers in Tsarist Russia were discovered in Helsinki at the end of 1913. They spread to other cities, primarily drawing members from malcontent Baptists and Evangelical Christians. Noting the origin of the Christians of Evangelical Faith, this work stated that a new

> wave of activity and growth of the sect was observed in 1922 after the arrival of Voronaev, the conspicuous Pentecostal preacher.[10]

Ivan Efimovich Voronaev was born in Russia in 1886 and served with the Cossacks under the Tsar.[11] Shortly after his conversion in 1908, he ministered in Baptist churches in Irkutsk and Krasnoiarsk. Religious persecution caused him to leave Russia with his wife and two children via Harbin, Manchuria in 1911. Arriving in San Francisco he pastored a Russian Baptist church and worked as a typesetter and proof reader. He later served a Russian Baptist group in Seattle, Washington, sharing the church building with its American pastor, Ernest Williams. It was he who introduced Voronaev to the Pentecostal doctrines.[12]

---

[9] Zhidkov, *loc cit.*, p. 62.

[10] *Kratkii nauchno-ateisticheskii slovar'* (Moskva: Iz-vo nauka, 1964), p. 469.

[11] Sources have been gathered from interviews with charter members of the Russian Pentecostal Church, New York City, on June 26, 1965, its 46th anniversary; taped interviews with Mrs. Katherine Voronaev, May 1964; interviews with Paul Voronaev, 1965; letter from Mrs. Anne Marusczak, nee Anne Siritz, etc.

[12] Ernest S. Williams served as the General Superintendent of the Assemblies of God, United States, from 1929–1949.

Three years later the Voronaevs moved to New York City and Ivan Efimovich became the busy pastor of the growing Russian Baptist Church on Henry Street. Their neighbors, a Pentecostal family named Siritz, often engaged the Voronaevs in discussions on the baptism with the Holy Spirit and the subsequent evidence of speaking in other tongues. However, it was not until Voronaev's young daughter Vera accompanied Anne Siritz to a Pentecostal service in Glad Tidings Hall on 42nd Street[13] and experienced the glossolalia, that Voronaev sought for a personal Pentecost. To avoid strained relations at his Baptist church, he kept his daughter from attending Glad Tidings, but several of his parishioners began visiting the Pentecostal meetings as investigators but remained to become participants in the glossolalia. Shortly thereafter, Voronaev himself "spoke in other tongues as the Spirit gave him utterance." Rather than complicate matters further, he resigned and founded an independent Pentecostal work. He was surprised to find almost twenty Baptists who became charter members of the first Russian Pentecostal Church in New York, for they had already become tongues-speakers. The group began worshipping in the Emmanuel Presbyterian Church on 6th Street on July 1, 1919. During the next two years many Russians, Ukrainians, and Poles were converted and baptized with the Holy Spirit. Among the baptized were some Slavic ministers.

During a cottage prayer meeting held in a member's home, an utterance in another tongue was followed by its companion gift, the interpretation of tongues in the Russian language stating, "Voronaev, Voronaev, go to Russia." This was repeated three times. Voronaev refused to accept this as a directive from God, reasoning that it was but a sincere human desire on the part of the hostess. She, Anna Koltovich, was grieved at his rejection of the message and fervently prayed that God would reveal the call personally

---

[13] Presently Glad Tidings Assembly of God, 33rd St.

to her pastor. Within days, while privately at prayer in his city apartment, Voronaev was quickened by the very same words, "Voronaev, Voronaev, go to Russia." He believed at once. Despite the obligations of a growing family and the lack of funds, in obedience to God he made preparations to leave America.[14]

On July 15, 1920, the Voronaev family departed for Varna, Bulgaria, where he had a brief but fruitful ministry before journeying on to Odessa. Monthly support came from the Glad Tidings Assembly of God in New York and from the Russian and Eastern European Mission in Chicago. From 1921 to 1930, continued financial assistance was mailed from the United States. This "capitalistic" aid and Voronaev's accounts of his stewardship in the form of correspondence were to be used against him by the Soviets as trumped up spy charges before his imprisonment.

Upon his arrival Voronaev was well received by the Baptists and the Evangelical Christians in Odessa. He preached for the "common" Baptists in the morning services, and for the "intelligentsia" Evangelical Christians during the evening services. He visited his relatives in the Orenburg region and preached there, winning his mother to Christ, but with little general success. Returning to Odessa, Voronaev decided to begin his own services and openly declared the Pentecostal message. Drawing half his congregation from the Baptists and Evangelical Christians who eagerly embraced the Pentecostal doctrines, Voronaev certainly could not hope to be popular with the local pastors. The movement grew rapidly and the work in Odessa alone was to reach a membership of almost 1000.[15]

---

[14] Interview with Mrs Anna Koltovich, February 5, 1965; taped interview by Rev. Paul Demetrus with Mrs. Katherine Voronaev, May 1964.

[15] Taped interview with Mrs. Voronaev, May 1964.

Voronaev traveled extensively, with an itinerary that included visits to Leningrad and Moscow. Pioneering for two to three months at a time while the Odessan church and the Pentecostal headquarters were administered by his co-workers, Voronaev opened new assemblies across Russia at a phenomenal pace. Among those who entered into the experience of glossolalia were some Baptist preachers such as D. I. Ponomarchuk and G. G. Ponurko, who later as Pentecostalists were to hold executive positions in the AUCEC. As word spread by mouth, all-day meetings were held in village after village as Voronaev preached and also ministered successfully in praying for the sick and afflicted.[16]

Soviet writer F. I. Garkavenko described Voronaev as a Pentecostal missionary who was disguised as a Baptist "planted" again in Russia by the "American imperialists."

With the aid of counter-revolutionary elements, he even founded the first Pentecostal sect in our country. The Pentecostalists conducted anti-Soviet activities as they propagated their provocative "prophets." In those years many of the Baptist communities . . . transferred to the Pentecostals.[17]

Another Soviet writer accused Voronaev of returning to Russia on a special assignment by the American General Council of the Assemblies of God in order to spread Pentecostalism in the USSR. He declared that

. . . Voronaev and his closest assistants were paid collaborators of the General Council and the Russian Eastern European Mission in Chicago. Voronaev received $100 per month and his assistant $50. The Pente-

---

[16] *Ibid.*

[17] F. I. Garkavenko, *Chto takoe religioznoe sektanstvo* (Moskva: Nauchno-populiarnaia biblioteka, 1961), p. 83.

costal leaders in the USSR regularly dispatched accounts of their activities to the USA.[18]

Voronaev, under missionary appointment by the American Assemblies of God, did send routine reports regarding funds received for himself and his co-laborers. The Baptists and Evangelical Christians viewed Voronaev's activities from another vantage point. *Bratskii vestnik* maintained that as early as 1923 the rise of Pentecostal churches, primarily organized from members of the existing evangelical churches, caused a division which

. . . left some churches in feeble condition and the majority of believers truly grieved about the schism.[19]

In 1926 the publication *Baptist* warned its readers against Voronaev and his followers, labeling them "deceivers" who went about sowing seeds of doubt by stating that it was necessary for believers to perform healings and to speak in tongues.[20]

It may not have been a causative factor, but neither could it be discounted that the disappointments which resulted from the failure to merge in 1920, and the subsequent cleavage between the Baptists and Evangelical Christians in 1923, left many evangelicals susceptible to the Pentecostal challenge of speaking in tongues.

Voronaev's son Paul, present in Russia with his father during this period, reported that initially about half of the Pentecostal congregations consisted of believers who left the Baptist and Evangelical Christian churches, while the remainder was made up of new converts. After the first three years of the Pentecostal movement, 90 per cent

---

[18] G. M. Livshits, *op cit.*, p. 135.

[19] *Bv*, No. 5, 1955, p. 67.

[20] "The Shaker's Work" and "False Prophets," *Baptist*, Nos. 11–12 (Moskva: 1926) , pp. 26, 27.

of the increase in membership was drawn from new converts.[21]

iii. Pentecostal Headquarters in Odessa

It was in 1924 that the Union of Christians of Evangelical Faith was organized in the Odessa oblast, and by 1926 it was extended throughout the Ukraine. Voronaev, in his shortlived Pentecostal magazine *Evangelist*, listed over 350 assemblies with a membership of about 17,000 drawn from the Baptists, the Evangelical Christians, the Orthodox, and others.[22] Donald Gee, for many years the editor of *Pentecost*, wrote of available statistics which claimed that there were 80,000 Pentecostal believers in Russia.[23] He wrote this in 1936 when, more than ever, statistics of any kind emanating from the Soviet Union were impossible to verify.

In 1928, the editor of *Baptist* published an article designed to expose an opportunistic strategy of Voronaev who attempted to gain additional readers for the Pentecostal periodical *Evangelist*. Accompanying the article were the cover pages of both magazines photographed side by side, revealing several striking similarities such as

> . . . identical texts are on the top of the cover page, the same symbol of our World Alliance (misappropriated without permission), the same type, size, the same seal with slight modification . . . the specialty of this magazine is imitation. . . . Be careful! Do not play with fire . . .[24]

---

[21] Interview with Paul Voronaev, New York City, March 18, 1965.
[22] *Evangelist* (Odessa: 1928, No. 1), p. 1. (Published only during 1928).
[23] Donald Gee, *Upon All Flesh* (Springfield, Mo.: The Gospel Publishing House, 1947), p. 31.
[24] N. V. Odintsov, "A Serious Warning," *Baptist*, No. 8 (Moscow: 1928), pp. 31, 32.

The luxury of striking at each other in their publications, of vying for the confused sheep who strayed in and out of Baptist and Pentecostal folds, at first permitted by the Soviets, was unexpectedly discontinued at the height of its indulgence. Not realizing that the days of unprecedented freedom enjoyed by most of the evangelicals were numbered, the expectations of continued expansion and extended ministries were greater than ever. For instance, at the 1928 Baptist World Congress, Ivanov-Klyshnikov, one of the twenty-eight Russian delegates present, boasted of the many opportunities for ministry and stated optimistically:

> The Russian people represent the most fruit-bearing spiritual ground among the peoples of the whole world. It is a people of God-seekers. . . . We observe signs of a great awakening . . .[25]

However, most conspicuous by their absence at the following Congress held in 1934 in Berlin were the Russian delegates. Optimism was replaced by deepening anxiety for it was learned that the Russian Baptists had

> . . . returned from the Toronto Congress of 1928 to find their government preparing measures of repression and early in 1929 these took the form of law . . .[26]

---

[25] W. T. Whitley (ed.), *Fourth Baptist World Congress* (Toronto: Stewart Printing Service, 1928), p. 77.

[26] J. H. Rushbrooke (ed.), *Fifth Baptist World Congress* (London: Baptist World Alliance, 1934), p. 25.

PART II

THE 1944 MERGER OF THE EVANGELICAL CHRISTIANS AND THE BAPTISTS

6

The Repressive Law of 1929

i. Patriarch Tikhon's Losing Struggle
Against the Soviet Regime

Prior to the enactment of the Law of April 1929 religious as well as antireligious propaganda was permitted. The evangelicals grasped every opportunity to spread the gospel across the Soviet Union for more than a decade. The years leading up to 1929 were most fruitful for all evangelicals except the Mennonites.

The terrible famine that followed the Civil War forced the Soviet Government to introduce the New Economic Policy, a temporary expedient which would increase the nation's food supply and stabilize its economy. This was necessary despite foreign aid, which included $66 million worth of food and medicine supplied by the American Relief Administration. The American Mennonites alone helped to feed up to 38,600 Russians daily.[1]

Meanwhile, a death struggle was in progress between the Soviet rulers and Patriarch Tikhon concerning his refusal to relinquish consecrated church articles that were to be sold, supposedly to provide added state funds for the purchase of food. Arrests and the execution of priests assumed a mass character from 1921-23. Following the arrest of Patriarch Tikhon, in hopes of further dividing the

---

[1] E. G. Kaufman, *The Development of the Misionary Interest and Philanthropic Interest Among the Mennonites of North America* (Berne, Indiana: The Mennonite Book Concern, 1931), p. 21.

Orthodox Church, the government supported the ecclesiastical movement called the "Living Church." Led by the ambitious Metropolitan Aleksandr Vvedenski, the movement was launched briefly by a number of bishops who temporarily controlled most of the churches.

It was at this time (1922-23) that Prokhanov felt it most opportune to challenge the movement to begin a national reform based upon New Testament principles. He printed and distributed 100,000 copies of "The Gospel Call" as a special appeal to the Orthodox leaders. On March 15, 1923, Prokhanov addressed the Congress of the Ancient Apostolic Church, chaired by Vvedenski. He impressed many of the clergymen, but brought on hostility from others whose unfavorable report caused his brief imprisonment in Putirski prison.[2]

After declaring that he was no longer an enemy of the Soviet regime, Tikhon was released in June 1923 and was able again to assume the reins of the Orthodox Church.

ii. The Soviet Toleration of the Sectarians

The sectarians enjoyed some toleration, by courtesy of the Soviets, since they conceivably could weaken the unity of the Russian Orthodox Church. From 1921 to 1928 the Communist Party employed the tactics of divide and ruin without departing from its basic long-range policy.[3]

The Soviet Government hoped that the evangelicals would be more successful against the power of the Orthodox Church than the state could be.

In accordance with its policy, the Soviet Government welcomed the Evangelicals' support, and paid for it by

---

[2]Prokhanoff, *op. cit.,* pp. 210–225.

[3] Boleslaw Szczesniak, *The Russian Revolution and Religion* (Notre Dame: University of Notre Dame Press, 1959), p. 23.

handing over to the Evangelicals a number of Orthodox Churches, and by permitting their ministers to preach in the market places and on the steps of cathedrals.[4]

W. Gutsche, who worked for years in the midst of the Russian Protestant sectarians, felt that they exhibited little sympathy toward the Orthodox Church during its early collisions with the Soviets.[5]

Hecker, a member of the Living Church, stated that the evangelicals took advantage of the unlimited freedom for religious propaganda from 1917 to 1929 and spread rapidly, building efficient organizations and publishing departments.[6]

At the 1923 Baptist World Congress, the Russian Baptists report stated that 5,000 Baptist Sunday Schools were attended by approximately 300,000 boys and girls.[7]

In 1927, the Russian Baptists published the following statement:

We are free to preach the Gospel in overflowing halls . . . we baptize openly in rivers and seas before great crowds of people. Of course, if some one of us would try to show that the monarchy is the best form of rule . . . or if one carries on antimilitaristic propaganda . . . then such a preacher will not be in grace with the Soviet power.[8]

The believer's position concerning military obligations received critical analysis by the Soviets. Emelian Iaros-

---

[4] Sidney Dark, *The War Against God* (New York: The Abingdon Press, 1938), pp. 113, 114.

[5] Blane, *op. cit.*, p. 179 citing W. Gutsche, *Religion and Evangelism in Sovietrussland* (Kassel: 1959), p. 21.

[6] Julius F. Hecker, *Religion and Communism* (London: Chapman and Hall), p. 72.

[7] W. T. Whitley, *Third Baptist World Congress* (London: Kingsgate Press, 1923), p. 147.

[8] "Our Present Condition," *Baptist*, No. 1 (Moskva: 1927), p. 22.

lavski, chairman of the League of Militant Godless, charged the Baptists and the Evangelical Christians with disloyalty to the Soviet Government since the records indicated that many of them had served loyally in the army under the Tsar.

... this is not a question of religion, but a question of politics, and counterrevolutionary politics at that![9]

Soviet writer P. Kaushanskii accused the Baptists of serving with the White Army after refusing, on religious pretenses, to serve in the Red Army during the Civil War.[10] Pro-Soviet British clergyman Hewlett Johnson wrote:

The outbreak of pacifism as a result of war-weariness complicated the position at a time when the Red Army of National Defense was being organized. It savored a tacit obstruction at a dangerous moment and many young Baptists were shot. Then came relief: both groups repudiated pacifism; whilst the State on its side made conscientious objection permissible.[11]

iii. Military Conscription and the Evangelicals

In 1923, *Izvestiia* published Prokhanov's letter directed to all believers in which he called upon their loyalty to Soviet rule and to military conscription. Finally, in 1926, at the Tenth All-Union Council of Evangelical Christians,

Prokhanov's unconditional authoritativeness and clear position regarding military service helped all the breth-

---

[9] E. Yaroslavski, *Religion in the U.S.S R.* (London: Modern Books Ltd., 1932), p. 52.

[10] Kaushanskii, "The Harm of the Baptists," *Agitator* No. 20 (Moscow: November, 1960), pp. 41–44.

[11] Hewlett Johnson, *Soviet Russia Since the War* (New York: Bone and Gaer, 1947), p. 122.

ren to follow the sound and proper road of Christian service to the homeland.[12]

Soviet writer Iartsev claimed that this directive made the believers suspect that Prokhanov was demon-possessed.[13] However, Prokhanov's position on military service was also adopted by the Baptists,[14] predicated on their thirteenth Doctrinal Article which declared:

> We believe that government, even in the New Testament period, did not carry the sword in vain, but has the right and obligation granted by God's law, to use it against the workers of evil in the defense of the offended, so that we hold ourselves obliged to bear arms when this is demanded us by the government.[15]

In this manner, military service was interpreted as the fulfillment of love in disarming evil, while the Biblical injunction to love one's enemies applied only to personal enemies.

Baptist leaders such as Pavlov, Timoshenko, and Ivanov-Klyshnikov were of the conviction that if all Baptists sought freedom from military service they would engender hostility against their denomination, and even more, they would plague the Baptists with an influx of insincere people whose only goal would be to dodge military service.[16]

Voronaev and the Pentecostal followers were accused by the Soviets of insubordination to the laws of the state, one of which was the refusal of military service.[17] Accord-

---

[12] I.I. Zhidkov, "Ivan Stepanovich Prokhanov," *Bv*, No. 2, 1945, p. 26.

[13] A. Iartsev, *Sekta evangel'skikh khristian* (Moskva: Bezbozhnik, 1928), p. 18.

[14] Zhidkov, *loc. cit.*

[15] *Ibid.*

[16] "Letter of Council of the All-Russian Union of Baptists to all Baptist brethren in the USSR," *Baptist*, No. 1 (Moskva: 1925), p. 26.

[17] E. V. Maiat, *Brat'ia i sestry vo khriste* (Moskva: 1960), p. 23

ing to Voronaev's son Paul, his father held no particular position regarding conscription, but placed the responsibility of the decision upon the conscience of each individual believer. The authorities forced him to revise this at the close of his public ministry, before his arrest and imprisonment.[18]

The wealthiest Mennonites were charged with abandoning their time-honored rejection of military service, both in 1905 and again in 1917, when "armed with rifles and revolvers, they aided the Tsar in suppressing the revolutionary movements."[19] However, during the revolution and the Civil War, bands of brigands sometimes grew to the size of small armies and were attracted to the wealth of the Mennonites. So intolerable was the suffering, that in order to protect the women and children, many men, despite a binding tradition, joined colonies to provide adequate defense.[20] A Soviet accusation went further, suggesting that the Mennonites

. . . in the guise of fighting against the bandits, were able to recruit more people against the Red Army.[21]

The Militant Atheists accused them of aiding the enemy armies during the Civil War, reportedly having found a small arsenal in a Mennonite colony in Tokmak.[22]

iv. The Mennonite Petition

Before the repressive Law of 1929 proved itself to be a major blow against all believers in the Soviet Union the

[18] Interview with Paul Voronaev, March 18, 1965.

[19] Garvenko, *op. cit.,* p. 10.

[20] E. H. Broadbent, *The Pilgrim Church* (London: Pickering and Inglis, 1931), p. 337.

[21] Reinmarus and Friezen, *op. cit.,* p. 40.

[22] M. Enisherlov, A. Lukachev, and M. Mitin (eds.) *Voinstvuiushchee bezbozhie v SSSR za 15 let 1917–1932* (Moskva: Gosudarstvennoe antireligioznoe izdatel'stvo, 1932), pp. 140–142.

Mennonites appeared to be the key target in drawing the fire and wrath of the communists.

During the relaxed era of the New Economic Policy the Mennonite Congress convened in 1924, hoping to recover a measure of their former religious liberties. They submitted an eight-point petition which enraged the Soviets, who stated:

> ... they demanded "minimum promises" from the Soviet rulers; freedom from military service ... instruction in the "laws of God" in school ... for children and young people ... religious meetings, choirs, Bible courses, etc. This provocative "ultimatum" was calculated to draw reaction from "brethren" abroad, especially in the United States and Germany. But nothing came of this.[23]

The "provocative ultimatum" miscarried and only one of the eight demands was ever granted—permission to import some Bibles.[24] This triggered a second migration and 21,000 Mennonites left the Soviet Union for Canada between 1923 and 1927 before the Soviet Government discontinued granting passports and the emigration ceased.[25] Shortly after this exodus seventy Mennonites fled from famine conditions in Siberia and arrived in Moscow seeking relief.

> Strangely enough, and quite unexpectedly, perhaps because of their very audacity and persistency, the Soviet authorities granted them passports with permission to leave the country.[26]

Word spread rapidly and Soviet officials were amazed to

---

[23] P. Evin, "The Mennonites," *Nauka i religiia,* No. 5 (Moskva: May, 1963), p. 26. (The*Mennonite Encyclopedia* listed the year 1925 (p. 390) as did Reinmarus and Friezen.

[24] Smith, *op. cit.,* pp. 505, 506.

[25] *Ibid.,* p. 526.

[26] *Ibid.,* p. 511.

suddenly find about 1,000 Mennonite families in the Moscow outskirts. Press reports told of the arrival of six, ten, and finally 13,000 refugees. Many of them were urged to sign statements that they were returning of their own free will. These were herded into freight cars and shipped back to Siberia. On November 19, 1929, the German Cabinet made intercession for the refugees still in Moscow, offering to provide a temporary haven in Germany and to finance the project. About 4,000 Mennonites actually left the Soviet Union in this manner.[27] A similar event occurred in 1963, when thirty-two evangelicals arrived in Moscow from Eastern Siberia, requesting aid at the American Embassy in order to emigrate to Israel. The Soviet Government promptly shipped them back to Siberia.[28] It was an awkward situation and the Soviets received a bad world press, but they dared not repeat their blunder of a generation past, when a mass of 13,000 believers converged upon Moscow after permission to emigrate was granted to seventy souls.

Before the crippling Law of 1929 was enacted, the obvious success of the Christian communes also embarrassed the Communists. The People's Commissariat of Agriculture, accused of being motivated by its narrow departmental interest, was scored by the League of Militant Godless for supporting the evangelicals. Another *Bezbozhnik* publication took issue with Vladimir Bonch-Bruevich, a Soviet leader who favored the government's utilization of the drive, zeal, and experience of the sectarians who worked in communes. Komsomol, the Young Communist League, feared the "Khristomol" (Evangelical Christians youth groups) and "Bapsomol" (Baptist youth groups) competition. They were charged with receiving aid from

---

[27] *Ibid.*, pp. 512–514; see Reinmarus and Friezen, pp. 75, 76; *Mennonite Encyclopedia*, p. 391.

[28] J. C. Pollock, *The Faith of the Russian Evangelicals* (New York: McGraw-Hill Book Company, 1964), pp. 180–184.

wealthy American Baptists such as Ford and Rockefeller, who donated millions to Protestant activities.

It is no surprise after this that Khristomol spent nearly twelve million rubles on its counterrevolutionary activity in the USSR.[29]

v. The Law of 1929—Death Blow to Church Legality

The Law of April 8, 1929, denied legal existence to all churches in the Soviet Union and allowed no activity other than the performance of worship. An elaborate codification of the laws on religion was decreed and more than sixty Articles were issued by the Commissariat of Justice.

The decade preceding 1929 saw 2,000 churches closed, whereas in 1929 alone 1,370 churches and synagogues were closed. According to law, if a majority of persons in a community desired a church building for some purpose other than religion, it was converted to that use. Members of the League of Militant Godless adopted a method of house to house recruitment with this goal in mind.[30]

The religious instruction of any person under eighteen years of age became a criminal offense, calling for corrective labor of up to one year. A. B. Lunacharski, the Commissar of Public Education, indicated the prevalent need for the Soviets to clean house within its own school system:

... Believing teachers are an absurd contradiction; the Sections of Public Instruction should take every opportunity to replace them by antireligious teachers.[31]

---

[29] *Putintsev,* op. cit., pp. 72, 95.

[30] George A. Foster, "The Attitude of Russian Communism to Religion" (unpublished B.D. thesis, School of Religion, Duke University, 1933), p. 109.

[31] *Izvestiia,* (Moscow, June 26, 1929) quoted in *The Religious Persecutions in Russia* (Geneva: 1930), p. 14.

The only substantial charge pressed against the Baptists and Evangelical Christians referred to their acceptance of financial aid from abroad. This was not unknown to the Soviet authorities, for these funds reached the Soviet State Bank and brought in valuable foreign currency.[32] This charge, as stated earlier, was also brought against Voronaev and other Pentecostal workers, called in 1927 "one of the most reactionary anti-Soviet sects."[33]

Under a wave of persecution initiated before the Law of 1929, Baptist Fetler's 2,000 seat Dom evangeliia was confiscated by the Soviets in 1928 and turned into a dance hall and Soviet club.[34] Hewlett Johnson admitted that

Fresh trouble arose when, in the winter of 1928-29, the collective farms were in process of formation. The natural desire of the Baptists to form collectives out of their own members led to a misunderstanding and produced the repressive enactment of 1929 . . .[35]

Baptist World Alliance President Rushbrooke maintained that the sectarian struggle against collectivization was interpreted by the Soviet government as counterrevolutionary action and led to the Law of 1929, a legislation "directed primarily against the evangelical churches."[36]

As early as 1927, in an interview with an American labor delegation, Stalin declared:

The Party cannot be neutral towards the bearers of religious prejudices. . . . Have we suppressed the reactionary clergy? Yes, we have. The unfortunate thing is that it has not been completely liquidated. Anti-

---

[32] Kolarz, *Religion* . . . , p. 302.
[33] Aleksandr P. Kurantov (ed.), *Znanie i vera v boga* (Moskva: Izdatel'stvo "Znanie," 1960), p. 128.
[34] Blumit, *op. cit.*, p. 12.
[35] Hewlett Johnson, *op cit.*, p. 122.
[36] Rushbrooke, *op. cit.*, p. 13.

religious propaganda is a means by which the complete liquidation of the reactionary clergy must be brought about.[37]

Before the evangelical Bible schools were forced to close and prior to the suspension of all religious publications estimates of the evangelicals' numerical strength during the twenties range from 500,000[38] to 4,000,000.[39] Perhaps the most reasonable total for the 1928 membership is 2,200,000, derived by comparing the statistics printed in *Bratskii vestnik*[40] with the Soviet estimate of a decimation of 78 per cent of the evangelicals since 1928.[41]

---

[37] Joseph Stalin, *Leninism*, Vol. I (Moscow: Cooperative Publishing Society of Foreign Workers in the USSR), p. 387.

[38] F. Putintsev, *op. cit.*, p. 449.

[39] Quaker Report, *Meeting the Russians* (Philadelphia: American Friends Service Committee, 1956), p 69.

[40] "Celebration of the 90th Year Jubilee of the Russian Evangelical-Baptist Movement," *Bv*, No. 1, 1958, p. 29.

[41] A. Klibanov, "About Religious Sectarianism," *Nauka i religiia*, No. 4 (Moskva: 1961), p. 75.

7

The Terrible Thirties

i. The Kulaks and Collectivization

At the same time that the churches were denied legal existence the first Five Year Plan was adopted by the Sixteenth Party Conference with staggering objectives both in industrialization and in the collectivization of agriculture. The plan was to convert the nation's labor force, both urban and rural, into workers of state-controlled projects.

The peasantry was to be allied with the proletariat by means of the collectivization of agriculture. The temporary reversion to capitalism under the New Economic Policy (1921-1928) enabled the Communist regime to regain enough strength to launch a "Second Revolution"—the forced collectivization of agriculture.

The *kulaks* were the greatest foes standing between the Soviet regime and success. In Lenin's *The Agrarian Question* (1908) he made his analysis of the peasantry by dividing them into three classes: the *kulak* or rich peasant; the *sredniak* or middle peasant, who farmed his own land in a small way; and the *bedniak* or poor peasant, who owned nothing.

The *kulak* has been defined in various ways; the earliest connotation applied to a grasping and profiteering peasant who loaned money, goods or implements to his pooorer neighbors at high interest rates.[1] A *kulak* rented land,

---

[1] L. E. Hubbard, *The Economics of Soviet Agriculture* (London: Macmillan and Co., 1939), pp. 307, 308.

hired labor, possessed a mill or other home industry, and engaged in trade or usury.[2] The Communists asserted that the *kulaks* were "the most brutal, callous and savage exploiters . . ."[3]

As late as 1929 the value of production of a *kulak* family averaged $700 a year, yet he was considered a "capitalist" in his village.[4] Still another researcher suggested that the

> . . . kulak was a kulak because he was more intelligent and enterprising and a better business man than the average peasant, and no doubt he generally made a good bargain for himself.[5]

The Communist Party transferred its policy from one of restricting the "exploiting" tendencies of the *kulaks* to one of the "liquidation of the kulaks as a class."[6] The Soviet agronomist, V. A. Karpinsky, maintained that the *kulaks* were hostile to the collective farms (kolkhozes) from the very beginning and agitated against them. Pressured by the alternative of being subjected to ruthless liquidation as a class, the *kulaks* were reportedly charged with treacherously murdering people active in the organization of collective farms. They

> . . . set fire to the grain filled barns of the kolkhozes, damaged their tractors, harmed and poisoned the kolkhoz cattle.[7]

---

2 "Russia's Agrarian Problem," *Foreign Policy Association Information Service* Vol VI, No. 10, (New York: American Russian Institute, 1930), p. 191.

3 *History of the Communist Party of the Soviet Union* (Moscow: Foreign Languages Publishing House, 1960), p. 290.

4 "Russia's Agrarian Problem," *Foreign Policy* . . . , *op. cit.*, pp. 190, 191.

5 Hubbard, *op. cit*, p. 92.

6 K. N. Abrikosov (ed.), *Angliiskaia khrestomatiia po sel'skomu khoziaistvu* (Leningrad: Tsentrizdat, 1930), pp. 18, 19.

7 V. A. Karpinsky, *What Are Collective Farms?* (London: Lindsay Drummond Ltd., 1944), pp. 21, 22.

The Soviets, who admitted that the *kulaks* had grown one-fifth of the country's grain for marketing, indicted them with the charge of refusing to sell to the State (in the crop-failure year of 1929) at prices fixed by the Soviet Government.[8] They

> ... terrorized the middle peasants who sold grain surpluses ... tried in every way to weaken and undermine the building of collective farms.[9]

Considered the bitterest enemies of Socialism and the last mainstay of capitalist restoration in the Soviet Union, the *kulaks,* who comprised 5 per cent of all the peasant farms,

> ... were completely expropriated. These measures fully met the interest of Socialist reconstruction and insured the success of the collective farm movements and the consolidation of the collective farms.[10]

The poor peasants, supported by local Party members, were released across the countryside for wholesale pillaging and they forced the surrender of the *kulak's* cattle, implements, and machinery. The confiscated *kulak's* property totaled 15 per cent of the collective farmland.[11] Finally,

> ... probably not less than five million peasants, including families, were deported to Siberia and the Far North.[12]

---

[8] *History of the C.P* ... , *op. cit.,* p. 424.
[9] *Ibid.*
[10] *Ibid.,* p. 447.
[11] Hubbard, *op. cit.,* p. 102. (According to the People's Commissar of Agriculture in 1930.)
[12] *Ibid.,* p. 117

The Communist Party admitted overstepping its goal by

. . . applying the emergency measures intended for the kulaks to some of the middle peasants.[13]

The Party's excessive "errors" were labeled as the causative factors in instigating the peasants to slaughter their animals before entering a collective farm. In the economic year 1929-30 the number of cattle had decreased by 14.6 million, pigs by one-third, sheep and goats by more than one-fourth.[14]

By the end of February 1930 the Central Committee of the Communist Party had introduced amendments which would place collective farming on a voluntary basis. On March 2, 1930, the Soviet newspapers published J. V. Stalin's article *"Golovokruzhenie ot uspekhov"* ("Dizziness from Success").[15] Stalin placed the blame and reproach on zealous Party members who were tactless and impetuous in advancing "dekulakization" (purging the villages of the *kulaks*). The fundamental error was the use of repressive measures against the middle peasants too often identified with the *kulaks*.[16]

When the peasants who were forced into collectivization were granted permission to withdraw from the kolkhozes, the high mark of 60 per cent of all peasant households which had been collectivized dropped sharply to 23.4 per cent. However, since the peasants were unable to recover former holdings, most of them returned before the year's end. No *kulaks* were eligible for membership.[17]

---

[13] *History of the C.P. . . . , op. cit.,* p. 425.
[14] *Ibid.,* p 449.
[15] *Ibid.,* p. 450.
[16] "Russia's Agrarian Problems," *Foreign Policy . . . , loc. cit.,* p. 198.
[17] Hubbard, *op. cit ,* pp. 118, 119.

During the chaos of collectivization an untold number of evangelical believers were included as targets by the Party members who saw a *kulak* in any person better off than his neighbor, or any individual who resisted inclusion in a collective farm. Even in legislative practice "every one unwilling to join was declared a kulak."[18]

Soviet accusations fell upon church and sectarian organizations, declaring them to be the staunch allies of the *kulaks,* throwing their entire weight and means in order to support these "enemies" of the Party. Their

> . . . counterrevolutionary activities assumed the nature of a direct attack against the kolkhoz, against Socialism.[19]

Soviet writer B. Tikhomirov claimed that despite the "poor-middle" hue of the Baptist laymen, at the head of their churches stood former traders, *kulaks,* and merchants. He placed the strength of the *kulaks* in the Ukraine (the stronghold of evangelicals) at 10 per cent of the farmsteads. Tikhomirov saw in the believer's collectives a strategic organization wherein the *kulaks* ruled.[20]

Another Soviet source claimed that a majority of farmhands (batraks) and the poor peasants

> . . . united in the struggle to decisively liquidate the kulak power in the Mennonite colonies.[21]

In the losing struggle, the Mennonites suffered greatly,

---

[18] Naum Jasny, *The Socialized Agriculture of the USSR: Plans and Performances* (Stanford: Stanford University Press, 1949), p. 307.

[19] S. Kogen (ed.), *Antireligioznyi sbornik* (Moskva: Moskovskii rabochi, 1940), p. 107.

[20] B. Tikhomirov, *Baptizm i ego politicheskaia rol'* (Moskva: Gosudarstvennoe izdatel'stvo, 1929), pp. 20, 59.

[21] Reinmarus and Friezen, *op. cit.,* p. 75.

being numbered among the more prosperous and inalterably religious. Their model 175 acre farms had been reduced to sixty-five, then thirty-five acres, and finally to "dekulakization." The

> . . . ruthless destruction of the Mennonite religious and cultural life was a part of the total program of dictatorship. . . . Many families were disrupted by exile and death, particularly among leaders as ministers and teachers.[22]

Also included among the worst sufferers were the Evangelical-Baptist groups in the rich agricultural regions.[23] Many industrious, sober, successful evangelical sectarians were driven from their farms and in some cases entire villages were surrounded and brutally attacked.

On March 14, 1930, commenting on the struggle in the kolkhoz movement, the Party openly admitted the administrative closing of churches without the agreement of the village majorities, and revealed that such action usually led to the strengthening of religious prejudices.[24]

Between 1929 and 1933 half of the livestock on which the country depended had been slaughtered as a direct consequence of collectivization. In the process, and the resultant famine of 1932-33, some five million peasants died. Other millions swelled the Siberian labor camps which, fed by mass additions from the Great Purges of 1934-38, made the NKVD "the largest single employer in the Soviet Union."[25]

---

[22] *Mennonite Encyclopedia, op. cit* p. 391.

[23] Paul B. Anderson, *People, Church and State in Modern Russia* (New York: The Macmillan Company, 1944). p. 112.

[24] *Kommunisticheskaia partiia i sovetskoe pravitel'stvo o religii i tserkvi* (Moskva: Politicheskoi literatury, 1961), p. 78.

[25] Donald W. Treadgold, *20th Century Russia* (Chicago: Rand McNally and Company, 1964), p. 289.

ii. Voronaev's Reported Apostasy

During these dark years, every religious faith suffered under severe and hostile restrictions. The atheists declared that the success of the building of socialism in the thirties was accompanied by a mass exodus of believers from religion.[26] Ivan Voronaev, the leading Pentecostalist, was charged with forsaking his denomination, and in 1930, he was supposed to have written the following:

> I decided to give up the religious ministry, to renounce all religious propaganda, to unshackle myself from the name of an evangelical preacher and presbyter, and to be occupied with physical labor, helping the working class in its energetic building of socialism. . . . I greatly regret and blame myself for not beginning to see it sooner.[27]

The Soviet author also indicated in his narrative that the leaders of the Pentecostals elaborately hid the fact of Voronaev's apostasy from the rank and file of the believers. Another account of his renunciation of religion, both of which were published thirty years after its alleged occurrence, included a photocopy of his handwritten statement of apostasy. These two accounts, although similar, are by no means identical confessions; yet each purportedly quoted his disavowal of faith. Voronaev is described as joyfully reading daily accounts of the progress of socialism in Moscow's *Pravda* and *Izvestiia*.[28]

Contrary to this account, is the testimony of Mrs. Katherine Voronaev, the wife of Ivan Voronaev. Through the persistent negotiations of her son Paul with Washington officials, and his direct appeal to President Eisenhower,

---

[26] *Kratkii nauchno-ateisticheskii slovar'*, *op. cit.*, p. 469.
[27] G. M. Livshits, *op. cit.*, pp. 135, 136.
[28] *Nauka i religiia*, No. 5 (Moskva, 1960), p. 28.

she was able to receive permission to leave the Soviet Union. On July 18, 1960, she arrived in New York City.[29] She recounted the arrest of her husband in 1930 and of her detention in an Odessa jail for two years before being shipped to Karaganda. Her persistent request to join her husband was finally granted, and from 1933-35, the two were together in a labor camp in Siberia. Exiled believers sought out Voronaev and he ministered to them. Released in 1935, the Voronaevs made their way to Kaluga, south of Moscow, and both preached among the Baptists in 1935 and 1936, where their message was received by some and rejected by others. They were rearrested on October 6, 1936 by the NKVD and placed in the Kaluga jail. On December 5, 1936, Ivan Voronaev was removed to the Peter-Paul fortress in distant Siberia, while Mrs. Voronaev was later sent to Alma-Ata where she was able to gain employment. The last word received from Voronaev reached his son's tutor in Odessa, in the beginning of 1937.[30] Aleksander Karev, editor of *Bratskii vestnik,* shared his belief with me that Voronaev died in exile. Ever clinging to the hope that her husband was yet alive, Katherine Voronaev died in 1965, at the age of seventy-eight. There is no doubt that had Ivan Voronaev apostatized as reported in 1930, instead of imprisonment a heavy schedule of personal lectures and a stream of his articles would have been propagated in order to demoralize many members of the Christians of Evangelical Faith. A. A. Osipov, an Orthodox theologian who apostatized in 1959, has been used in this manner. Kolarz reported that there was

. . . no evidence of Pentecostal activities in the thirties but it is certain that many congregations built up by

[29] Ruth Demetrus, "Back from Siberia," *The Pentecostal Evangel,* November 27, 1960, No. 2429, p. 4.

[30] Taped interview by Rev. Paul Demetrus with Mrs. Katherine Voronaev, May 1964.

Voronaev's evangelistic fervor continued to exist. The Pentecostal movement in the Soviet Union was strengthened in 1939 when a number of small but very active Pentecostal groups of Eastern Poland came under Soviet rule.[31]

iii. Cessation of the Baptist Union Headquarters

In William Fletcher's doctoral study on the survival of Orthodoxy between 1927 and 1943, he suggested that Soviet data on the churches are not always accurate, by admission of B. Kandidov. Many of the parishes

. . . appear to have held illegal services quite openly in "closed" churches. Some of the churches listed as closed were holding services twice a week, and many active churches were not registered at all.[32]

In this unpredictable milieu the Evangelical Christians and the Baptists managed to conduct a joint conference in Moscow in 1931 to discuss the system of the appointment of the overseers of the united churches. The delegates agreed to grant increased responsibility and authority to these presbyters who were tested and tried in the ministry and who could provide leadership in civic as well as spiritual matters, for good rapport with the government was important. Such leaders were to have the power to make decisions without "wasting the time and energy on interminable seasons of debate" such as constantly occurred during the earlier united councils. This system was incorporated because it was "expedient and useful for the times" in which they lived. Appointments were to be

[31] Walter Kolarz, *Religion in the Soviet Union* (New York: St. Martin's Press, 1962), p. 332.

[32] William Catherwood Fletcher, "The Russian Orthodox Church in the USSR, 1927–1943" (unpublished Ph.D. dissertation, University of Southern California, 1964), pp. 190–191.

effective on a territorial and republic scale. This decision was later endorsed at the merger of 1944.[33] In this manner, normal democratic procedures were dismissed and the way was paved for greater centralization of power, with the appointments of the senior presbyters emanating from the top presidium members of the Protestant merger.

Bratskii vestnik withheld the reason for the cessation of the activity of the Baptist Union in 1935, when, according to pastor Orlov, the majority of the members of this union transferred to the Evangelical Christian Union.[34] The Baptist Church in Moscow could not retain its house of worship in 1936, whereas the Moscow community of the Evangelical Christians never missed a service throughout its years of existence in Moscow, assembling in a former Reformed Church building.[35] It is possible that the Soviet Government, refusing to permit two separate headquarters among the closely identified evangelicals, favored the Evangelical Christians as the more urbanized, adaptable, and less provincially rigid of the two.

The following account is given in *Nauka i religiia* ("Science and Religion," the official anti-religious monthly of the Soviet Union) :

In the 1930's, the fall of the sects continued. The one-time large-scale, rigid centralization of the Baptists crumbled into many small, weakly-related societies. They naturally united with the societies of the Evangelicals and with groups of Pentecostals.[36]

Meanwhile, the anti-religious forces anticipated that religion would perish from the minds of millions with greater rapidity and thoroughness. On June 9, 1935,

---

[33] *Bv*, No. 1, 1945, pp. 35, 36.
[34] *Ibid.*, p. 15.
[35] *Bv*, No. 3, 1957, p. 64.
[36] A. Klibanov, "About Religious Sectarianism," *Nauka i religiia*, No. 4 (Moskva: 1961), p. 78.

Emelian Iaroslavski stated that not less than fifty million persons, and perhaps more, had cut themselves off from religion. Despite the large number, out of a total population of 168 million, 118 million yet remained under the influence of religion.[37]

At the height of the mass purge, a national census was taken in 1937 to celebrate the twentieth anniversary of the revolution. Of the fourteen questions listed, the ninth queried, "Are you or are you not a believer?" in order to ascertain the position of the individual concerning faith in God. Leopold L. S. Braun, an American Roman Catholic priest in Moscow under the Brest-Litovsk Agreement, personally answered the long census blank and later learned that 70 per cent of the population dared to declare themselves as believers. A large number refused to answer the question for fear of reprisals. After eight months of rechecking, in order to avoid all possibility of error, official statements declared the census null and void. The discomfiture of the Party was great, for the optimism of the atheists had been trumpeted in many editorials.[38] Conspicuous by its omission in the 1939 census was the question relating to religious faith.

In contrast to the antireligious approach within the Soviet Union, Hitler meanwhile was patronizing the Russian Orthodox faithful in Germany, helping to repair nineteen churches.[39]

At the 1939 Baptist World Congress which convened in Atlanta, Georgia, a special resolution was adopted, appealing to the Soviet Government to grant believers religious freedom, including the liberty of private and public wor-

[37] Paul B. Anderson, *Russia's Religious Future* (London: Lutterworth Press, 1935), pp. 4, 5.

[38] Leopold L. S. Braun, *Religion in Russia* (Paterson: St. Anthony Guild Press, 1959), pp. 37–39.

[39] Robert Magidoff, *The Kremlin vs. the People* (New York: Doubleday and Co., 1953), p. 69.

ship, of preaching and teaching.[40] Compared with the
3,219 Evangelical congregations still functioning in 1929,
only 1,000 remained active in 1940.[41]

iv. The New Religious Policy

Faced with the increased threat of the Third Reich, the
Soviet Government found it expedient to introduce a New
Religious Policy, an about-face inaugurated in the critical
year 1939, when merely offending the religious sentiment
of the believers was to be avoided. Oleshchuk, aide to
Iaroslavski of the League of Militant Godless, humbly
attested that

> Our League has committed many blunders in regard to
> Christianity . . . Marxist atheists must realize that the
> church has not always been a harmful influence.[42]

The Great Patriotic War prompted the Communist
Party to channel the nation's religious forces to serve general Communist policies. Concessions granted to religious
groups were matters of expediency and not of law. In
September 1941, three months after the German invasion
of Russian soil, the publications *Bezbozhnik,* the newspaper of the League of the Militant Godless, and *Antireligioznik,* the League's monthly organ, were discontinued. Maintaining that these publications were not
managed by them but by a special agency, the Soviet Government disclaimed its antireligious propaganda activity.
Thus, without admitting any change in government policy
toward the churches, the despised antireligious movement

---

[40] J. H. Rushbrooke (ed.), *Sixth Baptist World Congress* (Atlanta: Baptist World Alliance, 1939), p. 15.
[41] Serge Bolshakoff, *op. cit.,* p. 4.
[42] *Antireligioznik,* January 5, 1942.

could be terminated conveniently. By accepting this questionable logic Russian church leaders voiced their rationalization in declaring that there had been no persecution by the Soviet Government. To illustrate, the Russian Orthodox Church published 50,000 copies of a book entitled *The Truth About Religion in Russia,* in an attempt to prove that there never was any persecution of religion as such by the government. Understandably, the book was unavailable to the Soviet public but Dean Hewlett Johnson received 500 copies of the English translation. The Patriarchate insisted that after the October revolution, church workers were judged not for their religious activities, but for anti-Soviet hostilities which amounted to counterrevolution. The book did manage, however, to acknowledge the ideology of the Communist Party as anti-religious ideology. Warnings of Hitler's hypocrisy regarding his "defense of Christianity" were outlined, reminding the readers that Hitler's race theory openly taught that the Slavic race, including Ukrainians and Belorussians, was the lowest race, destined to serve as work beasts.[43]

Hitler's "Crusade" in the Soviet Union temporarily proclaimed liberation from atheistic oppression. Notably in the Ukraine, the invading armies were received with "bread and salt" as liberators. On the first Sunday after the Nazi occupation, mass meetings were held in the public squares solemnly proclaiming freedom of worship without molestation, under the protection of the Third Reich. All church property confiscated by the Soviets was returned at first to its rightful owners. The German quartermaster had even prepared packages of perfume and silk stockings for the wives of Russian priests. From the refurnished Smolensk Cathedral, a service was broadcast through the portable German army Telefunken transmitters.[44]

---

[43] *Pravda o religii v Rossii* (Moskva: Moscow Patriarchate, 1942), pp. 26, 108, 109.
[44] Braun, *loc cit.,* pp. 51–53.

Contrary to the hopes of the people in the liberated Soviet areas, the Germans failed to abolish the collective farm system. Instead, early in 1942, Nazi demands and brutality began to turn many civilians into active partisans who defended the homeland against the hated invaders.

The momentum toward unity among the Evangelical Christians and the Baptists was greatly accelerated during the Nazi invasion. Joint services of both groups in Moscow, Leningrad, and Novosibirsk were already in practice prior to the war.[45] Then in May of 1942, M. I. Goliaev and N. A. Levindanto, as representatives of the Baptist Union, appealed to the legally existent Union of Evangelical Christians to assume the guardianship and care of the Baptist societies, even as it served its own Union. This proposal was met with great joy and the unofficial united effort commenced.[46] That month they jointly appealed to the world to rally behind the Soviet Union in the struggle against Fascism.

Common patriotic activities united the believers more closely in spiritual relations. During the War, many evangelicals served with distinction, some as officers, decorated with medals and orders. More than 300 members of the Moscow church alone were killed in action. I. I. Zhidkov, first president of AUCECB, lost three sons in the war. Many civilian believers built trenches, anti-tank and anti-aircraft defenses. In 1943, the evangelicals raised 400,000 rubles for a medical plane called the "Good Samaritan."[47] Multiplied homes of believers were opened for the adoption of war orphans and all evangelical churches were requested to contribute monthly offerings through the local State Bank for this specific need. Strict accounting of records was kept as the amount and receipt number were required from the Moscow church headquarters.

---

[45] *Bv.*, No. 1, 1945, p. 31.
[46] *Ibid.*, p. 17.
[47] *Ibid.*, p. 18.

A quarter of a million war orphans already have been adopted, many of them into the homes of believers as a result of the direct appeal of their churches.[48]

Thousands of present-day evangelical members probably have emerged as a result of this response. This project actually bypassed the restrictions of the Law of 1929 which prohibited church activity in any area not specifically connected with the performance of the cult.

---

[48] W. H. Melish, *Religion Today in the U.S.S.R.* (New York: The National Council of American-Soviet Friendship, 1945), p. 12.

8

The Merger Decade

i. Mennonite Evacuations

It was the intention of the Soviet Government to deport the entire German-speaking population, including the Mennonites. However, due to the rapid advance of the German army, only twenty-one of the fifty-eight Mennonite villages of the Molochna region could be evacuated. In September and October of 1943, there were 35,000 Mennonites in the Khortitsa and Molochna areas who forsook their homes to accompany the retreating Germans.

Many old and sick people and children perished on the way, others were overtaken by the advancing Soviet armies and deported to Siberia. . . . Of the survivors 8,000 were absorbed by Canada and 5,000 by Paraguay.[1]

In two evacuations, first eastward, then westward, all the Mennonites disappeared from the Ukraine. Those who remained in the Soviet Union were scattered over the vast areas of Siberia and Central Asia, with Karaganda becoming one of the largest new Mennonite centers. In 1956, two visiting American Mennonite leaders reported a total population of close to 20,000 in about 125 Mennonite villages.[2] These Mennonites were not officially registered as religious groups, and in certain localities, when not worshipping independently, their services have been held

---

[1] Walter Kolarz, *Religion* . . . , p. 281.
[2] *Ibid.*, p. 282.

in conjunction with Baptist churches.[3] *Bratskii vestnik* omitted any mention of the Mennonites during the merger years of 1944 and 1945.

ii. The Exile of Zhidkov, Successor of Prokhanov

Under the German occupation, the Nazi authorities pressured the Pentecostal organizations in the Ukraine and Belorussia to amalgamate with the Baptists and the Evangelical Christians.[4] From this information, Kolarz concluded that the Soviets had accepted and continued this phase of the Nazi religious policy. However, in 1940, prior to the German invasion there was some evidence that the Soviet Government had already attempted to enlist all evangelicals into a single Union. A Soviet representative from Moscow was commissioned to secure information from the evangelical pastors in East Poland, the segment already absorbed by the Soviet Union. He attended their meetings, accumulating information and addresses. Following his return to Moscow he sent the pastors questionnaires encouraging membership in a nonexistent Russian Evangelical Union, whose president bore a name completely unknown to the evangelical pastors. Most of the questionnaires were burned instead of returned. From this report it was assumed that the Soviet Government, convinced that a centralized, easily observed evangelical union would necessitate the selection of a well-known leader who would be both acceptable and able to command respect, released I. I. Zhidkov from exile shortly before the 1944 merger.[5] During my visit to Poland in

---

[3] Smith, *op. cit.,* p. 526.

[4] Gutsche, *Westliche Quellen* . . . , p. 120 cited by Kolarz, *loc. cit.,* p. 332.

[5] Interview with a Slavic Baptist minister (name withheld) , 1964. Substantiated by an executive from the United Evangelical Church, Warsaw, Poland.

1959 the exile of Zhidkov was mentioned by several executive ministers of the United Evangelical Church. The whereabouts of Zhidkov from 1938 to 1943 is confusing, whereas M. A. Orlov, the only top executive not exiled, presided over the Union of Evangelical Christians until the merger of 1944. At this point, the *Bratskii vestnik* accounts are contradictory. It was Zhidkov who succeeded Ivan Prokhanov, the founder of the All-Union Council of Evangelical Christians, when it was obvious that Prokhanov could not reenter the Soviet Union in 1928 without being arrested. Two reports declared that Zhidkov remained its president uninterruptedly until 1944.[6]

With greater detail and clarity four separate accounts in *Bratskii vestnik* instead listed Orlov as the president and the key person engaged in convening the Council of 1944.[7] No intimation of the exile of Zhidkov had been either published or admitted in interviews with Russian pastors.

Preceding the official merger of 1944, the Moscow church headquarters maintained regular correspondence with both the Baptists and the Evangelical Christians. During the terrible days of the war a spontaneous unity was born among the well-known leaders of both unions. In many locales, before any official organizational aid was rendered by elder presbyters, the lay members had already united, dropping denominational barriers in order to evangelize more effectively.[8] There was an irresistible striving, an on-going process toward full unity which was difficult to restrain.[9]

---

[6] *Bv*, No. 2, 1945, p. 39 and Nos. 5–6, 1960, p. 45.

[7] *Bv*, No. 5, 1947, pp. 68, 69; No. 3, 1947, p. 22; No. 6, 1957, p. 49; No. 3, 1961, pp. 64–74.

[8] *Ibid.*, No. 1, 1945, p. 18.

[9] *Ibid.*, No. 4, 1957, p. 30.

iii. The Historic Merger of 1944

Finally on October 26-29, 1944, the historic Council met in Moscow, attended by forty-five delegates, including seven women. Each delegate's authorization was verified; twenty-one were Muscovites, six arrived from Kiev, and the balance represented believers in thirteen other cities, from Leningrad to Odessa, and from L'vov to Novosibirsk. In defense of the relatively small Council its validity was based upon three premises. First, it was alleged that the delegates gathered in response to the basic command and prayer of the Lord Jesus Christ "That they all may be one" (Jn. 17:21). Second, the Council was the natural result of the 1884 and 1920 conferences that convened in order to unite the two groups. Finally, the oldest and most experienced leaders of the two denominations were in attendance. Twelve of the preachers had been delegates in the important conference of 1920, and several had ministered to their people for over forty years.[10]

Harmony and unity prevailed throughout the sessions. On October 28, eight leading men from both unions were unanimously elected to the Presidium and M. A. Orlov was named president. During the recess, assignments of portfolios were defined among the Presidium members, which later received unanimous ratification by the Council. Addressing the delegates after the recess, M. A. Orlov surprised them by announcing his resignation from the presidency. His explanation for this action was that his responsibility of pastoring the large Moscow church and the added duties as elder presbyter of the Moscow area were already too burdensome. He presented I. I. Zhidkov as the first president of the All-Union Council of Evangelical Christians and Baptists, possibly the Soviet Government's choice. Orlov retained the post of vice-president along with M. I. Goliaev; A. V. Karev was appointed sec-

---

[10] *Bv*, No. 2, 1945, pp. 18, 19.

retary, and **P. I.** Malin became the treasurer. The non-resident executive members were A. L. Andreev, F. G. Patkovskii, and N. A. Levindanto.[11] The Council received congratulatory messages from the Baptist World Alliance and the All-American Union of Russian Evangelical Christians. On November 10, 1944, *Tass* published the following comment in *Izvestiia*:

> In the creation of the new All-Union Council of Evangelical Christians and Baptists the most prominent and popular leaders of the Evangelical Christians and Baptists emerged.[12]

Zhidkov's name headed the published list of executive officers. *Bratskii vestnik* referred to the confirmation of the Soviet newspaper as a further argument for the validity of the AUCECB,[13] but this may have erased the three favorable premises in the minds of many believers who distrusted the atheist government.

Commenting on the unanimous passage of the joint resolution on the merger, Aleksandr Karev stated,

> Having buried into oblivion all the former differences of opinion, out of two unions one is now created . . .[14]

Many delegates wept for joy as they embraced each other. The word "and" (Evangelical Christians *and* Baptists) in the denominational name was considered necessary during the transitional period, but this was replaced subsequently by the hyphenated Evangelical Christians-Baptists. Two rods in one hand were replaced on the Union seal by the encircled words "One Lord, one faith, on baptism."

---

11 *Ibid.*, No. 1, 1945, p. 37.
12 *Bv*, No. 2, 1945, p. 20.
13 *Ibid.*
14 *Bv*, No. 1, 1945, p. 33.

iv. Bases of the Merger

Compromises were necessary on the part of both unions in order to solve the issues that had divided the two denominations for six decades. The solutions (especially numbers nine and ten) were incorporated in the following "Ten Points of Agreement":

1. From two unions, the Union of Evangelical Christians and the Union of Baptists, across the entire territory of the USSR one union is formed, the Union of Evangelical Christians and Baptists.

2. The executive organ of the Union of Evangelical Christians and Baptists is the All-Union Council of Evangelical Christians and Baptists (AUCEC and B).

3. From within the membership of the AUCEC and B, which constitutes the Presidium, the president, two vice-presidents, a secretary and a treasurer are elected.

4. The AUCEC and B has its seal and inscription: "All-Union Council of Evangelical Christians and Baptists" and in the circle the words "One Lord, one faith, one baptism."

5. The Evangelical Christians and the Baptists, having existed separately before the merger of the unions, henceforth merge into a single community. Communities that existed separately as Evangelical Christians or as Baptists, will henceforth enter into one Union.

6. Each community, upon entering the Union of Evangelical Christians and Baptists, will bear the name of Community of Evangelical Christians and Baptists.

7. All communities of Evangelical Christians and Baptists, insofar as possible, must have ordained presby-

ters and deacons, in accordance with the Word of God: Titus 1:5; Acts 6:1-6; and I Timothy 3:1.

8. In each community, baptisms, the breaking of bread, and weddings are conducted by ordained presbyters. However, in the absence of such, these rites may be performed also by non-ordained members of the community, but only by commission of the church.

9. A baptism and wedding, performed both with the laying on of hands or without the imposition of hands on the baptized and the wedded, have identical validity. However, for the attainment of full unity in the practise of the church, it is recommended that a baptism and wedding be conducted with the imposition of hands, viewing this as a type of sacred prayer of blessing. If there be more than two persons for baptism, henceforth instead of the laying on of hands, the hands will be extended over the baptized as prayer is pronounced.

10. The Lord's Supper, or the breaking of bread, may be served both by breaking the bread in many minute portions or by breaking the bread in two, three, or several large portions. The bread and wine are received by the members in a standing position, which expresses our reverence before the commandment of the breaking of bread.[15]

No stated reason was given by the Soviet Government for its recognition and approval of the AUCECB. As the war progressed Stalin acknowledged the loyalty and practical aid rendered by the believers in the Soviet Union. A friendly posture toward religion also helped to improve public relations in the western world. As early as September 27, 1941, "Russian War Relief" held a successful rally in Madison Square Garden in its drive for one million dollars, the first of a long series of "Help Russia—

---

15 *Bv*, No. 1, 1945, pp. 33, 34.

Hasten Victory" drives. Shipments worth $25,064,651 were sent out by March 31, 1943, indicating the good will of America on a grass roots level.[16] The Southern Baptist Convention overfulfilled its project by dispatching household kits to Soviet families. Over 200,000 kits were packed in this single gesture of friendly concern.[17]

Soviet writer G. Spasov, treating religion in the Soviet Union, declared that all the religious societies of the USSR

> . . . acted in complete unanimity with all the Soviet people. . . . During the war, many representatives of the different religions received personal messages of gratitude from J. V. Stalin, for the assistance rendered to the Soviet Army.[18]

v. Who Initiated the Merger?

Whereas the Evangelical Christians and the Baptists would probably have merged officially early in the war, the consummation was impossible without government approval. The initiative appears to have come from the Soviet Government and not the evangelicals in that four months prior to the historic merger the Communist regime created the Council for the Affairs of Religious Cults (CARC) on June 30, 1944. The CARC included KGB agents and was directly responsible to the Council of the People's Commissars of the USSR, dealing only with recognized, approved religious societies other than the Russian Orthodox Church which received its own council.[19]

---

[16] Edward C. Carter, "Russian War Relief," *Slavonic and East European Review*, XXII (London: University of London, August, 1944) , pp. 61–73.

[17] Letter from W. O. Lewis (August 10, 1944) cited in *Bv,* No. 1, 1945, p. 23.

[18] G. Spasov, *Freedom of Religion in the USSR* (Washington, D.C.: The Soviet Embassy, 1951) , pp. 17–19.

[19] The Council for the Affairs of the Russian Orthodox Church was created on October 8, 1943, exclusively for the Orthodox.

The Soviets realized the value of loyal support from religious groups during the New Religious Policy of the war years and preferred to deal with united sectarian bodies under leaders who promised to be cooperative and compatible with the regime. Denominational centralization in Moscow was feasible and desirable since CARC, as the liaison body, would maintain contact with various religious headquarters in order to best observe the activities of the religious sects down to the local level.

The declared function of the Council for the Affairs of Religious Cults was to see that the correct practice of the laws and decrees directed for the constant realization of the principle of the separation of the church and state, and of the school from the church, was carried out. The new Council was to assist the religious unions in the solution of problems which the unions placed before the various state institutions.[20]

Immediately after the merger and formation of the All-Union Council of Evangelical Christians and Baptists its Moscow headquarters communicated with thousands of churches and presbyters (pastors), requiring them to complete the local mergers while allowing the churches no choice other than non-recognition and closure. Further, the AUCECB requested detailed monthly reports from each member church, it issued official credentials to each member pastor, and together with the CARC carried out the registration of each church community willing to comply with the rules of the AUCECB. Doubtless the Soviet Government found such efficiency of church administration a welcome apparatus in maintaining more complete and accurate records for its files on the sectarians.

Complete harmony and unanimity in every vote cast during the merger sessions of October 1944 suggested less the free democratic actions of individualistic Protestant

---

[20] "Sovet po delam religioznikh kul'tov," *Bolshaia sovetskaia entsiklopediia* (Moskva: 1949), pp. 522, 523.

believers than the obligation of forty-five pressured delegates to emerge with positive plans for a government-approved working union of evangelicals.

The churches in the Soviet Union did not enjoy the rights of a legal entity since they could not own anything or enter into a contract in their own name. The registration of believers in a "religious association" enabled them to obtain a license for existence, which could be granted or denied at the discretion of the local Soviet. At least twenty parishioners had to sign the contract and assume full personal liability for the maintenance of the house of prayer and the objects needed for religious services. The status of the churches remained unchanged under the policy of the Soviet Government.[21] Any tolerance in attitude by the government was a compromise it found to be expedient, but no statutory provisions had been repealed.[22] Whatever the concessions made by the Soviet Government, no laws were promulgated to give them the authority of law, nor would any laws be necessary to cancel the concessions.[23]

From the Soviet Embassy in Washington G. Spasov asserted that the Council for the Affairs of Religious Cults did not interfere with the internal life of religious societies, nor with the canonical and dogmatic aspects of their activities.[24] It became apparent that as the liaison council members became more involved in various aspects of church administration, they disregarded the Soviet Constitution's principle of the separation of the church and state. However, in the honeymoon year of 1945, Orlov

---

[21] Vladimir Gsovski (ed.)   *Church and State Behind the Iron Curtain* (New York: Frederick A. Praeger, 1955), xviii, xix.

[22] Casimir C. Gecys, "The Soviet Bill of Rights" (unpublished Ph.D. dissertation, Dept. of Political Philosophy, Fordham University, 1952), p. 133.

[23] Alex Inkeles and Kent Geiger, *Soviet Society* (Boston: Houghton Mifflin Company, 1961), p. 417.

[24] Spasov, *loc. cit.,* p. 24.

expressed his pleasure in the new relationship of AUCECB to CARC, acknowledging that the Council

> ... has its local representatives assigned to the provincial Soviets, who work out solutions to the problems of our congregations and are extremely attentive to our needs. This same Council helped us to solve the complex problem of convening our current All-Union Council under wartime conditions, for which we not only heartily thank our Lord, but the Soviet Government also.[25]

I. V. Polianski, president of the CARC, flattered I. I. Zhidkov with cordial greetings and a gift of an artistic antiquarian watch on his sixtieth birthday in September of 1945.[26]

Various reasons were suggested by the Soviets for the merger of the two Protestant unions. The *Atheist's Companion* declared that in the

> ... resulting victory of socialism in our country the roots of religion were essentially undermined, and a mass of workers began to leave the sects. With the aim of preserving the remnants of their communities, the Baptists proceeded to create a single organization with the Evangelists in 1944 to be better adapted at that time to the changing conditions . . .[27]

Six Quakers from America visited the Soviet Union in 1955 and reported that the number of Baptist and Evangelical Christians' congregations had decreased from the 1928 figure of 3,200 to less than 1,000 communities in 1940.[28] Garkavenko, a Soviet writer, saw in the decline a crisis for the Baptists:

---

[25] *Bv*, No. 1, 1945, pp. 21, 22.
[26] *Ibid.*, No. 3, 1945, p. 3.
[27] S. I. Kovalev (ed.), *Sputnik ateista* (Moskva: Gos. izd-vo polit lit-ry, 1959), p. 155.
[28] Quaker Report, *Meeting the Russians, op. cit.*, p. 69.

The Baptist Union, as *Bratskii vestnik* witnesses, almost completely discontinued its work by 1935. A large portion of believers broke entirely with religion; another part began to transfer to the Evangelicals, who were stronger, and at that time better adapted to the new conditions . . .[29]

The antireligious leaders described one of the reasons for the merger as an assumption by the sectarian leaders that their joint forces could translate their religion into practice more effectively.[30]

The evangelical believers who formed the All-Union Council of Evangelical Christians and Baptists had long ceased to defy the Soviet Government on matters pertaining to military conscription. They had refrained from speaking candidly and critically concerning economic and political problems since the nightmare of the collectivization of agriculture. Though apparently neutralized, the testimony of a consistent Christian life by any member of the legally recognized religious communities served to recruit new members among the agnostic, and even atheist neighbors. A refusal to merge in 1944 would have resulted in the burial instead of the birth of the AUCECB, the denial of the privileges of government recognition, the loss of the securement, building and rental of churches which would be open to the general public. Severely persecuted throughout the thirties, the Baptists and Evangelical Christians gladly accepted the opportunity to unite officially and exhibited a willingness to cooperate fully. However, faced with the constant possibility of losing the privileges gained at the merger, the Protestant administrators have found it increasingly difficult to resist the insidious Soviet pressures to compromise principles in the process of cooperative endeavors.

---

29 F. I. Garkavenko, *op. cit.,* p. 13.
30 *Kratkii . . . , op. cit.,* p. 196.

PART III

THE ADDITION OF THE PENTECOSTALISTS

9

The August Agreement Regarding
Tongues Speaking

i. The Non-Joiners

Feeding the Soviet appetite for the centralization of the evangelicals was the unexpected addition of the Christians of Evangelical Faith (Pentecostalists) to the AUCECB on August 24, 1945. This move was uncourted by the Baptists and Evangelical Christians and many of them were resentful. Long indoctrinated against the Pentecostal doctrines the registered members exhibited their bias against Pentecostal believers, stereotyping them as religious fanatics. Many were convinced that the new members would prove detrimental to the welfare of the union churches.

General Secretary Karev brought attention to the important similarities in the evangelical beliefs shared by the Pentecostalists concluding that

> . . . for the existing merger . . . only one thing remained —to resolve the question of the glossolalia, that is, unknown tongues. The question of the glossolalia was solved in a manner acceptable to both sides, and the triumphant act of unity was accomplished . . .[1]

Karev proudly proclaimed that such a union had not been attained in any other country. He was not ignorant of the problems that a working relationship between the

---

[1] *Bv*, No. 3, 1945, p. 7.

117

Baptists and the Pentecostalists involved when he re-marked,

> Of course the extremists among the Pentecostalists are unwilling to make a rapprochement with the Baptists, yes, and the Baptists do not aspire to unite with them, but the moderates in the Pentecostal church can be united with the Baptist church for the joint labor in God's great harvest field, as has been attained in the USSR.[2]

Soviet writer Kalugin revealed that a significant part of the Pentecostal believers accepted the conditions required for their membership in the Union, but

> . . . another part did not, and they exist independently, continuing to perpetrate their fanatical practices. In distinction, these Pentecostalists are not registered with the local government organs and their activities are prohibited in the territory of the USSR.[3]

Torbet, a Baptist historian, suggested that there were as many as 700,000 Baptists who did not join the Union merger. He based this on the assumption that between 1941 and 1947 the membership of the "United Baptists" declined from one million to 300,000.[4] The same statistics are mentioned by Dr. W. O. Lewis, the Secretary of the Baptist World Alliance.[5] However, the number of Baptists—and for that matter Evangelical Christians and Pentecostalists—who remained outside of the government-recognized AUCECB is difficult, if not impossible, to ascertain. These believers were not registered by CARC and for more than twenty years a significant number of them have remained without the aegis of registered religious com-

---

[2] *Bv*, No. 4, 1957, p. 35.
[3] Kalugin, *op. cit.*, p. 19.
[4] Torbet, *op. cit.*, p. 203.
[5] Bolshakoff, *op. cit.*, p. 122.

munities. *Bratskii vestnik* estimates of their numerical strength tended to be minimal. Conversely, Southern Baptist Louie D. Newton, while in Moscow shortly after World War II, learned of revival growth instead of decline.

> ... during the first half of this summer (1946) 30,000 newly converted souls have already been baptized, and an equal number will be baptized during the second half of this summer.[6]

So rapid was the increase in membership that a minimum probationary period of one year was instituted before new members could be received into the local communities of the Evangelical Christians-Baptists.[7] The 350,000 members of 1948, all of whom were over eighteen years of age and had been baptized by immersion, increased to 530,000 by 1958.[8] Despite all the difficulties encountered within and without the Union, the AUCECB was a practical example of evangelical ecumenicity.

> ... we can also be an example to other countries of the world. The divisions of contemporary Christianity are a great evil, to a powerful extent throttling the evangelization of the world. ... With the help of God, lifting the banner of unity of all the contemporary churches adhering to the Evangelical-Baptist principles, we would like to say ... follow our example.[9]

ii. The Pentecostal Merger and the August Agreement

Several leading Pentecostal representatives met with the AUCECB executives at the Moscow conference of August 19-27, 1945. It was held in a peaceful, fraternal atmosphere, as discussions of the problems ensued. Each group attempted to clarify its own point of view, yet at the same

---

[6] Louie D. Newton, *An American Churchman in the Soviet Union* (New York: American Russian Institute, 1946, p. 44.
[7] *Bv*, No. 1, 1947, p. 6.
[8] *Bv*, No. 1, 1958, p. 29.
[9] *Ibid.*, No. 3, 1945, p. 8.

time sincerely strove to understand the other. This hastened full acceptance and complete agreement. The Christians of Evangelical Faith signed the "August Agreement," thus bringing the Pentecostalists into the Union of Evangelical Christians and Baptists; and by doing so, their denominational entity was forfeited. Four well-known Pentecostal leaders signed the agreement as representatives of 25,000 Pentecostal believers who entered the Union churches, mostly in Belorussia and the Ukraine.

Representing Belorussia was I. K. Pan'ko, who attained non-residence executive status in the AUCECB, and his aide S. I. Vashkevich. Both men had been trained in the Danzig Bible Institute, a Pentecostal school under the direction of such highly esteemed men as Nicholas Nikoloff of Bulgaria and Donald Gee of England. The four Russian ministers, as the Pentecostal representatives in the Soviet Union, were the pioneers responsible for giving full consent to the "August Agreement." The twelve points of this document mutually agreed upon during the August Conference were:

1. The communities of the Christians of Evangelical Faith (CEF) unite with the communities of the Evangelical Christians and Baptists in one union.

2. The single union has its general executive center in Moscow, as well as its one treasury in the same office.

3. Representatives of the CEF are also included among the executive staff members in the center.

4. The spiritual workers of the CEF are to remain in their spiritual calling which they held before uniting with the Evangelical Christians and Baptists, that is, elder presbyters, presbyters, and deacons.

5. Both sides recognize that the fulness of power from on high, spoken of in Acts 1:8, may be manifested with a sign of other tongues as well as without this sign. (Acts 2:4; 8:17, 39; 10:46, 19:6).

6. Both sides recognize, on the basis of Holy Scriptures, that diverse tongues are one of the gifts of the Holy Spirit, not given to all, but to some (I Cor. 12:4-11). This is also corroborated by the words of verse thirty of this chapter. "Do all have the gifts of healing? Do all speak in tongues? Do all interpret?"

7. Both sides acknowledge that unknown tongues without interpretation is fruitless, concerning which the apostle Paul explicitly states, "If there be no interpreter, then keep silent in the church" (I Cor. 14:6-9, 28). Both sides uphold this as a rule given by God, through apostle Paul.

8. Considering the words of apostle Paul about the fruitlessness of unknown tongues in the absence of an interpreter, both sides agreed to abstain from unknown tongues in general meetings.

9. In conjunction with the operation of the Holy Spirit in the services, recognizing that there may be manifestations leading to the destruction of the decency and the decorum of the service (I Cor. 14:40), both sides agreed to provide an educational program against this type of manifestation, recalling that God is not a God of confusion, but of peace (I Cor. 14:33).

10. In view of the fact that the Evangelical Christians and the Baptists do not practice footwashing, the present Agreement recommends that the CEF conduct an educational work designed to achieve a common understanding with the Evangelical Christians and Baptists on this question, aiming toward unity and the uniformity of public worship.

11. Both sides are to utilize all means, so that among the Evangelical Christians and Baptists on the one hand, and the Christians of Evangelical Faith on the other, there will be established the most sincere fraternal and mutual relations for reciprocal joy and blessed joint labor.

12. Following the signing of the present Agreement, both parties will announce the event of unity to their communities and will call for a prayer of gratitude for the great and praiseworthy work of concord in our country by all Christians, born-again by faith.[10]

Antireligious accounts of this merger left no doubt as to the Soviets' opinion of independent Pentecostalists, Baptists and Evangelical Christians. For instance,

. . . the union with the Pentecostalists was completed after their repudiation of the so-called speaking in other tongues . . . which deranges the mind of a person. The most stagnant, fanatical elements from all three sects did not acknowledge this merger and they continue to exist independently.[11]

Two of the four signatory members, representatives of the Christians of Evangelical Faith, abandoned the AUCECB shortly after the August Agreement of 1945. A. I. Bidash, due to his dissatisfaction with the Union compromise, led in an exodus movement. S. I. Vashkevich, at the time of the arrest of Ivan Pan'ko, hastily emigrated to Poland in 1947, where he remains to this day a leading executive of the United Evangelical Church, an ecumenical union of five denominations. As secretary and aide to Pan'ko, Vashkevich would have shared certain exile.

Ivan Pan'ko, the assistant elder presbyter of all Belorussia, erred with the best of intentions by assisting several aspiring young preachers in securing Soviet credentials which granted them military exemption during World War II. Shortly after the hostilities ceased, some of these young men exposed themselves as opportunists, completely forsaking the ministry for secular pursuits. Pan'ko's wartime intercession, which shielded these young men from active service, was judged to be treasonable. He received

---

[10] "The August Agreement," *Bv*, No. 4, 1957, p. 36.
[11] *Kratkii slovar'*, p. 95.

a twenty-five year sentence and was exiled to Irkutsk, Siberia, in 1947.[12] Stalin's death made possible the halving of his sentence in the program of amnesty. The pardon may also have been granted because of Ivan Pan'ko's influence in inducing the independent Pentecostalists of Belorussia to join the AUCECB. When he assumed the position of presbyter of the Minsk Evangelical Christians-Baptists' community, large groups of Christians of Evangelical Faith were added to the Minsk church and to many communities in Belorussia.[13]

It was believed that more than 50 per cent of the members of the Christians of Evangelical Faith joined the Union of Evangelical Christians and Baptists shortly after the August Agreement of 1945. In areas such as the Ukraine and Belorussia, the percentage ran higher. D. I. Ponomarchuk, a minister who had worked with Pentecostal founder Ivan Voronaev, was instrumental in convincing many Pentecostal members to make the transition. Having ministered both as a Baptist and as an Evangelical Christians pastor before joining forces with Voronaev, Ponomarchuk was in a key position to state that he was

. . . convinced that the division of these three unions was devoid of substance, since all three did preach the same Word of God—that of one God, one faith, and one baptism. I led in the discussions of unity with all believers.[14]

He was elected a member of the AUCECB and received an appointment as the aide to A. L. Andreev, the elder presbyter over the entire Ukraine, with residence in Kiev. As Ponomarchuk traveled across the Ukraine, the Moldavian SSR, and elsewhere, members and entire churches of the Christians of Evangelical Faith followed his example and joined the merger Union. In his appeal to the

---

12 Interview with Rev. Maxim Maximovich, February 8, 1965.

13 "Reports from Locales," *Bv*, No. 1, 1959, p. 8.

14 D. I. Ponomarchuk, "On the Unity of the Children of God," *Bv*, Nos. 5–6, 1960, p. 74.

Pentecostalists, Ponomarchuk described this step to unity as one granting them full rights as equal members in the Union, an evangelical fellowship in which there were no stepsons, but all were the sons of God by faith in Christ. He assured them that the merger was not created for the purpose of upbraiding one another over personal convictions, but to invite God to purify all within the membership from the negative forces which could destroy the unity.[15] Those who did not respond to the invitation of Ponomarchuk, Pan'ko, and other Pentecostal leaders, to enter the Union of Evangelical Christians and Baptists were left without a government-recognized religious union and their activities in the USSR were prohibited.[16]

iii. The Entry of the Baltic Nations

In addition to the Pentecostal representatives present at the Council of August 19-29, 1945, denominational leaders of the Baptists and the Evangelical Christians from the Latvian, Estonian, and Lithuanian Soviet Socialist Republics participated. Beginning with the treaty stage of September and October of 1939 and followed by trade agreements, these brave but helpless little nations finally found themselves under Soviet military control which extended to the Baltic nations after the ultimatums of June 1940. Accusing the three small countries of anti-Soviet actions, the USSR demanded the addition of Soviet troops in these nations as Hitler was occupied with the vast conquest of Western Europe. The Baltic states were forced to become Soviet protectorates and were expected to form governments friendly to the USSR. In August 1940, the 5,400,000 citizens of the three Baltic states were granted their "requests" to be incorporated into the USSR as Union Republics.[17]

---

[15] *Ibid.*, p. 75.

[16] Kalugin, *op. cit.*, p. 19.

[17] Basil Dmytryshyn, *USSR: A Concise History* (New York: Charles Scribner's Sons, 1965), pp. 211–213.

Meanwhile in Latvia, the Baptist seminary at Riga was closed and the building was converted to the headquarters of the Russian Secret Police.[18] At the 1950 Baptist World Congress held at Cleveland, Ohio, Latvian and Estonian delegates recounted how thousands of their people had fled to Scandinavia by means of small, open fishing boats, in order to flee from Soviet rule.[19] *Bratskii vestnik* reported nothing but mutual respect and the most cordial relationship between the Baltic believers and the Moscow headquarters of the AUCECB. However, the appointment of the elder presbyter over these countries was issued not to a Baltic leader, but to Nikolai Aleksandrovich Levindanto, born in the Caucasus of exiled Baptist parents. This action was taken despite the fact that highly esteemed, mature leaders were available in the Baltic area. Johannes Lipstok, former president of more than one hundred churches of the Estonian Baptist Union, capable and worthy of the position of elder presbyter, was bypassed. Another outstanding leader, also an Estonian, was O. A. Tiark, who received an M. A. degree from Columbia University in 1929.[20] He pastored Tallin's famous Olevist (St. Olaf's) Church, composed of seven former evangelical churches totaling 2,000 members, who now worship in a Gothic cathedral built seven centuries ago. Apparently the Baltic brethren did not meet the qualifications set by CARC as necessary for the elder presbyter over all the Baltics, and the most expedient selection was Levindanto, a Slavic minister who had spent many faithful years in Moscow. Twenty years later, in 1964, the Baltic believers still looked up to Levindanto as the authorized appointee from Moscow.

---

18 Torbet, *loc. cit.*, p. 206.
19 Arnold T. Ohrn (ed.), *Eighth Baptist World Congress* (Philadelphia: The Judson Press, 1950), pp. 102–104.
20 *Bv*, No. 6, 1955, pp. 26–28.

10

Church Polity and the Presbyters

i. The Russian Elder Presbyters

Soviet writers insisted on describing the AUCECB as representing a sham "democracy" that concealed the fact that presbyters were not elected, but appointed from the top echelon.[1] However, as stated earlier, *Bratskii vestnik* openly indicated that as early as 1931, a joint decision was made, and again endorsed in 1944, to entrust a greater degree of responsibility into the hands of each elder or senior presbyter, all of whom were appointed to this position by the AUCECB. The same procedure did not apply to the posts of local pastors, who were called presbyters. During local elections, usually in the presence of the regional elder presbyter, qualified men were permitted to be candidates for the available pastorates.

At the inception of the AUCECB in 1944, the leaders were faced with the difficult task of renewing contacts with many groups of evangelical believers whose whereabouts were unknown. The war had disrupted countless lives in the Soviet Union, and the evangelicals were no exception, especially the Mennonites. A primary task was to bring the merging churches to order and to register them. The All-Union Council organized a centralized system whereby all the preachers of its far-reaching fellowship were held in strict account to its Moscow office. By a "Schema" the AUCECB knew each presbyter's place of

---

[1] Kalugin, *loc. cit.,* p. 9.

ministry, his chronological and "spiritual" age, the length
of his pastoral ministry, his spiritual qualifications, etc.
The appointments of the elder presbyters to oversee the
assignments in the republics, regions, and oblasts, demanded a search for men who possessed the greatest
breadth of experience, both sacred and secular.[2]
The idea of supplying elder presbyters for the Evangelical Christians-Baptists communities was first stated at the
All-Russian Council of Baptists which was held in Moscow in 1911. Not until the plenary council of the Fed-
erated Union of Baptists, which was held in 1930, did the
proposal to authorize its leadership receive adoption. The
plenary council of the Evangelical Christians also adopted
a similar proposal. This system was acknowledged as the
one most expedient at the 1944 merger. The title of "representative" given to this office was replaced by "elder
presbyter," as originally designated in 1911. The term
was familiar to believers and better understood by the
secular world. The elder was a first among equals, a spiritual servant in his province or republic, serving not one,
but many churches, and responsible to the AUCECB for
his activities. An ordained, experienced minister, he was
to create greater depth in the spiritual life of the churches
and jealously guard the Christian unity within their
multi-national fellowship.
As early as 1946, President Zhidkov reported over 3,000
local communities united in the single Union. The Moscow headquarters employed an office staff of fifteen, which
issued nearly 12,000 letters that year in correspondence
with the elder presbyters and the local churches. Nearly
3,000 presbyter's certificates were prepared and mailed to
its member pastors.
In 1947, close to seventy elder presbyters were engaged
in labors similar to that of the co-workers of Apostle Paul

---

2 *Bv*, No. 5, 1948, p. 32, 33.

—Timothy and Titus. In oblasts such as Kiev, Roven, and Kur, the elder presbyters superintended from 120 to 200 churches. In areas such as Tadzhikistan, Kirgiz, and Uzbekistan, fewer communities were under their charge, but each elder presbyter had a difficult and responsible ministry. They were mature men, averaging from fifty to seventy years of age, required to be examples to all the presbyters under their charge, as well as proven master teachers and administrators.[3]

These authoritative representatives of the AUCECB maintained constant contact with the local churches by means of regular correspondence and personal attendance at services. They were careful to guard against any departure from doctrinal purity and evangelical simplicity in the services and activities of the local communities. Assistance, including support, was given where needed, while the established churches were encouraged to support the AUCECB. A "reminder system" was employed to educate the churches to remit five offerings per year for the support of the Council headquarters. General Secretary Karev outlined a statement regulating the work of the AUCECB, elder presbyters, presbyters, deacons, council of brethren, auditing committee, choir, etc., in his abstract of the first four years of the Union's progress.[4]

Elder presbyters were invited to attend the business sessions of the local church communities, and they made a special effort to be present during the election or the removal of any local presbyters. As overseers, they ordained presbyters and deacons, conducted baptismal and communion services, and assisted local church councils in the reconciliation of conflicts. They exerted their influence over the presbyters in promoting the proper ministry of pastoral duties and in the fulfillment of the regulations of the AUCECB.

---

[3] I. I. Zhidkov, "A Look Backward," *Bv*, No. 1, 1948, p. 8.
[4] A. V. Karev, "Report of the General Secretary of the AUCECB," *Bv*, No. 5, 1948, pp. 32–37.

In solving the complex affairs of the churches, especially in the case of the removal of a presbyter or his excommunication from the church, the elder presbyter selected two or three experienced presbyters to assist and support him in arriving at an authoritative decision. The elder presbyter assumed the initiative in making immediate decisions on overt misdeeds. He used his investigatory powers to ascertain the objectivity of reports and received counsel from other experienced presbyters and officers of the church, without which his success as a spiritual leader would be found wanting.

The elder presbyter was expected to be on constant vigil to keep his character pure and to uphold the honor of his high calling. His tongue was not to be a scourge, nor ever to be used in destroying fraternal unity or church order. He was never to be dictatorial, or guilty of projecting the fear of punishment upon his subordinates. The elder presbyter was also subject to regional church discipline as well as being subordinate to the AUCECB. If he was discovered to be an unworthy overseer and guilty of misconduct, he was subject to dismissal, lest the AUCECB be accused of granting a blameworthy elder presbyter continued endorsement. However, as Levindanto explained, the judgment of such cases was most complex and subjected the churches to the possibilities of strife and divisions. Therefore an accusation was

. . . not to be received against an elder except it be before two or three . . . the competency of the AUCECB alone is sufficient in order to view all sides, since some may enlarge upon the errors or be false witnesses because of the elder's insistence in defending church discipline.

The elder presbyter is dismissed from his work solely by the decision of the AUCECB.[5]

---

[5] N. A. Levindanto, "About the Ministry of Elder Presbyters," *Bv*, No. 1, 1956, pp. 48–52.

ii. Local Church Discipline

The AUCECB instituted guidelines for disciplinary measures which were to be taken in the local churches in a fifteen-page treatise published in the *Bratskii vestnik*.[6] In defining the penalties for the violation of church discipline, a distinction was made between those who ignorantly erred and those who erred by design. According to the instructions given in Matthew 18:15-17, an individual believer was enjoined to approach the offending member, and if unheeded he was to return accompanied by two or three witnesses. If the offending member remained unrepentant, he was then required to appear before the church, and excommunication followed where guilt was ascertained. The more obvious, damaging, and widespread the misdeed, the swifter the action.

Depending upon the nature and gravity of the accusation the guilty party could be admonished without further penalty, be prohibited from partaking of communion, or be disqualified from engaging in church activities and holding offices such as preacher, deacon, choir member, church council member, etc. During the period of observation (2 Thess. 3:14), a maximum of six months, the member under discipline was required to acknowledge his error and rectify the same before being eligible for removal from "observation." The guilty member was dismissed from the church if he remained non-repentant. Minor offenses did not require an appearance before the church, but sincere apologies were accepted before the exhorters.

Excommunication was defined as the full disassociation from, and the loss of all rights of membership in the church. Even as the ordinance of water baptism did not grant a person salvation or the spiritual new birth but

---

[6] N. A. Levindanto, "Local Church Discipline," *Bv,* Nos. 3–4, 1955, pp. 10–24.

only symbolized the inner work of grace, even so did excommunication outwardly attest to the spiritual separation of the person from the Lord. The AUCECB maintained that such a person had already departed from the "Church Universal" and that this disciplinary action properly severed him from the ties of the local church (Isaiah 59:2, Jn. 15:2, Rom. 11:22).

In the event of excommunication, the door was still open for his return to the church and even his possible candidacy to a church office. In order for this to occur, his former life and work were taken into account prior to an election, and if found eligible he could be elected to a particular office without a new ordination being required.

Upon genuine repentance, that is, the actual forsaking of sin, the open confession of the misdeeds, and a reconsecration to God, the offender was again received into the church. So long as life remained, no person was beyond the possibility of repentance. The AUCECB seldom needed to discipline members who repeated their errors a second time, but even these cases received a hearing attended by great concern. Appeal of the decision was possible, especially if the decree of excommunication was not unanimous. The elder presbyter was required to dispatch neutral, mature brethren to these hearings and decisions were binding on both sides. Such cases applied only to actions which were subject to differences of opinion.

Levindanto explained that the evangelical churches were unable to forgive sin, for this was in God's jurisdiction alone; but they granted the offender full restoration if sincerity and restitution were evident.

Without forgiveness and reconciliation, there can be no full pardon, and the self-willed, proud, errant one remains under church condemnation. If he moves, he may apologize by letter to state his repentance, and submit himself to the correction of the local church. Where there is no church, the excommunicant is forgiven by letter if repentance is acceptable.[7]

Levindanto brought attention to the cumbersome method of engaging the entire membership to examine all church affairs, especially in the larger churches "numbering many hundreds." General church action on the excommunication of members was frowned upon. He advised instead that these decisions be authorized by the church council together with its local presbyter. Evidently there was no explicit ruling, for Levindanto explained:

> In churches where the practice of summoning the church council does not exist, it is better for the decisions to be left to the presbyter and the church council, together with the active members of the church rather than leaving it to a chance minority.[8]

For all practical purposes, the local church activists consisted of the presbyters, members of the council and auditors, members of the twenty, deacons, the contingent of preachers, and the most mature members not already involved in office. The responsibilities of the local believers included the election of its ministers and their removal, the construction and major repairs of the houses of prayer, and the election of the members of the church council and the auditors committee.

Claiming no specific Biblical instructions concerning the reception of church members, the Russian evangelicals instituted a one-year minimum period of probation for applicants who desired water baptism, the door to membership. During this trial period, the applicants received private instructions from the presbyter and his staff, who,

---

[7] *Ibid.,* p. 15.
[8] *Ibid.,* p. 22.

in turn, became knowledgeable of the candidates' convictions and conduct. The final test arrived when the catechumen appeared before the church council. Upon approval, he was publicly presented before the church as worthy of full membership.

The probationary period of one year was not in effect at the time of the creation of the AUCECB. After a postwar avalanche of new members, which resembled revival proportions, the above measures were adopted. Pastors were urged to seek qualitative results rather than a sharp rise in membership, with its attendant shallowness and lack of dedication. Unstated, but possibly implied, was the Soviets' alarm at the phenomenal growth of the evangelicals.

By the close of 1947 growth was so rapid that there were nearly 4,000 Evangelical-Baptist communities and admission was made that positions of leadership were held by those who had brief preparation for the ministry. Nevertheless they were diligent and wholehearted and some of the churches were led by women, spiritually mature and wise.[9]

In some of our small churches where there is a need of brethren, a deaconess, if qualified conducts the prayer meeting and preaches, as did the daughters of Philip (Acts 21:9). But the Lord's Supper and other ordinances of the Lord are to be administered by presbyters of the neighboring churches who visit periodically for this purpose.[10]

iii. Pastoral Self-Discipline

Shortly after the mergers General Secretary Karev published a handbook of twenty-four rules for presbyters to serve as a self-disciplinary guide for each undershepherd

---

[9] Zhidkov, "A Look Backward," *Bv*, No. 1, 1948, p. 7.
[10] N. A. Levindanto, "About Ministers of Local Churches," *Bv*, No. 6, 1957, p. 17.

of a union church. They would serve well for Christian pastors of any parish in any country.

1. The first quality of a presbyter must be a fervent love for Christ . . .

2. Your personal life must be pure and holy. You must strive for victory over every sin. Let your heart be the purest in the community.

3. In all relationships be an example to your entire church . . .

4. Pray much for your church. Be an intercessor for individuals.

5. Improve yourself! Sutdy the Bible—you must know it better than everyone in the community. Study spiritual literature. Ceaselessly raise your cultural level.

6. Develop a sense of responsibility for the entire work of God in your community. If it is in decline, seek the fault in yourself.

7. Be faithful. Do not forsake the work of God due to the absence of earthly goods.

8. Live modestly. Learn to be content with little.

9. During success in your ministry, humbly thank the Lord. Often repeat the words, "He must increase, but I must decrease!"

10. Read more often: I Tim. 3:1-7 and Tit. 1:6-9.

11. Fear pride and conceit! Do not lord it over the church, but be a servant to all.

12. Love all your sheep! Beware of having favorites! Love the disagreeable ones!

13. Know all your sheep! Know their number; have an exact membership list. Know each one individually! Know their spiritual condition, their gifts, their joys and trials, and their family life.

14. Visit church members in their homes! Render personal love to the weak, the needy, the mournful and afflicted.

15. Share with your members all of their joys and sorrows! . . . Where one hears of grief—be there first!

16. Love the backslider! Remember Christ's parable of the lost sheep (Lk. 15:4-6).

17. Attend the funerals of your deceased members! This will be a balm for the grieving family.

18. Be the last to leave the service!

19. Do not censure other churches!

20. Be serious, but at the same time always be affable to everyone!

21. Guard your physical health, but do not begrudge it for the work of the Lord!

22. Be clean and tidy in your appearance! A clean body and clean clothing contribute to your authority.

23. Be an example in fulfilling civic obligations and train your members to do likewise. Your church must fervently love its country and its people.

24. Read these rules regularly and examine yourself to see if your life measures up to them.[11]

The presbyter of a local church served in a position that demanded dedication and guaranteed little if anything in the way of remunerative returns. Evangelical Christians-Baptists' pastors were not permitted to accept fees for weddings, baptisms, funerals or sick calls. Free will offerings, permitted by the Soviet Government, were justified by the AUCECB and were standard in all the churches. The offerings met the operating costs and maintenance of the houses of prayer, or rental of same. Speci-

---

[11] A. V. Karev, "A Handbook for Presbyters," *Bv*, No. 3, 1946, pp. 28, 29.

fied offerings were received for Moscow's AUCECB headquarters and for the elder presbyters. Presbyters who
served in the larger churches where the responsibilities
demanded a full-time ministry received support by free
will offerings. The apologetics for the support of the elder
presbyters were explained in order to remove the expected
Soviet charge and stigma of religious parasitism.

> If in our fellowship the presbyters of large churches
> are free from labor in industry, then all the more the
> elder presbyters are unable to labor in industry, for they
> are over a number of churches in the oblast, even sev-
> eral oblasts . . . constantly travelling to all of these
> churches. By what means could they do so if not by
> voluntary offerings?[12]

In 1947, Zhidkov noted that one-third of the local presbyters received some form of material assistance from their
churches.[13] There were cases of consolidation of small
neighboring churches into one larger church, which made
it easier to maintain the premises and to partially support the presbyter. Some churches had no choice but were
required by the government to join other sister churches
located within a seven-mile radius, especially in the Baltics.

iv. Church Statistics

With evident enthusiasm President Zhidkov shared an
optimistic report with Dean Hewlett Johnson when the
latter visited Moscow's AUCECB headquarters and church
in 1947. The Russian stated that under the Soviet regime
the evangelicals received precisely the same consideration
as did the vastly greater Russian Orthodox Church, a
treatment previously unknown.[14] However, of the only

---

[12] V. S., "Pastor or Hireling," *Bv*, No. 5, 1963, p. 44.
[13] I. I. Zhidkov, "A Look Backward," *Bv*, No. 1, 1948, p. 7.
[14] Hewlett Johnson, *Soviet Russia Since the War* (New York:
Bone and Gaer, 1947), p. 123.

two religious magazines published in the Soviet Union for nationwide distribution—the *Journal of the Moscow Patriarchate,* started in September of 1943 and the *Fraternal Messenger,* the organ of the AUCECB, first printed in early 1945—the Orthodox organ circulated 20,000 copies monthly compared with the 3,000 bimonthly copies published by the Evangelicals. In 1946, at a time when Zhidkov's optimistic list of expected blessings was growing, he told the President of the Southern Baptist Convention, Louie D. Newton, that AUCECB would be

. . . publishing the Bible, the New Testament, and religious hymnals. We shall continue to publish these until we have satisfied the entire need for this material. . . . We shall soon open a school to train our preachers. The Orthodox Church has anticipated us in this respect, but we shall soon catch up to it.[15]

The AUCECB's cherished desire for a preacher's school never did materialize. Other than receiving 7,000 Russian Bibles from the Latvian Baptists, ten long years passed before a limited publication of 10,000 Bibles was printed in 1957. None has followed since, but ever-increasing numbers of Russian Bibles enter the USSR via concerned tourists, and this may place the Soviets under psychological pressure to print another edition. Perhaps for this reason the believers were expecting a new publication of Bibles in 1968.[16]

Despite irregular and incomplete reports from the thousands of local churches *Bratskii vestnik* often published the available church membership statistics until early 1958, when Soviet antireligious pressures increased. The communities that submitted figures indicated an average membership of less than one hundred, or to be more

[15] Louie D. Newton, *An American Churchman in the Soviet Union* (New York: American Russian Institute, 1946), p. 44.

[16] *Bv,* No. 1, 1968, p. 64.

precise, 90.5 per church. In 1958, *Bratskii Vestnik* listed the total membership of its 5,400 communities at 530,000.[17] From the given statistics tabulated over a period of ten years,[18] only 168 communities were listed with memberships exceeding one hundred, accounting for 56,276 members. The remainder of 473,724 were found in 5,232 communities, an average of less than one hundred members per church.[19] The Mennonites joined the union in 1963 and the first numerical account listed 18,600 members who merged.[20]

Most of the presbyters were self-supporting, engaged in secular work. They could be found among mechanics, crane operators, carpenters, chauffeurs, tractor drivers, etc. They labored in construction projects, in factories, and on collective farms. Many pastors became pensioners at sixty-two years of age, receiving monthly financial assistance from the Soviet Government, and by this means were enabled, paradoxically, to render full-time service to their spiritual communities by courtesy of an atheistic regime!

In 1944, it was apparent that a very large majority of the Evangelical Christians and the Baptists participated in the historic merger although no statistics or percentages were disclosed in *Bratskii vestnik*. In the case of the Pentecostal merger, however, both figures and percentages were available, but with obvious discrepancies. In the 1955 report of the AUCECB presidium, it was stated that 80 per cent of the Pentecostalists had already united with the Evangelical Christians-Baptists.[21] D. I. Ponomarchuk, a former leader of the Christians of Evangelical Faith and

---

17 *Bv*, No. 1, 1958, p. 29.

18 *Bratskii vestnik* was not published during 1950–1952.

19 See Appendix A for the leading churches among the Evangelical Christians-Baptists.

20 "Evangelical Christians-Baptists and Mennonites," *Bv*, No. 3, 1968, p. 14.

21 "Report of the Work of the Presidium of the AUCECB in Moscow," *Bv*, No. 2, 1955, p. 71.

the only Pentecostal member in the presidium, published the figure of 25,000 as the total number of Pentecostalists that entered into the Union.[22] He firmly stated that the Pentecostal believers who remained independent and aloof comprised an inconsequential minority.[23] However, by admission of the presidium Council, 14,000, or a significant 36 per cent of the tongues-speaking Pentecostalists rejected the August Agreement of 1945.[24] The *Atheist Handbook* suggested that the Pentecostal believers who had already become members of AUCECB were withdrawing in increasing numbers.[25] The inner pressures and conflicts experienced within the church communities of the Evangelical Christians-Baptists provided some of the reasons for the exodus.

---

[22] *Bv*, Nos. 5–6, 1958, p. 28.
[23] D. I. Ponomarchuk, "About the Unity of the Children of God," *Bv*, Nos. 5–6. 1960, p.75.
[24] *Bv*, No. 1, 1960, p. 87.
[25] Kovalev, *op. cit.*, p. 155.

11

Controversies Between the Baptists and the Pentecostalists

i. Speaking in Tongues and the August Agreement

Due to the fact that there is no evidence of disagreement or dissension between member Baptists and the Evangelical Christians since their official unification in 1944, and because almost no information is submitted by *Bratskii vestnik* concerning the Mennonites during this period, special attention will be focused upon the problems encountered between the Baptists and the Pentecostal members.

Despite the August Agreement of 1945, in which the merging Pentecostal members pledged to abstain from the glossolalia (or speaking in other tongues as recorded in Acts 2:4) in the general worship services, evidence clearly indictes that tongues speaking continued to be manifested.

Although the glossolalia was an integral part of the primitive Christian church and was instrumental in fusing the early Christians into a powerful missionary force, the twentieth-century renewal of speaking in tongues has been misunderstood, misused, and abused to the extent that it has served as a divisive doctrine, separating evangelicals from each other in many countries of the world. Despite the general polarity of Baptist and Pentecostal views on this critical issue, a degree of success has been achieved in the Soviet Union for more than twenty years as thousands upon thousands of Baptists and Pentecostalists have worshipped and worked together, a record duplicated nowhere else in the world.

In some countries other than Russia the Pentecostal movement did not start as a separate church, but existed for some time among established denominations. For instance there was some degree of a working relationship between the Swedish Baptist Union and the Pentecostalists from 1907 to 1913, at which time the Baptist District Association decided that the Filadelfia congregation should be ousted from its membership. Lewi Pethrus, leader of the Pentecostal movement and former pastor of the 6,500 member Filadelfia church in Stockholm, hoped to reach an informal settlement which would permit a loose fellowship. Instead, the schism developed and in 1919 there was a formal division. The Pentecostal Swedes advanced three reasons for reacting against restrictive denominational organizations: It could not be supported from New Testament evidence; denominations served not merely as missionary organizations but also as pressure groups; and they obstructed the work of the Holy Spirit in the world.[1] Since that time the Pentecostal Swedes have practiced local church autonomy and an inter-church fellowship among glossolalists.

This chapter will include Soviet writers' criticisms that bear directly upon the doctrinal issues of the evangelicals. Attention given by the antireligious press to any adverse social effects reportedly emanating from the doctrinal position of the AUCECB will be analyzed in the following chapter. Soviet charges levelled against the non-union evangelicals will also be treated in a later sequence.

The basic doctrines held by all the members of AUCECB stem from the belief in the plenary inspiration of the canonical Scriptures which, they believed, supplied

---

[1] "The Pentecostal Movement and the Swedish Baptist Union 1907–1920," World Council of Churches *Bulletin,* Vol. VI, No. 1 (Lausanne: 1960), pp. 9–12.

all things necessary in faith and in practice. They were
in agreement that the essence of the Gospel consisted
mainly in its doctrine of man's sinful condition and his
need of salvation, the revelation of God's grace in Jesus
Christ, the divine Son of God, the necessity of a spiritual
new birth followed by the ordinances of believer's baptism, and monthly participation in the communion service.

Aleksandr Karev, General Secretary of the AUCECB,
cautioned the three-member denominations that the
merger was but the beginning of a process in which ex-
ternal organizational unity would require true inner unity,
a unity that

> . . . must be monolithic, without any fissure in it. . . .
> The divisions of living Christianity are a great evil,
> greatly hindering the evangelization of the world.
>   Lifting the banner of unity . . . adhering to the Evan-
> gelical-Baptist principles, we would like to say to all
> likeminded churches of the world: follow our example.[2]

The August Agreement of 1945 discontinued the practice of footwashing, which affected those in the Pentecostal ranks, and in 1963 the merging Mennonites. There
appeared almost no evidence of the infraction of this new
regulation, whereas in the practice of the glossolalia, violations increased rather than diminished during the first
years of unity. By 1948 and 1949, President Zhidkov found
it necessary to instruct the presbyters to control the public
prayers in each service by assigning selected members to
pray audibly, followed by the presbyter's concluding
prayer. It was found necessary by Zhidkov to

> . . . foresee the objections of individual believers who
> quote the apostle's expression "Do not quench the
> Spirit." They say, "The Spirit arouses us to prayer and

---

[2] A. Karev, "Another Step in the Work of Unity," *Bv*, No. 3,
1945, p. 8.

you quench our spirits and thus destroy the Word of God." We do not quench the Spirit, but we strive to suppress noise and disorder.[3]

The August Agreement forbade the utterance of tongues in all public services but the intimate sharing of one's experience of the glossolalia with other members as individuals was not prohibited. However, nine years later, *Bratskii vestnik* altered part of the Agreement of 1945 by inserting the stipulation that no Pentecostal members could exercise the liberty of personal persuasion upon their fellow members. This was referred to as a major condition of the August Agreement, despite its nonexistence! Rather, it replaced the proviso to abstain from footwashing which was originally stated in 1945.[4] The persistency and the degree of effectiveness of the Pentecostalists within the Union probably forced the substitution in order to halt the infiltration and spread of this doctrine among the Union churches.

ii. Early Baptist Charges Against Tongues

As described earlier, Ivan Voronaev spearheaded the phenomenal growth of the Christians of Evangelical Faith during the nineteen twenties. Within a few short years 350 Pentecostal assemblies were founded, containing 17,000 active members in the Ukraine. Donald Gee placed the growing membership at 80,000,[5] which apparently included aherents.

The attitude of the Baptists toward Voronaev greatly resembled the hostile articles of Soviet writers that maligned the Pentecostal leader. Both charged Voronaev

---

[3] I. I. Zhidkov, "In the School of Prayer," *Bv,* No. 2, 1949, p. 8.

[4] I. I. Zhidkov and A. Karev, "To All Presbyters of the Communities of the Evangelical Christians-Baptists," *Bv,* No. 1, 1955, p. 5.

[5] Donald Gee, *The Pentecostal Movement* (London: Elim Publishing Company, Rev. ed. 1949), p. 159.

and his followers with the teaching of error, using the powers of hypnosis upon believers weakened by prayer and fasting to engage in monosyllabic utterances.[6] They described their manifestations as a form of pure *Khlystism*, and called them Shakers. The Baptists accused the Pentecostalists of implanting fear into the hearts of Baptist and Evangelical believers by causing them to doubt the efficacy of their salvation on the basis of lacking the gifts of the Holy Spirit. Baptist Z. Pavlenko, much concerned, wrote that the time had arrived

> . . . when Satan must take the form of an angel of light in order to scatter the ranks of the people of God. I deem it necessary to write some words about this terrible error being spread by Voronaev and his followers . . .[7]

Another Baptist, N. Turkov, described the religious ecstasies of the Pentecostalists as mad orgies of debauchery. He warned fellow Baptists not to follow them, lest they give added credence to the atheist's definition of religion as the opium of the people. He enjoined believers to carry out a tenacious struggle against any appearances of Pentecostalism in their communities. "Let us begin then with the help of God to fight this diseased growth on the body of our Church. . . ."[8]

Baptist leader M. Timoshenko, probing for the cause of Voronaev's success in introducing so many Baptist men and women to "experience this aberration," concluded that it was the chastisement of many Baptists who had grown lukewarm in their devotional lives. He also interpreted the inroads made by the Pentecostalists upon the ranks of Baptist churches as a warning against vanity and petty sins which called for self-examination. He asked for

---

[6] *Baptist,* No. 2 (Moskva: 1925), p. 20.
[7] *Ibid.,* Nos. 5–6, 1926, p. 13.
[8] *Ibid.,* Nos. 7–8, 1926, pp. 11, 12.

a greater commitment and consecration in the form of a
new promise of faithfulness.[9] This candid commentary indicated the impact made upon an increasing number of
evangelicals by the fervent, probably over-zealous followers
of Voronaev. Dissatisfaction and disillusionment may have
been sown by the Baptist feud with Prokhanov and the
Evangelical Christians, thus opening the door to the glossolalia, an experience that seemed to fuse people of diverse backgrounds into one accord in an atmosphere of
love.

The Pentecostal merger of 1945 did not eliminate the
problems encountered in the twenties, but by endeavor-
ing to work together, a greater degree of understanding,
and to some extent appreciation for each other's views,
was attained.

iii. Pentecostal Doctrines

Evidence of glossolalia, or the spontaneous utterance of
a language that the speaker himself does not know, occurred on the Day of Pentecost.[10] Since its inception in
the first century there have been evidences of glossolalia
down to the present century, although in limited instances
and for brief periods of time. The glossolalia was discussed
by the historians Irenaeus and Tertullian and was practiced by the Montanists, Little Prophets of the Cevennes,
Jansenists, Irvingites, Shakers, early Mormons, converts of
Whitefield and Wesley, and in the Welsh and Scottish re-
vivals. Not until the turn of the twentieth century, however, did the Pentecostal experience become known and
activated in the lives of millions around the world. Since
1900, when the Bible students of Charles Parham's school
in Topeka, Kansas, discovered that the glossolalia phenomenon was the evidence of the baptism with the Holy

---

[9] *Baptist,* No. 1, (Moskva: 1925), p. 15.
[10] Acts 2:1–4.

Spirit, approximately two million North Americans have spoken in other tongues. World estimates vary considerably, running as high as ten million persons.

As early as 1907 Estonian Christians were among the tongues speakers.[11] Except for a few outbreaks of the utterance in tongues among the Oneness Pentecostalists shortly before the arrival of Voronaev, no significant impact was made upon the Russians in the twentieth century. Bringing the fire of the New York City revival with him, Voronaev not only attracted the Baptists and the Evangelical Christians to his message, but elements of the Jesus Only (Oneness), the *Khlysti*, and a variety of mysticals ever abounding in Russia, were probably attracted to the mushrooming Pentecostal assemblies which he founded. Without adequately trained leadership during so rapid and extensive a growth, the perils of fanaticism were multiplied, but the power potential could not be dismissed.

Henry Pitney Van Dusen, former president of Union Theological Seminary, shared his response to the current Pentecostal movement in the world in this manner:

> I have come to feel . . . that the Pentecostal movement with its emphasis upon the Holy Spirit, is more than just another revival. It is a revolution in our day. It is a revolution comparable in importance with the establishment of the original Apostolic Church and with the Protestant Reformation.[12]

In our present decade, the glossolalia experience has become widely known in the historic Protestant churches across America. Some of the notable clergymen of these churches who have spoken in tongues and remain with their denominations are Dennis Bennett (Episcopalian),

---

[11] Nils Bloch-Hoell, *The Pentecostal Movement* (New York: Humanities Press Inc., 1964), p. 85.

[12] John L. Sherrill, *They Speak with Other Tongues* (New York: McGraw-Hill Book Company, 1964), p. 27.

Harald Bredesen (Reformed), Howard M. Ervin (Baptist), James H. Brown (Presbyterian), John L. Peters (Methodist), and Larry Christenson (Lutheran). Morton T. Kelsey, a Episcopal clergyman who has not spoken in tongues, conducted a research of the glossolalia movement and concluded that

> Speaking in tongues . . . as one of the gifts of the Spirit, is a true Christian phenomenon. It is one entrance into the spiritual realm; by giving access to the unconscious, it is one contact with non-physical reality, which allows God to speak directly to man . . .[13]

Denominational acceptance was not expected by Voronaev when he edited the *Evangelist* in 1928. During its single year of publication Voronaev made the Pentecostal position of the Christians of Evangelical Faith explicit. In an article on "The Call to the Ministry," his magazine contrasted the ineffectiveness and failure of contemporary Christians with the power and success of the early apostles. Non-Pentecostal ministers were berated for producing little fruit after decades of preaching. They were subjected to the charge that the

> . . . labor of those who minister and work without the power of the Holy Spirit, by carnal, envious zeal as do the professionals, will not be recognized by the Lord. He will say to them "I never knew you. Depart from me." (Mt. 7:23; 25:11, 12).[14]

Even more damaging than the derisive remarks against all the ministers who had not experienced the glossolalia was the personal doubt of salvation which was implanted in the minds of the Baptist and Evangelical Christian laity.

---

[13] Morton T. Kelsey, *Tongue Speaking* (New York: Doubleday and Company, 1964), p. 231.
[14] *Evangelist*, No. 1 (Odessa: 1928), p. 12.

If the assurance of one's salvation was contingent upon the experience of the glossolalia, then the finished work of Christ's redemption upon the cross of Calvary was virtually denied. In order to arrive at a better understanding of the doctrinal positions held in disagreement among the Russian Pentecostalists and the initial members of the Union, let us focus our attention upon these problem areas.

The Russian Baptists do not adhere to the doctrine of the eternal security of the believer as do their fellow Southern Baptists in the United States, largest of the twenty-seven different Baptist bodies in America. Instead, they accept the Arminian position as do the Russian Pentecostalists and their American counterpart, the Assemblies of God, largest of twenty-two different Pentecostal bodies in the United States.[15] The Evangelical Christians-Baptists of the Soviet Union acknowledged and taught the real possibility of the eternal loss of a believer's salvation if he departed from the faith and remained unrepentant. This is all the more surprising since their Confession of Faith in 1928 supported the Calvinist doctrine of eternal security, stating: ". . . it begins from the first moment of the new life and will never come to an end."[16]

The late E. Y. Mullins, eminent Southern Baptist theologian and former president of the Southern Baptist Theological Seminary in Louisville, Kentucky, was convinced that the New Testament avoided the "pantheistic tendency of extreme Calvinism and the deistic tendency of the extreme Arminianism."[17] He believed that God's method in the Scriptures

. . . clearly taught that no one in Christ will ever be lost. It also explains the passages which seem to imply

---

[15] Klaude Kendrick, *The Promise Fulfilled: A History of the Modern Pentecostal Movement* (Springfield: Gospel Publishing House, 1961), p. 4.

[16] *Ispovedanie very Khristian-Baptistov* (Moskva: 1928), p. 25.

[17] Edgar Young Mullins, *The Christian Religion In Its Doctrinal Expression* (Valley Forge: The Judson Press, 1964), p. 434.

that some are in danger of being lost. These are exhortations to prevent the danger which is real from the human standpoint. To point out the danger and warn against it is the divine method of preventing it. It explains also cases of apparent apostasy in the Bible. These were either cases of backsliding which were followed by a return to God, or else they were cases of spurious conversion where the real spiritual life never existed.[18]

B. Hays maintained that if the doctrinal points which traditionally separated Arminians from the stricter Calvinists were placed before a random group of Baptists from the American Baptist Convention and the Southern Baptist Convention, the majority of them would agree with the Arminians on all points save one. That one was

> . . . the question of apostasy, or the possibility of "falling from grace." On this point, most of our people, apart from the Free Will and General Baptist groups, probably would still hold to the Calvinist view that denies such a possibility.[19]

Conversely, A. V. Karev, chief theological voice of the AUCECB, supported the Arminian position, stating that it was possible for a converted person to apostatize from Christ (Heb. 3:12; 6:4-6) .

> In this passage it is very clear that this concerns born again people. . . . how can one understand John 10:27-30 . . . "and they shall never perish, . . . no man is able to pluck them out of my Father's hand." Yet we know the question Christ gave to all his followers: "Will you also go away?" Even the apostles, chosen by Christ himself, were so asked. To what does this relate? . . . our free will . . .[20]

---

[18] *Ibid.,* p. 438.
[19] Brooks Hays and John E. Steely, *The Baptist Way of Life* (Englewood Cliffs: Prentice Hall, Inc., 1963) , p. 161.
[20] A. V. Karev, "What the Bible Teaches—Basic Bible Doctrines," *Bv,* No. 1, 1964, p. 59.

Karev maintained that apostasy, the severance of the branch (believer) from the Vine (Christ), produced eternal death.

Another AUCECB writer, V. Somov, placed backsliding Christians into two categories—the "prodigal sons" and the "Alexander coppersmiths" (2 Tim. 4:14). Only those who indicated sincere repentance by the resumption of daily Christian living were again accepted into the believers' community as prodigals. The Alexanders, or unrepentant evildoers, were left to God's judgment.

The truly repentant, even those guilty of gross sins such as adultery and drunkenness, were permitted reentry into the local churches, although previously excommunicated. The church members who resented this forgiveness-acceptance policy were satirically labeled "zealots of purity" by Somov, who saw a parallel in the elder brother of the prodigal and his unforgiving attitude. He listed Biblical examples of repentant King David and Apostle Peter as proofs of restoration and continued ministries.[21] Mitskevich bluntly illustrated the official AUCECB position by disclosing the sordid past of a former leader of a local church, who

> . . . went so far as to live worse than a filthy pig, but . . . with anguished conscience for his sinfulness, he repented before the Lord. After this, he came to a meeting and fully confessed. Within a year they received him into the church. . . . And we cannot but receive those who, having repented, depart from all sin.[22]

Ivan Voronaev, under missionary appointment of the American Assemblies of God, taught and preached from the Arminian position, and was therefore in full accord with the Russian Baptists on the real danger of a con-

---

[21] V. Somov, "Questions in the Life of a Christian," *Bv*, No. 4, 1964, p. 37.

[22] A. I. Mitskevich, "Prodigals," *Bv*, No. 1, 1954, p. 71.

vert's apostasy and ultimate lost condition. Ralph M. Riggs, former General Superintendent of the Assemblies of God, stated that a person

> . . . does not lose his freedom of will after being saved. He has the gift of eternal life but may return the gift and become as he was before receiving it. By faith he became saved and by subsequent unbelief he may become lost. No man is able to pluck one of Christ's sheep out of the Father's hand, but may definitely remove himself out of His hand. Unbelief and unconfessed sin persisted in will damn any soul (Heb. 3:19; Rev. 3:5) .[23]

Against such an argument and its Scriptural supportive references, Mullins earlier explained that the writers were dealing with principles and spiritual attitudes rather than the accounts of actual occurrences. Seen from the human perspective and from the standpoint of human weakness, they were real dangers which could occur. However, God's grace and power, and not man's weakness, were ultimately the decisive factors that enabled man to overcome.[24]

It must be noted that it is "impossible to present the Baptist position, for there is no such thing,"[25] but doctrinal articles written by persons who have gained the respect and confidence of Southern Baptists may be regarded as representative teachings.

Believing Jesus Christ to be as relevant to their generation as he was to the apostles (Heb. 13:8), the Russian Pentecostalists expected the operation of the gifts of the Holy Spirit in the twentieth century to parallel those of the first century.[26]

---

[23] Ralph M. Riggs, *We Believe,* Book Three (Springfield, Mo.: Gospel Publishing House, 1954) , p. 25.

[24] Mullins, *loc. cit.,* pp. 435–437; also Norman Wade Cox (ed.) , *Encyclopedia of Southern Baptists,* Vol. II (Nashville: Broadman Press, 1958) , p. 1088.

[25] Cox, Vol. I, xv.

[26] "Back to Pentecost," *Evangelist,* Nos. 3–4 (Odessa: 1928) , p. 1.

The members of the church of Christ were baptized with the Holy Spirit and endowed with the gifts of the Spirit of God (Acts 1:5-8; 2:1-4; 10:44-46). The following gifts were in the church: wisdom, knowledge, faith, gifts of healing, miracles, prophecy, discernment of spirits, divers tongues, interpretation of tongues (I Cor. 12:7-10; Mk. 16:17, 18).[27]

According to the doctrinal teachings of the Russian and American Pentecostalists, the glossolalia, or the "baptism with the Holy Spirit" was introduced in the preaching of John the Baptist as recorded in all four gospels of the New Testament: "he shall baptize you with the Holy Ghost" (Mt. 3:11); "I indeed have baptized you with water: but he shall baptize you with the Holy Ghost" (Mk. 1:8); "he shall baptize you with the Holy Ghost and with fire" (Lk. 3:16); "he that sent me to baptize with water, the same said unto me, Upon whom thou shalt see the Spirit descending, and remaining on him, the same is he which baptizeth with the Holy Ghost" (Jn. 1:33). This spiritual baptism was administered by the risen, ascended Christ on the Day of Pentecost, in an upper room located in Jerusalem where about one hundred and twenty disciples were assembled, according to Luke 24:49, Acts 1:5, and 2:1-4.

Voronaev insisted that the church recognize the speaking in tongues to be the contemporary as well as the primitive believer's sign of the baptism with the Holy Spirit, as heralded by John the Baptist. In his magazine, *Evangelist,* he scored the Orthodox, Old Believers, Roman Catholics, Lutherans, Adventists, Sabbatarians, Baptists, and Evangelical Christians when he stated the following:

... When you ask preachers and leaders of these churches if they believe in or have received the baptism with

27 "Christ and His First Church," *Evangelist,* No. 1, 1928, p. 9.

the Holy Spirit, they then respond affirmatively. It occurred to me to ask many of them when they received
the baptism with the Holy Spirit.
All answered in one accord: "When we were baptized
in water . . ." They received a spiritual baptism in a
mechanical manner. But I say . . . not one of them received the baptism with the Holy Spirit. . . . The first
Christians especially coveted it with fasting and unceas-
ing prayer . . . (Acts 1:14; 2:1-4; I Cor. 14:1-5; 12:31) .[28]

Voronaev made reference to Prokhanov's article in
Khristianin, (1924, No. 3, page 46) , in which the editors
reportedly acknowledged their need for the experience
which the apostles possessed, and they called for increased
ardor within their ranks.

Pay serious attention, dear reader, to this sincere acknowledgment by the very leaders and editors of the
Evangelical Christians' magazine! They did not make
this acknowledgment of themselves, rather the Lord con-
victed them . . . (Jn. 11:51) .[29]

Voronaev triumphantly proclaimed that the Pentecostal
message had permeated many of the Baptist and Evangelical Christians' churches to the extent that their membership rolls sharply declined. His pungent prophecy, not
without spiritual pride, also claimed that

Their structures of hay and stubble will burn (I Cor.
3:12), because they were built without the power of
the Holy Spirit.[30]

Evangelist reproved the leaders of the Evangelical-
Baptists for neither personally striving for the gifts of the

---

28 "About the Baptism with the Holy Spirit," *Evangelist,* No. 1,
1928, p. 22.
29 *Ibid.,* p. 23.
30 *Ibid.*

Holy Spirit, nor allowing their members to pursue such gifts unhindered. The pastors were described as scribes and Pharisees who were judged as hypocrites by Christ. During the twenties, the Soviets permitted religious publishers to entertain doctrinal disputes and indulge in railing accusations of other denominational leaders.

In contrast, ever since its first issue was published in 1945 *Bratskii vestnik,* the official organ of the AUCECB, has treated with courtesy and tact other religious groups whose doctrines were contrary to its own statement of faith. During the Korean conflict, however, sharp criticisms and barbed accusations were hurled against the United States as the Russian evangelicals became politically involved in promoting Soviet-approved world peace efforts, details of which shall be considered in a later chapter.

Bratskii vestnik has served essentially as a correspondence Bible school for the thousands of evangelical pastors. The 3,000 copies of the magazine have been published on Soviet presses in Moscow, usually six times annually. With some 500 copies sent abroad to satisfy its foreign readers, the remaining 2,500 copies somehow must meet the needs of more than 5,000 churches and over 25,000 preachers.[31] In the twenty years spanned in this study seventy-six issues totaling over 6,500 pages have been edited by Aleksandr Karev, the General Secretary of AUCECB. No copies of the journal were printed during 1950-52, the strained closing years of Stalin's reign, yet upon its resumption of publication in 1953 nothing was mentioned of the three-year lapse.

Through the decades the contents of *Bratskii vestnik* have spanned the sixty-six books of the canonical Bible, copies of which have been shared and recopied, compiling a voluminous commentary. While its literary approach is essentially simple, there have been ample sprinklings of

[31] *Bv,* No. 1, 1958, p. 29.

erudition. In its systematic theology, it has presented the doctrines of God, the nature and attributes of God, the Trinity, the deity of Christ, the personality of the Holy Spirit, creation, angels, the origin of man and his nature, miracles, the fall, the origin, nature and consequences of sin, the plan of salvation, the mediatory work of Christ, his vicarious death, resurrection and ascension, the justification and sanctification of regenerated man, the ordinances of baptism and communion, the personal return of Christ in his second advent, premillennialism, the judgment of believers and their rewards, and the future punishment of the unregenerate.

The magazine contains reports, statistics, and church photographs—many of which resemble small log cabins. The biographies of their evangelical leaders and the itineraries of the AUCECB executives both at home and abroad have been outlined. Christian ethics and church discipline have been treated in a pragmatic manner. Conspicuous by their absence are any statements which might be construed to question the program of the socialist regime.

Numerous articles have dealt with the perennial problem of the emphasis by Pentecostalists upon the gifts of the Holy Spirit, and especially the glossolalia. Leading AUCECB executives, such as President I. I. Zhidkov, Secretary A. V. Karev, I. I. Motorin, and A. I. Mitskevich have written polemically on tongues speaking. Recently, K. V. Somov was assigned to write frequently about the glossolalia controversy that has continued to plague the Union. In a twelve-page study on the Holy Sprit, he admitted that "More than any other truth of our confession are the differences that exist concerning the baptism with the Holy Spirit."[32]

---

[32] V. S., "Thoughts About the Holy Spirit," *Bv*, No. 3, 1962, p. 11.

Somov maintained, as did the Southern Baptist Convention, that one could not be a disciple of Christ without possessing the Holy Spirit. If a person was a recipient of Christ, he also had received the Holy Spirit.[33] Mitskevich believed that a person became a member of the universal church on the day of his conversion, at which time he was baptized by the Holy Spirit. He explained that the words

> . . . "by one Spirit are we all baptized into one body" (I Cor. 12:13) declares to us that it is impossible to be a member of the universal church without having experienced the baptism by the Holy Spirit. If you doubt this, you have no basis upon which to consider yourself a member of the body of Christ . . .[34]

It was at this point that a great gulf of misunderstanding separated the Baptists and the Pentecostalists, both in Russia and in America. Although most of the doctrinal authors of the Assemblies of God such as Myer Pearlman, Ernest S. Williams, Carl Brumback, and Ralph M. Riggs have been consistent in identifying the glossolalia experience as the "baptism 'with' the Holy Spirit" or the "baptism 'in' the Holy Spirit," the frequently used phrase identifying the experience has been the "baptism 'of' the Holy Spirit." Pentecostal laymen, evangelists, and pastors use the preposition "of" thoughtlessly, alternately with the prepositions "with" or "in." Even Dr. Klaude Kendrick in one and the same paragraph has referred to the glossolalia as both the "baptism 'of' the Holy Spirit" and the "baptism 'in' the Holy Spirit."[35]

Many Pentecostalists remain unaware of the importance of the misuse of the preposition "of" when speaking of the glossolalia experience which is effected by Christ, the

---

[33] *Ibid.,* p. 14.

[34] A. I. Mitskevich, "Thoughts about the Activities of the Holy Spirit," *Bv,* No. 2, 1959, p. 49.

[35] Kendrick, *op. cit.,* p. 2.

baptizer. Baptists generally understood the term "baptism 'of' the Holy Spirit" as one identical with the "baptism 'by' the one Spirit," meaning that the Spirit baptized every believer into the one Body of Christ. E. Y. Mullins, one-time president of the Southern Baptist Convention and Baptist World Alliance, declared that in regeneration, the new creation experience of a convert was the result of the direct action of the Holy Spirit upon man's spirit.[36] Quite apart from the physical baptism by immersion, the baptism "by" the Spirit denoted the believer's spiritual union with Christ in a vital relationship. In this baptism the Holy Spirit was the baptizing agent, while the Body of Christ became the receiving element (1 Cor. 12:13).

The four gospel writers, however, referred to a baptism in which Christ as the agent, "shall baptize you with the Holy Ghost." Yet Dr. Mullins wrote that "Pentecost was the historical fulfillment of the predicted baptism of the Holy Spirit (Acts 1:5)."[37] The Assemblies of God believed that the "indwelling of the Holy Spirit" occurred simultaneously at regeneration, that it equated the baptism "by" the Spirit into the Body of Christ. The Russian Pentecostalists departed from this tenet when they implied that all believers who did not speak in tongues did not possess the Holy Spirit and therefore were unprepared to meet Christ at his second advent. However, concerning the baptism which occurred on the day of Pentecost (Acts 2:1-4), both Russian Pentecostalists and the American Assemblies of God insisted that Christ was the baptizing agent and that the experience was then, and is now accompanied by the speaking in other tongues as a supernatural phenomenon, subsequent to salvation, whether it be moments, weeks, months, or years.

I. Motorin found it necessary to refute the charge made

---

[36] Mullins, *op. cit.*, p. 52.
[37] *Ibid.*, p. 360.

by the Russian Pentecostalists that whoever did not speak
in tongues did not possess the indwelling Spirit.

> . . . nowhere is it said that one having the gift of healing,
> the gift of tongues, or the gift of the interpretation of
> tongues has eternal life. The opposite is stated by Jesus
> Christ—"I never knew you" (Mt. 7:22, 23)—a warning
> for those Christians who think more about miracles,
> tongues, than of a wholesome life in Jesus Christ.[38]

The Russian Evangelical Christians-Baptists and the
Southern Baptists have readily agreed that the glossolalia
was a valid spiritual gift that appeared briefly in the early
period of the primitive Christian church for the purpose
of presenting the gospel to the many foreign Jews visiting
Jerusalem during the Feast of Pentecost (Acts 1:21). Foreign tongues, supernaturally given by God, they maintained, were also used to share the good news with the
Gentiles at the household of the Roman centurion Cornelius (Acts 10:44-48), and to reach the strategically located Ephesians (Acts 19:1-6). Mitskevich asserted that
the necessity for tongues had disappeared because the
Scriptures have been translated in over 1,000 languages.
He chided the seekers of this experience saying,

> . . . certain believers, doubting their primogeniture in
> the baptism by the Holy Spirit, call upon God with
> great strain . . . insistently demanding tongues . . . stub-
> bornly tarry for tongues.[39]

Using another approach, A. Karev wrote in a charitable
manner, making a statement that would be acceptable to
the Russian and American Pentecostalists, save for the
omission of speaking in tongues.

---

[38] I. Motorin, "The Day of the Descent of the Holy Spirit," *Bv*,
No. 3, 1961, p. 15.
[39] A. I. Mitskevich, "Thoughts about the Activities of the Holy
Spirit," *Bv*, No. 2, 1959, p. 52.

One must make a separation between being born of the Holy Spirit and being filled with his power. . . . Without the Holy Spirit, salvation, faith, and the new birth are impossible. . . . But after the new birth, we must strive to receive the power of the Holy Spirit . . .

The majority of Christians have life, but do not yet have abundant life; the power of the Holy Spirit gives abundant life. The new birth is not the equivalent of a small portion of the Holy Spirit, nor is the power of the Holy Spirit a larger portion. They are the initial and subsequent acts . . .[40]

In a memorial article, Karev attributed the successful merger of almost all the Pentecostal believers in Belorussia to the dynamic influence of the Pentecostal presbyter, Ivan K. Pan'ko. Karev maintained that the reason other Pentecostalists did not join the Union churches was due to the extreme view they held concerning all other Christians who were not tongues-speakers. According to the independent Pentecostalists, the absence of glossolalia denoted the lack of the power of the Holy Spirit in the convert's life and witnessed to his "carnal" state. Karev concluded that the independents exhibited spiritual pride and self-exaltation, especially those who viewed the Baptists and Evangelical Christians as unconverted people.[41]

For the Pentecostalists who overemphasized the manifestations of the Holy Spirit, Karev offered this indictment:

. . . there are preachers who so preach and teach about the Holy Spirit that He stands between Christ and the child of God . . . as a screen. . . . The person who speaks much about the Holy Spirit and little of Christ is not filled with the Holy Spirit, for the Holy Spirit glorifies Christ and leads us to the preeminent love for Christ . . .[42]

---

[40] A. V. Karev, "About the Holy Spirit," *Bv*, No. 3, 1960, p. 16.
[41] A. V. Karev, "Memorial of Ivan K. Pan'ko," *Bv*, No. 6, 1964, pp. 65, 66.
[42] A. V. Karev, "About the Holy Spirit," *Bv*, No. 3, 1960, p. 18.

However, Karev urged all believers to strive to receive the power of the Holy Spirit in order to follow in the footsteps of Christ and to be transformed into his image.

vi. Violations of the August Agreement

Three years after the Pentecostal believers joined the Union the AUCECB summoned all churches, presbyters and preachers to a Council in October of 1948, in order to deal with violations of the August Agreement. The conference outlined goals for the attainment of complete reverence in all services and a reserved form of preaching that would not produce emotional reactions.

> How often the noise and shouts of nothing more than nervous sobbing and moaning, which destroy the reverent quiet of the service, are received as a special blessing, as a move of the Holy Spirit. . . . These manifestations are . . . but the results of "wrought up" nerves of our hearers.[43]

The problem continued unabatedly in 1949 as President Zhidkov surveyed the constant and persistent struggle against vocal disturbances during congregational prayers. The continued corporate prayers left Zhidkov "embarrassed, troubled and astonished at the spiritual ignorance and piteableness, and often, even the perversion of the truth." This led to his recommendation that the

> . . . presbyter is to control the entire service, including the prayers. Such order will bring more satisfaction to everyone. . . . We do not quench the Spirit, but strive to quench noise and disorder . . .[44]

---

[43] A. V. Karev, "On the Stillness and Reverence in Our Ministry," *Bv*, No. 1, 1949, pp. 44, 45.
[44] I. I. Zhidkov, "In the School of Prayer," *Bv*, No. 2, 1949, pp. 6–8.

In 1946, AUCECB presidium members M. Goliaev and A. L. Andreev were the first evangelicals permitted to travel abroad after the War. They visited fellow evangelicals in Scandinavia and attended Pentecostal services, emphasizing in their reports that the doctrines and practices in Sweden and Finland were no different from their own.

We found out that the Finnish Pentecostalists practice neither footwashing nor choral prayer in their meetings, certainly no ejaculations during the pronouncement of prayer . . .[45]

I wrote to the Finnish pastor for his comment on the above statements. The reply written by the associate pastor, stated:

We were surprised to hear the statement made by Brother M. Goliaev. . . . The fact is however, that the Pentecostals in Finland differ . . .
a. The gifts of the Spirit, including prophesying, speaking in tongues and interpretation of tongues, are frequently manifested both in our assembly services and in our public meetings . . .[46]

Andreev toured many churches in the Ukraine, a stronghold of Pentecostalists, informing them that he heard no choral prayer in the Pentecostal churches in Scandinavia. This may have been the case during his brief visit, and he made full use of the report to convince Pentecostalists of the reasonableness of the August Agreement which forbade glossolalia in services.

The continued disregard and violation of the Agree-

[45] M. Goliaev, "My Impressions During a Visit to the Pentecostals in Sweden and Finland," *Bv,* No. 6, 1946, pp. 31, 32.
[46] Letter from Reverend Tapani Karna, Helsinki, Finland, April 8, 1965.

ment caused Zhidkov to take decisive, vigorous action against those who, after repeated warnings, continued to pray in tongues while services were in progress. He issued orders to

> . . . expel them from the church, not because they are Pentecostals, but for their violation of our fraternal agreement.[47]

The internal dissension caused by the Pentecostal practices in the churches increased to the extent that a special conference was held in Moscow on January 26-31, 1957. The key former leaders of the Christians of Evangelical Faith met with the AUCECB presidium. Representing the Pentecostalists were D. I. Ponomarchuk, G. G. Ponurko (successor to Voronaev after his arrest), M. I. But, N. V. Kuz'menko, A. M. Tesliuk, and S. I. Marin. The following principles were agreed upon:

1. All true children of God . . . have the indwelling Holy Spirit according to I Cor. 12:13, Rom. 6.

2. . . . before God, the decisive fundamentals are not spiritual gifts, but a life and walk in the Spirit (Gal. 5:16-25).

3. We must not direct our gaze on the gifts above all else . . . but the glorification of Christ must be pre-eminent . . .

4. Where spiritual gifts are regarded as most important, it is here that the unity of the Spirit is severed among all of God's people. Spiritual gifts are granted to edify everyone. They can be used with blessing only when believers do not place themselves above, nor force them upon others. All contrivances and insin-

---

[47] I. I. Zhidkov and A. V. Karev, "To All Presbyters of Communities of Evangelical Christians-Baptists," *Bv*, No. 1, 1955, p. 5.

cerity must be discarded as belonging to the provinces of darkness.[48]

The above guidelines probably were aimed at the local church leaders who persisted in ignoring the regulations of the AUCECB. Zhidkov admitted that church discords were caused by contentious leaders who

> . . . slander each other, while the lambs . . . are grieved and pained at the disorder . . . stubborn, proud, obstinate, disobedient ones cannot maintain their church posts.[49]

Members of local assemblies were informed of their prerogatives to appeal for action to their elder presbyter in case of unfaithful or deviant presbyters, deacons, or preachers, and if necessary, appeal directly to AUCECB. For the necessary order and well-being of the assembly, an errant worker could be replaced by a more suitable candidate upon approval of the church in the presence of the participating elder presbyter.[50]

By the end of 1958, the problem seemed to be arrested, although the task of silencing the Pentecostalists seemed ever incomplete. Soviet antireligious pressure had increased, especially against the independent evangelicals, which may have caused greater reservation in the behavior of restless Union members.

> Now we are united in Christ and together we labor in one sacred path and in the bonds of love. . . . Experiencing the special blessings of the Lord, but feeling the responsibility for those yet outside the union, the

---

[48] "AUCECB News," *Bv*, No. 1, 1957, p. 79.
[49] I. I. Zhidkov, "The Church of Christ and its Order," *Bv*, No. 5, 1956, p. 7.
[50] *Ibid.*

leading brethren gathered in Kiev in May 1958, in order to lift their mighty voice calling for unity.[51]

The stern approach gave way to the counsel of Mitskevich, who urged the brethren to guard the unity already attained, and to strengthen the spiritual merger by refusing to permit any derogatory remarks to escape from the pulpit. He recommended the development of long suffering, not merely patience, in order to realize the coveted goal of genuine unity. He called for the member churches to allay all fears in regard to the election of Pentecostal men to church offices provided that they observed the conditions of the August Agreement. Regret was voiced concerning the independent Pentecostals who still refused unity, and Mitskevich indicated that the continued rejection rose from a lack of proper leadership and the absence of basic spiritual training.[52]

[51] A. I. Mitskevich, "The Unity of the Children of God," *Bv*, Nos. 5–6, 1958, p. 37.
[52] *Ibid.*, p. 38.

12

Soviet Charges Against the
Pentecostalists

i. The Soviet Section of the History of Religion
and Atheism

In 1959, A. I. Klibanov led a Soviet Government expedition in Lipetsk oblast, in the city of Voronezh, to study the contemporary state of religious sects, the ideology and tactics of sectarianism, and ways of overcoming religious survivals. This was conducted under the auspices of the Section of the History of Religion and Atheism, a branch of the Institute of History, USSR Academy of Sciences.

The historical ethnographic method, combining the study of the activity of local sects, personal chats with believers, and an investigation of archives sources, was used in the work of the expedition. In describing the teaching of the Pentecostalists, Klibanov noted their extreme mysticism, expressed not simply in the admission of other worldly power or the "knowability of God" but rather in the assertion of the accessibility of God to man via the sense organs. He listed Pentecostalists among the most "virulent species of religious opium."[1]

Garkavenko, in writing on religious sects, referred to the leaders who followed Voronaev, the founder of the

---

[1] I. A. Malakhova, "Historians Study Modern Religious Trends," *Istoriia USSR*, No. 2 (Moskva: 1961), pp. 233–235.

Christians of Evangelical Faith, as epileptics and hysterical "prophets" and "prophetesses."

> Psychiatrists explain that shrill excitement of the centers of speech are in the cortex of the brain and inhibit the remainder of the cortices of the brain so that a person ceases to understand what he says . . . this incoherency is called "angelic" tongues by Pentecostals. People with sound nervous systems cannot enter such a state at all. . . . People with weak nervous systems, following the ritual of such nervous shocks, end up in a mental hospital.[2]

Garkavenko continued, claiming that the various miracles, healings, and prophesies were enacted in the prayer meetings in order to reinforce the religious rites on the psychology of the believers. They always had "prophets or prophetesses who interpreted the incoherent muttering of the glossolalia."[3]

ii. Pentecostal Polemics

The Assemblies of God author of a comprehensive work on the glossolalia apparently replied to Garkavenko's counterparts in the United States when he wrote:

> The critics are continually identifying them with abnormal personalities whose neurotic tendencies stamp them as . . . candidates for the psychopathic wards. . . . Every revival movement has its share of cranks, fanatics, neurotics and feeble-minded individuals; and Pentecost is no exception. . . .
> We do protest the charge, however, that *all* Pentecostal people are abnormal. . . .[4]

[2] Garkavenko, *op. cit.*, p. 82.
[3] *Ibid.*, pp. 95, 96.
[4] Carl Brumback, *What Meaneth This?* (Springfield, Mo.: The Gospel Publishing House, 1947), p. 104.

To answer the charge made by fellow evangelicals that this controversial doctrine provoked strife, division, and unrest in Christendom, Brumback replied that

> . . . these friends fail to realize that in our insistence upon tongues, we are not contending for a pet doctrine . . . but for that wonderful experience of which speaking with tongues is the initial, physical evidence. It is our sincere belief that without this evidence there can be no fully Scriptural baptism with the Holy Ghost.[5]

This view was shared by Pentecostal believers in the Soviet Union, both Union members and independents. They agreed with the American Assemblies of God members that this experience was available to all believers. Further, they made a fine distinction between the evidence of speaking in tongues, received when one was initially baptized with the Holy Spirit, and the recurring gift of tongues as described in 1 Cor. 14. They considered the gift of tongues twofold in its operation—devotional and congregational; the former was for private use and the latter for the public and therefore more spectacular.[6] The public practice of speaking in tongues was forbidden to all Pentecostalists who became members of the communities of Evangelical-Christians-Baptists. While the exercise of devotional tongues served to edify the individual it was necessary for the companion gift (the interpretation of tongues) to accompany the congregational use of tongues in order to edify the church. The August Agreement of 1945 allowed no place for congregational tongues, even when accompanied by the interpretation, the practice of which was approved by Apostle Paul (I Cor. 14:27, 39) . A contradiction in the AUCECB basic principles was readily apparent as illustrated by the following statement:

---

[5] *Ibid.,* p. 188.
[6] *Ibid.,* p. 291.

Each member of the church participates in the service with those gifts which he received from the Lord (1 Cor. 12:4).[7]

The gifts of the Spirit, according to the context of the reference above, included the nine gifts customarily accepted and practiced by the Pentecostalists, but their assent to the August Agreement denied their continued existence. For the Pentecostal believers the decision to merge with the AUCECB was a difficult one, but those who selected this path of government recognition by removing their distinctive denominational label were obligated to respect the August Agreement. Worshipping in tongues could be maintained only in private devotions or in small clandestine meetings.

The late Donald Gee, for many years the editor of *Pentecost,* and esteemed by Pentecostalists around the world, warned:

> Do not fail the purpose of God. Beware of making too much of "messages," whether through tongues and interpretation, or any other way. The Spirit of God is not so prodigal with these things as we, in our folly, would have Him to be. The Bible plainly teaches temperance in the use of inspirational gifts. . . .
>
> Never let your exercise of prophetic gifts cause your meetings to degenerate into what one writer caustically described as a "tongues club."
>
> . . . The greatest victories of the world-wide Pentecostal Revival have occurred where the Movement has been first and foremost an agency for fervent evangelism.[8]

---

[7] "Fraternal Epistle to All Evangelical Christians-Baptists, Christians of Evangelical Faith and Mennonites," *Bv,* No. 6, 1963, p. 53.

[8] Donald Gee, "To Our New Pentecostal Friends," *Pentecost,* No. 58 (London: Feb. 1962), inside back cover. *Pentecost* has been the official organ of the Pentecostal World Fellowship.

No doubt, many of the Russian Pentecostalists were intemperate, others exhibited zeal without knowledge, and some fanatical exponents of spiritual gifts invited the ire and reaction of the Soviet Government.

On the question of divine healing, the AUCECB acknowledged the healings and miracles as recorded in the Bible literally and without apology. Writing on the Book of Acts, Mitskevich reasoned that miracles were necessary in that day "for who would believe their words about the resurrection of Christ if their witness was not confirmed with signs . . . as healing." By means of dispensational treatment, Mitskevich declared that the confirmation signs had ceased, and that any attempts to duplicate similar deeds would mean certain failure and result in reproach before an unbelieving world. However, he allowed for the possibility of contemporary healings within church circles alone,[9] whereas K. V. Somov stated that "in later times, miracles already were excluded from the plan of God."[10] Earlier in 1954, Mitskevich had published the following dogmatic statement:

Signs ceased in the apostolic period . . . the first days of Christianity the Holy Spirit showed many signs, then day by day less and less appeared until they ceased entirely (1 Tim. 5:23; 2 Tim. 4:20 . . .).[11]

When the well-known American evangelist Oral Roberts visited the Moscow church in 1960, he was invited by the AUCECB executive leaders to dinner. For four hours they questioned him about the gifts of the Spirit and in particular about his ministry of prayer for the sick. After candidly answering their difficult, probing questions, Roberts asked them,

[9] A. I. Mitskevich, "Thoughts From the Book of Acts of the Apostles," *Bv,* Nos. 5–6, 1960, pp. 96–108.
[10] K. V. Somov, "The Holy Spirit," *Bv,* No. 3, 1963, pp. 15–19.
[11] A. I. Mitskevich, "On Signs," *Bv,* No. 2, 1954, p. 31.

May I ask you some questions? Why is it that you brethren have only a preaching ministry? Have you no hands?[12]

He had observed the sick in their midst, but saw no evidence of ministering to their needs for healing in the church services.

The Soviet antireligious press pointed out a similar discrepancy, stating that the presbyters

. . . devote much attention to miracles in their sermons . . . pouring from the pages of the Baptist magazine, *Bratskii vestnik*, as from a horn of plenty.

. . . as to where these signs are today, Mitskevich modestly points out: "The Holy Spirit . . . discontinued the phenomenon." Why? Only Mitskevich knows.

However, to spread religious superstitions without believing in miracles is very difficult even for the experts such as the Baptist theologians.[13]

A cartoon accompanied Kaushanski's article, depicting God as an aged, white-bearded man asleep on a cloud next to a sign which read "I no longer perform miracles."

The candid hours of sharing with evangelist Oral Roberts concluded with prayer as each Russian minister received the laying on of hands by the American. One of the pastors testified after prayer that God had been dealing with him to use his hands in a ministry of prayer for the sick, but an inner reserve had restrained him from doing so. He expressed his desire to be used of God in a contemporary healing ministry.[14]

---

[12] Oral Roberts, "My Trip to Russia for Christ," *Abundant Life*, No. 8 (Tulsa: 1960), p. 14.

[13] P. Kaushanski, "Miracles According to the Baptists," *Nauka i religiia*, No. 12 (Moskva: 1961), pp. 18–20.

[14] Roberts, *op. cit.*

Southern Baptist Mullins believed, as did the Russian Evangelical Christians-Baptists, in the Biblical miracles of the past, including healings.

> . . . God can work suddenly as well as slowly . . . his supreme interest is the realm of free personal beings, and that whatever is needful for their welfare he can and will perform.[15]

However, concerning the contemporary Christian's confrontation with suffering and pain, Mullins maintained, together with many Baptists,[16] that

> . . . in the New Testament suffering is glorified, not as a good within itself, but as a means of spiritual growth. Pain may and indeed often does follow as a result of holy living in a sinful world. In all its forms it is for the Christian a means of growth in the divine life.[17]

Contrary to a passive attitude, the Russian Pentecostalists and the American Assemblies of God preached that believers could be used of God in supernaturally ministering health to the sick by the means of prayer. Myer Pearlman explained that it

> . . . is not to be understood that the possessor of this gift . . . has the power to heal everyone; allowance must be made for the sovereignty of God and the sick person's attitude and spiritual condition. Even Christ was limited in His miracle-working ability by the unbelief of the people. Matt. 13:58.
> The sick person is not absolutely dependent upon one

---

[15] Edgar Young Mullins, *The Christian Religion in its Doctrinal Expression* (Valley Forge: The Judson Press, 1964), p. 273.
[16] Cox, *Encyclopedia . . .* , Vol. II, p. 1313.
[17] Mullins, *op. cit.*, p. 276.

possessing the gift. All believers in general, and elders of the church in particular, are empowered to pray for the sick. Mark 16:18; James 5:14.[18]

The Russian Pentecostalists taught by Ivan Voronaev were in accord with the doctrinal position taken by the Assemblies of God concerning the gifts of the Holy Spirit. The nine gifts, as recorded in 1 Corinthians 12, were classified in three categories: the three gifts of revelation (the word of wisdom, the word of knowledge, the discerning of spirits), the three gifts of power (faith, miracles, healings), and the three utterance gifts (tongues, interpretation of tongues, prophecy). In each of the classifications, Ralph Riggs emphasized one gift as the greatest: the word of wisdom (revelation), faith (power), and prophecy (utterance).[19]

Myer Pearlman, one of the most honored Assemblies of God authors of the past, distinguished between the gifts of the Spirit and the fruits of the Spirit (Gal. 5:22, 23) in this manner:

The fruit of the Spirit is the progressive development of the Christ-life implanted at regeneration; while the gifts may be bestowed suddenly to any Spirit-filled believer at any point in the believer's experience.[20]

Misuses and abuses of the gifts were acknowledged and genuine attempts have been made to adhere to the Scriptural use of the gifts. Pearlman distinguished between true and false inspiration by means of the practical test of love, without which the exercise of the gifts failed to achieve the intended benefit to everyone involved. Further, no

---

[18] Myer Pearlman, *Knowing the Doctrines of the Bible* (Springfield: The Gospel Publishing House, 1937), p. 324.

[19] Ralph M. Riggs, *The Spirit Himself* (Springfield: Gospel Publishing House, 1949), p. 113.

[20] Pearlman, *op. cit.,* p. 33.

amount of spiritual manifestations nor zeal in the ministry could satisfy the deficiency of the fruits of personal holiness.[21]

Donald Gee candidly and objectively criticized those who had developed a "gift complex." Groups that had boasted of their liberty with "the gifts" were urged to evaluate the Pentecostal revival, to see if it was fulfilling its high purpose of lifting Christ as the Savior of the world. He reminded the irresponsible elements within Pentecostalism that the exercise of the gifts of the Holy Spirit were "never intended to be the hobby of little religious clubs" and that the

. . . witness of history throughout all ages of the church is that inspirational movements that make too much of "messages" through spiritual gifts inevitably sign their own death-warrant.[22]

---

[21] *Ibid.*, pp. 332–334.
[22] Donald Gee, "Messages Through 'The Gifts' " *Pentecost*, No. 60 (London: 1960), inside back cover.

PART IV

THE EVANGELICAL'S RELATIONSHIP TO THE SOVIET GOVERNMENT

13

The Soviet Liaison Council

i. The Council for the Affairs of Religious Cults

We have considered the historical background and mergers of the denominations that are now members of one union and subject to the AUCECB headquarters in Moscow although they are spread across all fifteen republics of the Soviet Union. We shall now delve into the responsibilities of the evangelical believers in their relationship to the Soviet Government.

Ivan Vasilevich Polianski served as the Chairman of the Council for the Affairs of Religious Cults (CARC) until his death in 1956. Except for general background information indicating that he carried out important state assignments prior to his 1944 appointment, there was speculation that Polianski may have been a police agent as was Karpov, his counterpart for the Council for the Affairs of the Russian Orthodox Church (CAROC).[1]

Former American reporter Robert Magidoff was in Moscow at the time CARC was organized and he felt that the scores of council representatives functioned as "Stalin's eyes"[2] as well as contact men between the local Soviet officials and the local religious groups.

In addition to the Evangelical Christians-Baptists, the following religious bodies had similar relations to the CARC: the Roman Catholic Church (Lithuanian and

---

[1] Walter Kolarz, *Religion in . . . ,* p. 135.
[2] Magidoff, *op. cit.,* p. 75.

Latvian dioceses), the Jewish Communities of Moscow and Kiev, the Moslems, the Central Buddhist Council, the Old Believers, the Armenian Church, the Methodist Church of Estonia, the Evangelical Lutheran Church (Estonia and Latvia), the Reformed Church (Transcarpathian Province), the All-Union Council of Seventh Day Adventists, and the Molokans.[3]

The CARC could authorize these religious bodies to convene councils and conferences and to publish religious literature. It also had authority to grant them permission to teach religious doctrines in special theological academies maintained at church expense.[4] Although the Soviet Government claimed that the CARC fulfilled the same functions as the CAROC, the treatment was not entirely equal. Whereas the Russian Orthodox Church was permitted to operate several academies and seminaries, this privilege has been denied to the AUCECB despite its optimistic hopes shortly after the Great Patriotic War. Polianski assured a visiting clergyman, W. H. Melish, that all religious groups were given equal treatment and that the only reason for the existence of the separate CAROC was due to the fact that the Russian Orthodox Church adherents numbered considerably more than the total within the CARC.[5] CARC officials repeated the claim that the two councils performed similar functions, but that the CARC relationship was more complicated, for it dealt with twelve separate religious groups instead of one.[6]

CARC deputies in each of the regular districts of the Soviet Union managed all minor difficulties on a local level and turned to Moscow for the solution of infrequent

---

[3] *Conference in Defense of Peace of All Churches and Religious Associations in the USSR* (Moscow: Moscow Patriarchate, 1952), p. 135.

[4] Kovalev, *op. cit.*, p. 391.

[5] Melish, *op. cit.*, p. 22.

[6] Constantin de Grunwold, *The Churches and the Soviet Union* (New York: The Macmillan Co., 1962), p. 108.

serious cases. Whether the violations of some laws were caused by religionists or by what a Soviet official described as the "misplaced zeal of a local official or a group of undisciplined young atheists," necessary steps were taken promptly.[7]

Prior to 1943 the Soviet bureaucracy did not obligate itself to the detailed care of religious groups, such as making provisions in its state planning to include the multiplied needs of thousands of churches. The pre-revolution Duma Commission on Religious Cults maintained a relatively loose organization compared with the CARC, for once the Soviet State

. . . felt that the churches' services could be of advantage, it entered into the bargaining process, and from 1943 to the present the churches' existence in the Soviet Union has been in the context of the bargaining situation.[8]

In those early years after the War, flattered by its new relationship with CARC, AUCECB published greetings from Polianski in the *Bratskii vestnik,* and entertained high hopes for a grandiose plan of Bible and hymnal publications, confident that

. . . in 1948 we shall be able to publish a substantial hymnal containing our spiritual songs, since there is no hindrance of any kind.[9]

Nine years after this statement was written the hymnals were finally published. Similarly, optimism was expressed for the printing of Bibles; and the reward came in 1957, thirty years after a previous publication which was initi-

---

[7] *Ibid.,* pp. 107, 108.
[8] Fletcher, *op. cit.,* p. 256.
[9] "Eighty Years of Evangelical-Baptists Hymns," *Bv,* No. 5, 1947, p. 24.

ated by Prokhanov. However, the CARC did assist the conference delegates who arrived in Moscow in 1944 and 1945 by arranging for their room and board,[10] in distinct contrast to the Tsarist government's disruption of Pashkov's conference in 1884.

The modus vivendi established by the state during the Great Patriotic War reverted to a modified program of antireligious propaganda. The former League of Militant Godless was replaced by the euphemistic Society for the Propagation of Scientific and Political Knowledge. The official act of the establishment of the Council for the Affairs of Religious Cults was printed in the collection of laws and decrees, but no change in legal status was effected.[11]

The Law of 1929 remained in effect, circumscribing the religious organizations to religious duties alone and noninterference in the affairs of the state. Religious societies were forbidden to create mutual benefit clubs, cooperatives, render material aid to its members, organize special children's, young people's or women's meetings, or to maintain various kinds of circles and groups other than the staff which ministered the cult. Also forbidden were the organizations of sanitariums and hospitals, open libraries and reading rooms, excursions and children's circuses. Religious communities guilty of violating the Soviet law were to be suppressed by the State.[12]

Peter Kolonitski, editor of *Nauka i religiia* (Science and Religion, the offical antireligious monthly magazine of the Soviet Union), stated in an interview,

God has no place in the world we are living in. For the time being, we have no means of ridding our society of the clergy, who do their utmost to stand in our way.[13]

10 "We Were In Favor," *Bv*, No. 3, 1945, p. 15.
11 Gecys, *op. cit.*, p. 133.
12 Kovalev, *op. cit.*, pp. 391–392.
13 Grunwold, *op. cit.*, p. 70.

It is interesting to note that the Soviet Government's newspaper *Izvestiia* supported and patronized the church in its role as a useful ally of the Soviet regime. At the same time the Communist Party's paper *Pravda* counteracted any possible influence this support might have within the USSR by sponsoring antireligious propaganda.[14] However, when a religious group was suspected of duplicity, it was often berated by the Soviet press. At one time *Bratskii vestnik* proudly declared that the evangelicals were attempting to adapt their beliefs to socialist reality, claiming that communism and religion did not contradict each other. The evangelicals' article contained a greeting to President Nikolai Bulganin on the fortieth anniversary of the "great and sacred October" in which gratitude was expressed to God that the Soviet rulers practiced the great ideal found in the gospels, at a time when the Christians in the West "talked so much of Christian ideals, but failed to practice them."[15] Flattery from Christians was not appreciated by the Communist regime; it instead drew denunciatory replies.

ii. Soviet Legislation Regarding Religion and Communist Party Violations

The Soviet Government divided local religious bodies into two sizes[16]—a "community" consisting of twenty or more believers, and a "group" of less than twenty believers. Both were organized in order to satisfy their religious needs. A religious body was permitted to elect its minister and other church officers necessary to serve its needs in the performance of the religious services of the cult. Prayer meetings that touched on political purposes contrary to

---

14 Gecys, *ibid.*
15 *Bv*, No. 6, 1957, p. 3.
16 "Soviet Legislation on Cults," *Nauka i religiia*, No. 10, (Moskva: 1961), pp. 89–92.

the interests of the Soviet society were forbidden. Believers were not to be encouraged to deny the fulfillment of their civic obligations, nor could propaganda be disseminated to alienate them from active participation in state, cultural, and socio-political activities.

A religious community or group could safely initiate its limited activities only after registration with CARC agents. Upon violation of the Soviet law on cults, its right to function could be revoked. Sects that maintained anti-Soviet views and groups considered fanatical were barred from registration. The Pentecostal churches that chose not to join the local communities of Evangelical Christians-Baptists assumed an illegal status simply by continuing their worship activities.

Favorable conditions enabled registered believers to obtain some prayer houses and other cult property without charge by means of an agreement with the executive committee of the regional or municipal Council of Workers' Deputy. An agreement was signed by at least twenty members of the religious community, who then assumed the complete responsibility for the maintenance of the property. This included the payment of all expenses connected with the ownership and use of the property, and adequate compensation to the State for the deterioration or loss of the property. An inventory of all property was maintained, including the purchase of all new articles as well as articles transferred from other houses of prayer which were not the possessions of individual members. Officials from the executive committees of the Council of Workers' Deputies were to be allowed admittance for periodic inspections at any time other than the worship services. It became apparent that the CARC, overtly intended to be an official arbitration council, increasingly could persuade and possibly control local church groups and communities. Such intrusion by the CARC leaders in the internal life of the churches violated the Soviet legislation of April 8, 1929, which reemphasized the 1918 decree "On Separation of Church and State."

Two Moscow clergymen, boldly protesting the CAROC harassment of the Russian Orthodox Church, charged that

> . . . during the period 1957-1964, under personal pressure from Khrushchev, who permitted "subjectivism and administrationism in the leadership," which was finally condemned by the Communist Party of the USSR, . . . the council radically changed its function. . . .[17]

The two priests, N. I. Eshliman and G. P. Yakunin, further indicated that Communist Party ideology was more aggressive than the Soviet State law by declaring that government registration of the clergy had become illegal because it served as a sanctioning act instead of simply a formality. They protested and appealed to N. V. Podgorny, chairman of the Presidium of the Supreme Soviet of the USSR, stating that it was

> . . . well known that in our country, during the period 1961-1964, and under the personal initiative of N. Khrushchev, an active campaign was conducted for the massive closing of Orthodox churches.
> . . . the mass closing of Orthodox Churches was an outspoken infraction of the law based on a non-objective, arbitrary interpretation of Soviet law, and violated the freedom of participation in religious cults as envisaged by the Constitution of the USSR.[18]

The priests objected to the unwritten orders given to clergymen orally by the CAROC in 1961-1962, saying that

---

[17] "Appeal by Two Orthodox Priests, Moscow, December 15, 1965," *Religion in Communist Dominated Areas*, Vol. V, Nos. 9–10 (New York: 1966), p. 74.

[18] *Ibid.* p, 76.

services connected with a burial were no longer permitted without the written permission of local authorities. The priests declared that this was in violation of the decree presently effective "On Religious Associations."[19] They concluded their lengthy letter by courageously requesting that all the churches, monasteries and theological schools closed during the period 1961-1964 be "justly returned to the Russian Orthodox Church."

Soviet legislation limited the use of offerings received in the house of worship to purposes connected with the maintenance of its property, the support of its ministers and its denominational headquarters. No levies or compulsory collections were permitted under Soviet law.

The administration of church property and church funds was to be the responsibility of the laity, without any interference from the ministers. The local church elected three members of an executive council by means of an open election and was empowered to elect an auditing committee of three. These elected church officers could not be removed by the local ministers or denominational headquarters, nor could instructions be issued to them by the spiritual authorities. The functions of the presbyters and preachers were limited to the conducting of the religious services. The right to challenge anyone in the executive council or the auditing committee of a local religious community was the exclusive prerogative of the executive committees of the local State authorities.[20]

Although *Bratskii vestnik* was silent concerning these internal pressures by the Soviet regime, the relationship of pastor to people in all but the largest evangelical churches was so intimate that the presbyter's authority in all areas of church life was not easily abrogated. The infiltration of non-evangelicals or Soviet "plants" into the

---

[19] *Ibid.*, p. 78.
[20] "Soviet Legislation on Cults," *Nauka i religiia*, No. 10, 1961, p. 90.

local churches was controlled by the strict observation of prospective members during the one-year minimum probationary period preceding baptism. Only baptized members could be candidates for church offices.

This may have had a far more damaging effect in the Russian Orthodox Church. In a companion letter of complaint directed to Patriarch Aleksei, the two Orthodox priests reminded him that the church council of 1945 empowered the pastor to be the father and head of the local parish, concerned also with the "spiritual control over the administrative and economic life of the flock entrusted to him." The decree of 1961 directly contradicted the definition of the role of the priest in the parish and the scope of his pastoral service. Their complaint charged that the decree

. . . of the synod, which takes away from the priest the administrative and economic management of the parish, in actual fact lowers the priest to the level of an employee celebrating services and rites on a contractual basis, and makes him entirely dependent on the executive committee.

. . . only by putting an end to the intervention of "civil authorities" into the sphere of the sacred, . . . the "divine" Russian Church will be able to serve our country without hypocrisy and with effectiveness.[21]

The letter ended with a plea that the "anti-canonical decisions of the Council of Bishops of 1961" be rescinded. Shortly thereafter, the two priests were informed, on order of the Patriarch, that they were released from their posts and suspended from sacramental functions pending their complete repentance![22]

---

[21] "An Open Letter to His Holiness Patriarch Alexei, Moscow, November 21, 1965," *Religion in Communist Dominated Areas,* Vol. V, Nos. 11–12 (New York: 1966), p. 97.

[22] *RCDA*, Vol. V, Nos 15–16, 1966, p. 129.

Paul Anderson, editor of the National Council of Churches Bulletin called *Religion in Communist Dominated Areas*, noted the insistence of the two priests that they were loyal to both the church and the Soviet government, thus constituting a loyal opposition. He pointed out that living under a regime avowedly intent on liquidating belief in God, both those who resisted and those who sought accommodation were struggling to avert one and the same liquidation.[23]

---

23 *Ibid.*, Vol. V, Nos. 11–12, 1966, p. 89.

14

The Believers' Responses and Reactions to the Soviet Government

i. Celebrating State Holidays

President Zhidkov left no doubt in the minds of the members of the registered evangelical churches that not only religious, but state holidays also were to be observed by the constituency. They were members not only of a heavenly, but of an earthly land—the Soviet Union, a country to be loved and highly valued. Zhidkov listed the state holidays which were to be celebrated by the members of the communities of the Evangelical Christians-Baptists, including

> ... the great October Revolution, the greatest national holiday of our Soviet homeland. ... In the realm of religious law, the October Revolution brought to our country the basic true freedom of conscience expressed before everyone in the great act of the separation of church and state. ... Now there is equity for all ... it took France 125 years, whereas the Soviet regime enacted this great reform within a few years. ... All the above mentioned makes ... the Great October Revolution especially dear to all believers.[1]

The Stalin Constitution, celebrated in December, was termed 'the most democratic of all constitutions in the

---

[1] I. I. Zhidkov, "Our Holidays," *Bv*, No. 2, 1946, pp. 14, 15.

world. . . ."[2] Evangelicals found this difficult reading if
they were among the masses who "sat" in exile during
the purges which were at their apex immediately after
Stalin's Constitution was confirmed by the Eighth Congress in 1936. If indeed Zhidkov had been released after
nine years of exile to assume the leadership of the
AUCECB, it is difficult to explain his praise without sus-
pecting a position of compromise, possibly induced by
psychological reconditioning or impending threats upon
his family. Zhidkov claimed to be following the Scriptures
obediently in asking the churches to pray for all in authority, concluding that

> We must follow our country's order for all its citizens
> . . . by participating in community holidays, demonstra-
> tions, meetings, etc.[3]

If Zhidkov wrote in this manner with the hope that the
believers would understand his delicate position and not
take such instructions too seriously, then evangelical parents were still faced with a difficult and dangerous choice.
They could attempt to keep their children from joining
the Little Octobrists and the Pioneers, or risk the toll that
the anti-religious indoctrination would exact, since atheist
teaching was included in the many popular activities provided for Soviet youth groups.

ii. Soviet Youth and Evangelical Parents

Although the Pioneer rules included a love for the Communist Party, and its training program prepared the
youngsters for Komsomol candidacy, the members possessed a code of conduct resembling many qualities which
are compatible with the Christian ethic, such as obedience

---

[2] *Ibid.*
[3] *Ibid.*

to parents, care for the young and aid to the old, self-discipline, love for labor, and the care of public property.

In R. T. Fisher's study of the official reports of twelve Komsomol Congresses held from 1918 to 1954, he indicated the awareness on the part of the Komsomols that the controlling hand of the Communist Party left no phase of the youth organization or activity untouched. Throughout the years the Komsomol pattern has retained many of the same elements that it embraced in its formative years. Ever supplied by fresh reserves, the Komsomol membership is called upon to help the Soviet regime in its political indoctrination, general education, industry, agriculture, social relations, military activities, and world affairs. Impressionable youth, as yet idealistic and not disillusioned, were trained to acquire a certain quality of character which included a loyalty to Party chiefs, iron discipline, self-sacrificial bravery, ideological purity, unshaken conviction, incessant vigilance, uncompromising militancy, and a hatred toward enemies.[4]

A. V. Karev revealed the AUCECB headquarters' awareness of the concern and apprehension of Christian parents for their young. He subtly communicated a message of encouragement for Christian parents to faithfully train their children despite the trials of life in the midst of a Soviet society by drawing a parallel from the life of Moses. He reminded his readers that Moses spent the formative years of his life with his parents, during which time the fundamentals of faith, hope and love were deeply implanted.

> The time came to enter the palace . . . dangerous for the soul of Moses . . . but with such fundamentals . . . there was no alarm. The faith of his parents was such that the God who protected him in the Nile river, would

[4] Ralph Talcott Fisher Jr., *Pattern for Soviet Youth* (New York: Columbia University Press, 1959), p. 279.

protect even in the Pharaoh's palace, from its temptations and allurements.

Today, we see the power and greatness of God as indicated before Pharaoh and all the Egyptians, . . . the power of darkness contending with the power of light.[5]

Likewise, AUCECB presidium member Mitskevich called attention to the fact that the home of believers was a great school in which children were to be nurtured in honor, nobility, morals and culture. Sensitive to the charges of the anti-religious press so often aimed at sectarian parents, he warned the evangelicals against antagonizing their children by physically compelling them to read their Bibles or forcing them to pray at length. In acknowledging a believer's beating of a child which necessitated the attention of a physician, he advocated parental self-control, adding the following advice:

Train children to work. Spare them from indolence. See to it that the children read; keep them from immoral books. Instill the love for people and love for nation in your children. Let the light of the teachings of Christ be seen from the windows of a Christian home.[6]

Party members were alert for any such instances of sectarian beatings of children. A report was followed by the action of the Soviet People's Court, depriving believers of their parental rights and committing the children to a State Children's Home.[7]

In Margaret Mead's study, *Soviet Attitudes Toward Authority*, E. Calas, after observation concluded that parents

[5] A. V. Karev, "Lessons for Believers from the Life of Moses," *Bv*, No. 5, 1956, pp. 11–21.

[6] A. I. Mitskevich, "The Beauty of the Christian Life," *Bv*, No. 2, 1955, pp. 42, 43.

[7] Livshits, *op. cit.*, pp. 139, 140.

. . . must serve as models of political and social activities, industriousness, unselfishness, and optimism. Children become emotionally alienated from parents who do not act in accord with the precepts and ideals which the children learn in school and in the Pioneer or Komsomol organizations.[8]

Punishment as a form of correction was consistently emphasized in the Soviet Union but corporal punishment was outlawed and frequent warnings were issued against this abuse of punishment. Parents placed themselves "under the microscope" to search for inadequacies in their role of parenthood.[9]

The antireligious press published a steady stream of articles accusing the sectarians of negativism in the social upbringing of their children.

Baptists mutilate their children; they educate them in a reactionary spirit by not permitting them to wear the Pioneer tie, nor to enter the Komsomol. Children who have fallen into the Baptist net are made sullen, unsociable, depending upon God's will for everything, whereby they lose their capacity for independent thinking.[10]

The fact that children dared to think and act outside the context of molded thought in a communist society greatly disturbed the core of workers who constantly propagated scientific atheism. More involved than the independent Baptists and Evangelical Christians were the Pentecostalists who were often accused of forbidding their children to join the Pioneers, or wearing the "devil's sign," the red tie, or even attending school beyond the fourth year.

[8] E. Calas, "Conclusions of Research on Soviet Child Training Ideals and Their Political Significance," *Soviet Attitudes Toward Authority* (New York: McGraw-Hill Book Company, 1951), p. 107.
[9] *Ibid.,* p. 109.
[10] Livshits, *op. cit.,* p. 131.

The believers' violation of the Soviet Constitution as it applied to the separation of church and state, and the school from the church, invited the wrath of the officials.

> . . . the leaders understand that faith will die if parents do not rule the "souls" of the offspring . . . children of tender years sit with parents in prayer meetings . . . this weakens the psyche and cripples the children and young people in such a religious, fanatical atmosphere. . . .[11]

Dismayed by the impact the Communist youth group had made upon his youngsters a Pentecostal preacher named Godyshev removed his two sons from the Pioneers. Pressured by the Crimean school director Zharskaia, Godyshev boldly asserted:

> Your business is to teach my children, but I myself will train them as I need to. . . . I will give myself as a sacrifice if you unteach my son. You honor a struggle—then let's struggle.[12]

Pentecostal preachers were stereotyped as persons forbidding the reading of newspapers, journals, and books (except the Bible), the attendance at the cinema, theatre, concerts, dances, and social organizations. Some instructed members not to vote, nor work in government establishments, and to refuse service in the Red Army.[13] Pentecostal presbyter Oleg Klimok convinced his members not to remain in professional unions, or participate in Soviet holiday demonstrations, or join the Komsomol.[14]

iii. Non-Registered Pentecostalists

As a rule non-registered Pentecostalists gathered secretly and in small groups at the apartments of various members.

---

[11] Kalugin, *op. cit.*, p. 23.
[12] Maiat, *op. cit.*, p. 26.
[13] Livshits, *op. cit.*, p. 136.
[14] *Nauka i religiia*, No. 4, 1962, p. 39.

The uninitiated outsider had no access to such meetings, but descriptive information secured from former members who apostatized revealed that believers

> . . . gradually enter into a state of religious ecstasy . . . a spectacle of nervous, psychological stimulation artificially aroused, prepared by grim, ascetic fasting. Psychological exhaustion is induced by prayers, jumping, hopping, etc. . . . then they entirely lose self control. . . .
> . . . during prayer, they all take on some kind of mass psychosis, hysteria . . . as being a communion in the spirit . . . speech is replaced by incoherent mutterings . . . called "speaking in new tongues" (glossolalia).[15]

Soviet films such as "The Road from Obscurity,"[16] and "Clouds over Borsk"[17] have depicted the fanaticism of the Pentecostalists. The expressed goal of these productions was to illustrate dramatically the destructive toll due to the indifference of Soviet citizens in relation to anti-religious work. The influence of the sectarian preachers upon young people was admitted, even stressed.

The Pentecostalists were berated for refusing medical aid, clinging to the means of prayer alone to drive the "evil spirits" out of persons' bodies. In the Saratov oblast, a woman who held healing services was found guilty of breaking the Soviet law which categorically forbade similar kinds of "medical" activity.[18] A Pentecostal mother who lost her third child stated, "If God wills, He will heal the child; if not let Him take him." In this incident the president of the village soviet, the school director, and the local

---

[15] Garkavenko, *op. cit.,* pp. 86–88.
[16] G. Ul'ianov, "The Road from Obscurity," *Nauka i religiia,* No. 5, 1961, pp. 90, 91.
[17] E. Gromov, "Ideological Struggle," *Nauka i religiia,* No. 5, 1962, p. 89.
[18] "Freedom of Conscience and Lawfulness," *Nauka i religiia,* No. 9, 1961, p. 74.

obstetrician brought her to the hospital with the sick child, but it was too late.[19]

Difficult-to-believe charges were ascribed to fanatical Pentecostalists, such as a brutal murder by a grandmother,[20] child-sacrifice by a devout couple,[21] as well as mental derangements, family dissolutions,[22] and mutilation.[23]

To account for all these accusations as trumped-up charges would be an oversimplified attempt to eliminate the dangers of fanaticism. In the clandestine climate of fervent religious meetings self-appointed prophets with peripheral knowledge of the Bible inflamed ignorant devotees into frenzied prayer. The Episcopal clergyman Morton T. Kelsey, a student of Jungian psychology, listed the psychological criticisms of tongues speaking, none of which has been overlooked by Soviet writers. The unleashing of emotionalism, Kelsey asserted, was not a necessary part of speaking in tongues, but such outbursts have been linked to schizophrenia, hysteria, catalepsy, or an abnormal trance state. Tongues speaking has been identified with ordinary schizophrenia, one form of psychosis, in which some individuals have been overwhelmed by the experience to such an extent that they never again regained psychological equilibrium, and the weak ego disintegrated. Some tongues speaking experiences have been described as neurotic manifestations, associated particularly with hysteria, and where there was group, hypnotic, or auto-suggestion, feats normally impossible could be performed.[24]

[19] *Nauka i religiia*, No. 7, 1963, p. 75.
[20] Maiat, *loc. cit.*, pp. 18, 19.
[21] *Nauka i religiia*, No. 12, 1961, p. 31.
[22] N. Shtanko, "Behind a Heavily Curtained Window," *Izvestiia*, (Moskva), June 20, 1962, p. 6.
[23] *Nauka i religiia*, No. 10, 1962, p. 36.
[24] Mortin T. Kelsey, *Tongue Speaking* (New York: Doubleday & Company, 1964), pp. 206–211.

The Pentecostal meetings may indeed have attracted the mentally unstable, for in the mystical aspects and the little understood manifestations of the charismatic gifts, they were able to find opportunities for the disordered self-expression that they sought. Unless the meetings were conducted by mature leaders capable of dealing kindly but firmly with mentally abnormal persons, the services could be wrought with the perils of uncontrolled religious excitement, an atmosphere in marked contrast to those of joyous worship and praise or deep soul-searching, all of which met the criterion of edification for the entire congregation.

The Pentecostal glossolalia has disturbed both the AUCECB executives and the atheist cadres. Both groups wished it were nonexistent because its strange and inexplicable attraction seems to have drawn enthusiastic response from young and old alike. The *Komsomol'skaia pravda* graphically portrayed the frustration that I. Voevodin, Chairman of the Atheist's Club, experienced in dealing with the Pentecostalists. He attended a court in Krasnoiarsk, in which Leonid Shevchenko, a leader of the "barbaric Pentecostal sect" was on trial. He described their program as one of antagonism and hatred for human beings.

> Even with the full realization of all the savagery and immoral atrocities of the sectarians, it is difficult to answer the bitter question: "Why do the sectarians find so many followers? Where do they get their strength?"[25]

Acknowledging Shevchenko, an engineer, to be a "powerful, clever and devilishly shrewd man," Voevodin noted that he aided people in finding jobs and in securing practical advice.

---

[25] I. Voevodin, "Komsomol Leaders Must Play a Greater Role in Atheistic Propaganda," *Komsomol'skaia pravda* (Moskva) September 25, 1962.

Kindness and intimidation, financial help and black-mail, tearful prayers and fiery sermons were the methods which Shevchenko beautifully used.

. . . The people, poisoned by Shevchenko and his assistants, refused to fulfill their civic duties, burned pioneer kerchiefs, and trampled down the red flag with their boots. And what did we, members of the Komsomol do. . . . Almost nothing.[26]

Voevodin bemoaned the fact that in that city of a half-million, only one small group of fifteen Komsomol atheists were active!

Somehow it isn't even considered a defect in Komsomol circles, whether an activist conducts antireligious work or does not know how. . . . Why such irresponsibility and complacency among the Komsomol leaders? . . . people are lost . . . and it does not bother the Komsomol workers. . . .[27]

Yet the very next day, a *Pravda* editorial boastfully claimed an intensification of the scientific atheistic education in various areas, including the above mentioned city of Krasnoiarsk, stating that

. . . considerable experience in personal work with be-lievers was gained in the province of Zaporozhe and in the Krasnoiarsk (Siberia) region.[28]

Besides the independent Pentecostalists, Soviet sources revealed that despite the successful unity of 1944, there were unrelated independent groups of Evangelical Chris-tians in the Ukraine, Belorussia, Siberia, and the Urals.[29]

---

26 *Ibid.*
27 *Ibid.*
28 "Participation in the Battle on the Ideological Front," *Pravda* (Moskva) September 26, 1962.
29 Kalugan, *loc. cit.,* p. 17.

Some independent Baptists have been accused of conducting illegal anti-social activities, including the opening of illegal prayer halls.[30] Other independents called "Pure Baptists" and "Complete Evangelical Christians" actually divided twenty-two union churches by reviving old schisms as they condemned the AUCECB leaders for achieving the historic unity, calling it instead dirty work.[31] One of their strong objections to the union was its acceptance of the Pentecostal believers.

By the very nature of their illegal status the non-registered evangelicals appealed to fanatical and anti-Soviet elements as well as sincere believers who were convinced that the registered churches were composed of compromisers. This conclusion was drawn because of the apparent unwillingness of the AUCECB to ever criticize the government. Rather the evangelical headquarters consistently maintained a posture of respect for and subservience to the Soviet State and its imposed limitations.

iv. The Dissident "Initiative Group"

In August of 1961 the "Initiative Group" (also known as the "Organizational Committee" and "Church Council") emerged as a divisive force within AUCECB churches. At the height of its drive against AUCECB the dissident movement, led by A. F. Prokof'ev and G. K. Kriuchkov,[32] spearheaded the withdrawal of approximately 5 per cent of the membership[33] or some 26,500 believers.[34]

30 Livshits, *loc. cit.*, p. 134.

31 *Bv*, No. 6, 1963, pp. 36, 39.

32 *Bv*, No. 6, 1963, p. 13. (Their denominational background is not given).

33 "National Convention of Evangelical Christians-Baptists," *Novosti Press Agency* (Moscow: 1966) cited in *RCDA*, Vol. V, No. 21, 1966, p. 168; *Bv*, No. 6, 1966, p. 36 stated that 4% seceded, while p. 39 stated that in the beginning of 1966 there were 6,000 who sep-

The AUCECB summoned a major conference in Moscow on October 15-17, 1963, to which 450 ministers responded.[35] The agenda included the examination and confirmation of the AUCECB rules and regulations, the election of the presidium by the valid voting delegates, and the problem of unity.[36]

Researcher William C. Fletcher claimed that the convention was called specifically in response to the challenge of the Initiative Group. His findings caused him to declare that the schism

> . . . apparently began in response to an instruction issued by the AUCECB to its senior presbyters ordering them to avoid preaching when requested to do so by churches in their territory and to instruct their churches not to baptize candidates under thirty years of age, and no longer to seek new converts. . . .[37]

Bratskii vestnik shed little light on the accusations. The Initiative Group was described as a divisive movement that vilified the AUCECB leaders. Generalizations were stated, such as

> Errors and shortcomings exist both in the "Orgkomitet" and AUCECB. . . . We strive not only to acknowledge our errors and shortcomings, but also to correct them, that is, to bring fruit worthy of repentance.[38]

---

arated in the Ukraine. By mid-year, 2,000 of them returned to their churches.

[34] *Bv*, No. 1, 1958, p. 29 listed the membership of 5,400 churches at 530,000.

[35] *Bv*, No. 6, 1963, p. 7.

[36] *Ibid.*, p. 9.

[37] William C. Fletcher, "Protestant Influences on the Outlook of the Soviet Citizen Today," William C. Fletcher and Anthony J. Strover (eds.), *Religion and the Search for New Ideals in the USSR* (New York: Frederick A. Praeger, 1967), p. 68.

[38] *Bv*, No. 6, 1966, p. 39. (Orgkomitet' was another name for the Initiative Group.)

Admission was made by the AUCECB regarding the inadequate attention of the elder presbyters in serving the local communities.[39] The Moscow presidium members were requested to personally visit local churches more frequently in order

. . . to strengthen and deepen the ties of the churches of our fellowship with their headquarters.[40]

The presidium in Moscow remained the center of power, retaining the right to appoint the elder presbyters of oblasts, regions and republics. However, continued pressure by the Initiative Group probably precipitated a significant change at the next triennial Conference in 1966, when decentralization of AUCECB power was effected. The elder presbyters were to be elected at a conference of presbyters in their areas instead of receiving the appointment from AUCECB headquarters in Moscow.

Nothing in the examination and affirmation of the Statutes of the AUCECB indicated any increase in the minimum age of eighteen for church membership by means of baptism. As early as 1946, Zhidkov defended the Soviet law because it enabled a candidate for water baptism to be sufficiently mature for this important ordinance. He sought to strengthen his argument by this parallelism:

Let us not forget that our Lord Jesus Christ received baptism only when he was thirty, that is, full maturity.[41]

It is possible that a similar expression could have been misconstrued to mean that the minimal age for baptism had been increased to thirty.

The blunt assertion that the Evangelical Christians-

---

[39] *Bv*, No. 6, 1963, p. 37.
[40] *Ibid.*, p. 42.
[41] *Bv*, No. 5, 1946, p. 27.

Baptists' churches were no longer to seek converts would have resulted in the probable exodus of far more than 5 per cent of the evangelistically oriented believers from the membership rolls. Perhaps for appeasement, the delegates at the 1963 Conference were given the right to review, alter, and confirm the proposed new Statutes. The church delegates examined and adopted them finding that they ". . . in no way contradicted the Word of God and our Evangelical-Baptists confession."[42]

Insistence was made upon the continued obedience to the Soviet Government (Rom. 13:1, 2) as the Christian duty of each church.[43] All believers were warned against sending letters to the government that might place the entire fellowship in jeopardy with the Soviet regime and threaten the future work of the evangelicals in the country.[44] However, the unquestioned AUCECB support of the Soviets promised continued cleavage.

The Initiative Group, accusing the AUCECB of forsaking the defense of the believers' interests and principles, had organized and petitioned for registration as a separate religious union. The Soviet government saw it as an

. . . illegally born organ . . . implanting in the believers hostile views against the Soviet system both in Party's and government's policy towards religion . . . they instigate actions contrary to the laws.[45]

The dissident group justified its demands for full religious freedom and a change in the cult laws on the basis of the separation of church from state. They were refused permission to convene an All-Union conference on the

---

[42] *Bv*, No. 6, 1963, p. 98.
[43] *Ibid.*, p. 52.
[44] *Ibid.* See also *Bv*, No. 6, 1966, p. 32.
[45] "Who Are Those 'Initsiativniki' Among the Evangelical Christians-Baptists," *Nauka i religiia*, No. 7 (Moskva: 1966), p. 25.

basis that this would constitute government interference in inner-church affairs of the already established AUCECB.

There is evidence that the Initiative Group summoned groups of believers to Moscow in order to exert pressure on the government to satisfy their demands. Instead of yielding, CARC reproved the leaders, yet hesitated to take decisive administrative action against them.[46] Shortly thereafter, the Initiative Group leader, A. F. Prokof'ev, was sentenced to five years' imprisonment.[47]

In 1964, a letter of appeal reportedly signed by 120 believers in the village of Kulunda, Barnaul, was transmitted via Poland to New York City where it was published by a Russian newspaper, *Novoe russkoe slovo*. Four Baptists were summoned before the Altai Regional Court on December 24-27, 1963, and were found guilty as charged of conducting illegal meetings, of drawing teenagers into the sect, and of propagating against the AUCECB. The death of one of them, Nikolai Khmara, was reported after two weeks' imprisonment as a result of Soviet terror and mistreatment. Marks of wounds and bruises were found by the widow and relatives who had claimed his body.

The funeral service was held on January 16, 1964, with a procession of evangelical believers marching through the town singing hymns and carrying placards which read:

For to me to live is Christ and to die is gain.
Fear not them which kill the body, but are not able to kill the soul.
I saw under the altar the souls of them that were slain for the word of God.[48]

If this was a Stalin-type attempt by the Soviet regime to intimidate the Initiative Group it instead produced in

---

[46] *Ibid.*
[47] Fletcher and Strover, *loc. cit.,* p. 69.
[48] *RCDA,* Vol. III, No. 18, pp. 122–125.

them a greater determination to remain independent and to challenge more believers to secede from the AUCECB, a union they were convinced was a tool of the Soviet rulers. Mikhail Zhidkov, minister son of the late President Zhidkov,[49] offered some added illumination on the tensions between the registered and non-registered believers when he stated to me that CARC workers were "planted" among the independent believers in order to stir up hostility against the registered churches in an attempt to divide and disrupt the work of unity.[50] If this were the case, the work of the CARC boomeranged somewhat in producing greater zeal and animosity against the Soviet Government. On the other hand, what the antireligious forces could not openly achieve in their prolonged battle against the evangelicals, the believers themselves were accomplishing, as dissension, distrust, and hostility spread within their ranks.

v. Unity Efforts

To further strengthen the cause of unity, the AUCECB had consistently exercised the initiative in inviting the non-registered evangelicals to join the Union churches. Presidium members, elder presbyters, and local presbyters sought diligently to maintain the unity already attained, and offered an open hand of fellowship to groups and to individuals of like faith who would agree to be governed by the rules and regulations of the AUCECB.

Following an important council held in August of 1959, the AUCECB distributed a "Handbook" designed to assist all the local presbyters in their daily work of unity. On February 9, 1960, all the registered churches were polled by mail to ascertain the progress of the unifying work with non-registered Christians of Evangelical Faith.

---

[49] Iakov I. Zhidkov died on October 27, 1966 just three weeks after the Moscow Conference of 1966.

[50] Interview with Mikhail Zhidkov, July 5, 1965.

The responses indicated that the majority of the Pentecostalists expressed no desire for unity. They were considered

. . . extremists who, being fanatically trained in their views, do not have the desire to restrict themselves to the "August Agreement."[51]

This admission of failure was followed by a new regulation which opened the door for the return of members who had "left the ranks of our fellowship."[52] No statistics were offered on the number of Pentecostalists who withdrew after joining the Union churches, but mention was made of the fact that a number continued to leave the churches. Undaunted, a special fraternal letter was sent to all non-registered groups after the AUCECB Congress of 1963, appealing to them to remove all the causes hindering full unity.[53]

More recently, in a report at the expanded plenum, consisting of forty-five members of the AUCECB held in Moscow on September 2 and 3, 1964, emphasis was placed again upon the work of strengthening the relations with the non-registered Evangelical Christians, Baptists, Pentecostals, and Mennonites. The Presidium introduced a special division dedicated to the unity of the AUCECB with the two branches of the Mennonites in the Soviet Union, the "Church Mennonites" and the "Brethren." The first week of 1965 was proposed as a "Week of Prayer" for unity.[54]

---

[51] "The Work of Unity with the Affiliated and Non-Affiliated Christians of Evangelical Faith (Pentecostalists)," *Bv*, No. 6, 1963, p. 22.

[52] *Ibid.*

[53] "Notice to All Brothers and Sisters of the Christians of Evangelical Faith (Pentecostals) Found Outside of Unity," *Bv*, No. 2, 1964, pp. 70, 71.

[54] "Expansion of the Plenum of the AUCECB," *Bv*, No. 6, 1964, pp. 41–43.

15

Soviet Antireligious Activities

i. Scientific Atheist Propaganda

Be it a government-recognized, registered body of believers, or a clandestine non-registered group of worshippers; be they Orthodox, Protestant, Catholic, Moslem, Buddhist, or Jewish, Soviet moralists considered all religions a distraction from the real purpose of living, and potentially dangerous. They provided too much competition for communist ideological designs.

In an interdisciplinary approach to the problems of Soviet character, Margaret Mead held that the degree of contrast felt by young Soviets between Bolshevik moral indoctrination and the real world of political dishonesty and evasion would be a factor in selecting youth most capable of making the necessary moral compromises. A premium was placed upon the individuals who could stay on top by devious means in order to survive within the system, rather than those who possessed responsible moral behavior and meticulous honesty.[1]

In nine essays written by former Soviet citizens who spent years as both students and teachers in Soviet educational institutions, the accounts indicated that the majority of Soviet persons in the educational milieu was unsympathetic to the regime. They concluded that if as many anti-Bolsheviks were among other strata of the

---

[1] Margaret Mead, *Soviet Attitudes Toward Authority* (New York: McGraw-Hill Book Company, 1951). pp. 99, 100.

population as among the teachers, then the overwhelming majority would be against the regime. Very few students doubted the slogan "Religion is the opium of the people," yet few desired to be engaged in any active participation against religion or in the denial of God. Younger people were effectively estranged from religion, and the Pioneers and the Komsomol members, as a rule, were atheists.[2]

In his doctoral study, R. Kramer pointed out that

... reason fully justifies the rejection by Soviet moralists of religion conceived as they conceive it. What they reject is "God" as a catch-all explanation for otherwise unexplainable natural phenomena which must be jettisoned as soon as the phenomena are explained naturally. What they reject is "God" as confirmer of injustice and supporter of inhumanity and hypocrisy.[3]

Although Communism rejected religion, children in the Soviet Union were taught to distinguish right from wrong, but on the basis of Soviet doctrine. Teachers-in-training found it necessary to complete specific studies in the historical background and theories of atheism. The Communist Party's fundamental and avowed opposition to religion has been one of the norms of the law, so that anyone attempting to maintain or strengthen evangelism could be considered counter-revolutionary. Their actions, although entirely legal, could be made to appear counter-revolutionary if so desired. A candidate of Philosophy, I. Kichanova, wrote in *Izvestiia* that the

... "exclusiveness" of the believer raises a wall between man and society, between man and the world. The reli-

---

[2] George L. Kline, *Soviet Education* (New York: Columbia University Press, 1957), pp. 44, 50, 76, 130.

[3] Richard Kramer, "Practical Morality Taught to Soviet Children as Illustrated in Four Official Soviet Periodicals 1937–1951" (unpublished Ph. D. dissertation, Faculty of Political Science, Columbia University, 1953), p. 196.

gious "microbrotherhood," is just brotherhood with a minus sign. It is against: against those of different beliefs and against non-believers. Its group morality, its totems and taboos will come into conflict . . . with the general concept of good. . . .[4]

The Communist "good" demanded that scientific-atheistic propaganda be conducted among the parents as well, especially with those who compelled their children to attend church services. In order to be successful the work had to be carried on skillfully, systematically, persistently, and with determination, without offending the feelings of the believers. Religious persons were to be influenced by example, conviction, and the dissemination of scientific knowledge, as the basic tasks of the educational work and upbringing in the schools.[5]

At the Twentieth Party Congress (1956) the plan to create boarding schools for virtually the entire school-age population was announced. The purpose was to reinvigorate the indoctrination of Soviet youth and effect a totally controlled environment during the early formation of the basic attitudes and values of the new generation. Within six years more than 1000 boarding schools had enrolled 400,000 pupils.[6]

The Young Pioneer organization, founded in 1922, involves twenty-one million children from ages nine to fifteen. Their traditional wearing of the triangular red necktie symbolized the unity of three generations—Communists, Komsomols, and Young Pioneers. Its Central Council labored under the guidance of the Central Com-

[4] I. Kichenova, "In the Name of Mankind," *Izvestiia* (Moscow) December 19, 1965, p. 5.

[5] I. Kairov, "Fundamental Problems of Educational Work for the 1954–55 School Year," *Uchitelskaia gazeta* (Moscow: August 18, 1954), pp. 3, 4.

[6] Allen Kassof, *The Soviet Youth Program* (Cambridge: Harvard University Press, 1965), pp. 165, 166.

mittee of the Komsomols. Its variety of activities included the organization of recreation, the promotion of initiative, the development of love for work to accustom them to socially useful activities, and the provision of happy hours in thousands of Young Pioneer palaces and clubs, country camps, libraries, and technical hobby centers.

In this Soviet setting a bold stand for religion became increasingly difficult for young believers as they passed through their adolescent years. I asked one of the younger Moscow pastors if his twelve-year-old daughter was a member of the Young Pioneers. She was, but after each meeting she reassured her parents that her faith was unchanged, and that she did not accept their anti-religious teachings.[7] Articles in *Bratskii vestnik* encouraged social participation of evangelical young people rather than isolation. Clashes between sectarian parents who were not members of the Union churches and the Soviet youth organizations were repeatedly reported in *Nauka i religiia*. Mitskevich encouraged believers to take a reasonable and socially acceptable stand concerning education, culture, and physical exercises. He reminded them that they lived

. . . in a century of great achievements of science and technology and in this century Christ wants to call souls.

Among us there are individual believers who, regretfully, are strangers to all that is new and useful in the area of culture. They are accustomed to count all that is worldly to be sin.[8]

However, the task of the Soviet teacher was to educate the young generation in the spirit of Marxist-Leninist science, in the spirit of a materialistic and scientific world outlook, which was incompatible with any religion. The *Teacher's Gazette* declared that a Soviet teacher

---

[7] Interview with V. L. Fedichkin, July 22, 1963.
[8] A. I. Mitskevich, "Hold Fast the Form of Sound Words," *Bv*, No. 1, 1960, pp. 53, 55.

. . . is under obligation not only to be an unbeliever himself, but also he is to be an active propagandist of godlessness among others, to be the bearer of ideas of militant proletarian atheism.[9]

Since the teacher was the closest aid of the Communist Party in rearing the New Soviet Man, the demands on a teacher's time greatly exceeded the actual classwork. All were expected, as a matter of policy, to make visits to the homes of their pupils and to attend parent-teacher meetings, as well as to take part in extracurricular work. Daily, in school and out, the teacher was expected to expose and to overcome religious prejudices, skillfully and calmly, tactfully and persistently. However, problems abounded. A. A. Shamaro complained that Soviet young people laughed and jested if they came across religious people, shrugged their shoulders and said, "It's not my affair, I haven't any time . . ." as they turned away from any discussion with believers.[10] The *Sputnik ateista* ("Atheist's Companion") complained that the dissemination of atheist propaganda was not simply the task of the specialists; teachers, doctors, librarians, engineers, agronomists, etc., were also urged to struggle with religious fanatics whenever their paths crossed.[11]

Molodoi kommunist (Young Communist), disturbed by the complacency of Komsomol members, illustrated unconcern and apathy within the membership by an incident in which a former Komsomol member turned in his membership card, explaining,

. . . I don't need it any longer. I joined a Baptist sect over a year ago. . . . I was bored. . . . No one was inter-

[9] F. Oleshchuk, "Religion—A Reactionary Ideology," *Uchitelskaia gazeta* (Moskva), November 26, 1949, p. 2.

[10] Aleksandr A. Shamaro, *Neprimirimost'* (Moskva: Znanie, 1963), p. 4.

[11] S. I. Kovalev, *Sputnik ateista, 2nd ed.* (Moskva: Gosudarstvennoe izdatel'stvo politicheskoi literatury, 1961), p. 440.

ested in me. Nobody ever asked me what my interests are, what I think about, what my needs are, but the Baptists are interested in what kind of feelings I have. They display attention upon me.[12]

On the other hand, many teachers and youth workers were persuaded that it was unnecessary and even harmful for Soviet children to be exposed to antireligious propaganda in school, believing that it resulted in needless curiosity about religious matters. The teachers were censured for their incompetent use of, or worse, the complete failure to use the program material designed for the atheistic training of children.[13] This complaint was shared by I. Kairov, the Minister of Education in the Russian Republic[14] because an inseparable part of the ideological political work was the atheistic training of students in and out of classrooms in order to develop and nurture a materialistic world outlook.

Nauka i religiia conceded that the majority of believers were honorable Soviet people not to be censured because they were "shackled" by their religious ideology. The struggle against religion required ideological weapons alone, since compulsory tactics increased religious fervor to fanaticism, provided material for religious propaganda, and caused a distrust in the Soviet system.[15]

Scientific-atheistic propaganda formed a vital part of the Communist education of the masses of the people. The scientific-atheistic training was introduced to children at an early age in order to combat the influence of religious adults upon those tender years. Lectures were supple-

---

12 S. Khudiakov, "More Atheist Books, Good and Varied Ones!," *Molodoi kommunist,* No. 3, 1957, pp. 118–121.

13 "For thinking Through and Building a System of Scientific-Atheistic Education," *Nauka i religiia,* No. 1, 1962, pp. 5–7.

14 Kairov, "The Basic Tasks . . . , *Uchitelskaia gazeta, op. cit.*

15 "For Thinking Through . . . ," *Nauka i religiia,* No. 1, 1962, pp. 5–7.

mented with visits to the planetaria, television quizzes, and films. The practice of open debates with evangelical ministers was discouraged, admittedly because the Soviet "Houses of Culture should not be turned into temples, nor the lecturer's chair into a pulpit."[16]

The USSR Ministry of Higher and Secondary Specialized Education and the similar ministries of the Union Republics took organized measures to increase scientific research and pedagogical work in the field of atheism.

The granting of academic degrees required the approval of a special committee attached to the Council of Ministers of the USSR, which examined the candidate's political loyalty to the Communist Party and inquired about his zeal in advancing the Party's program. The constitutional provision on behalf of education served as a powerful instrument in the hands of the Party in the propagation of communism and atheism. Their aims were supported by granting stipends and scholarships, screening candidates for university training, controlling the teachers and professors, limiting the freedom of thought, and denying the parents' associations the right to influence Soviet educational policy.[17]

In 1958, after Khrushchev's educational reform, entrance to higher educational institutions was dependent upon proof of having spent two or three years at work, and on the recommendation of a Komsomol, Party, or trade union organization. Those who qualified obtained their education tuition-free. Passive believers filtered through, and unknown numbers have studied in numerous universities. Precaution against permitting active believers to enter universities was expressed in an article that exposed a liberal professor who was on good terms with Kiakhr, a student recognized as an active Baptist and a gifted preacher. Another professor tested Kiakhr on the

---

[16] *Nauka i religiia*, No. 2, 1960.
[17] Gecys, *op. cit.*, pp. 281, 296.

Marxist criticism of Godseekers, and upon failure the student was dismissed.[18] Students majoring in teacher training, philosophy, and history were obliged to complete specific studies in the historical background and theories of atheism.

ii. Antireligious Conferences

In February of 1963, nearly 400 communication workers across the Soviet Union—members of the press, radio and television, gathered in Moscow to discuss the problems of atheism. Almost all of the participants spoke of the shallow, poorly written, primitive atheistic publications. They stressed the importance of material accurately presented without the use of sensationalism.

> . . . The majority of believers are honorable Socialist citizens, and some are even active socially. Not all Pentecostalists are fanatics . . . one must separate the honorable kind.
> Journalists constantly have . . . fully alert readers—the believers. For this reason, the author of an atheistic article must be completely accurate in relation to the facts, and must know the subject thoroughly. For a minor inaccuracy, the error invites distrust in the entire article. . . .[19]

In June of 1964, over 1200 delegates of the All-Union Society of Knowledge heard similar warnings. The director of the House of Atheists in Rostov-on-Don reported that the work began

> . . . with massive antireligious propaganda. Analyzing it, we realized that it was weak . . . we found that due

---

[18] "Believers in Tartuski University, Estonian SSR," *Nauka i religiia*, No. 3, 1962, p. 51.
[19] "Journalists Discuss the Problems of Atheism," *Nauka i religiia*, No. 5, 1963, pp. 3–6.

to the lack of understanding believers nothing would
enlist them. . . . Activists need to pay special attention
. . . visit the churches, prayer halls, listen to the sermons. Atheist education is hard work and demands
preparation. . . .[20]

The training of Soviet antireligious workers on a mass
scale was contrasted by the almost nonexistent formal
training of the ministers of the Evangelical Christians–
Baptists. In a radio message to British believers in 1958,
Zhidkov joyfully announced the fact that six of their Russian young men were studying theology in Baptist colleges located in London and Bristol.[21] Nine long years
passed before three additional young ministers were permitted to follow in their steps.[22] No evangelical Bible
school in Russian has been functioning since Prokhanov's
school was closed. However, the AUCECB announced
plans to initiate a limited Bible correspondence school for
young preachers in 1968.[23]

At a service held in the Russian Baptist Church in New
York City, several visiting ministers from Moscow shared
with the small congregation brief glimpses of their uphill
battle.

You ask, have we no seminary, no Sunday School? That
is true, but in the book of Acts the believers were scattered, yet the Word grew. . . . No, we have no missionary society, but there are 5,000 preachers who have
75,000 workers ready to go forth.

We have 1,300 meeting places in the Ukraine . . .
with blessings as well as difficulties. We see the fruit,

---

[20] "The Fourth Conference of the All-Union Society of Knowledge," *Nauka i religiia*, No. 8, 1964, pp. 3–5.
[21] Iakov Zhidkov, "Radio Message to Christians of the British Isles,"
Bv, No. 2, 1958, pp. 9, 10.
[22] *Bv*, No. 1, 1968, p. 64.
[23] *Ibid.*

not the hardships. . . . Pray for us that the great revival may become greater. Pray for those who cannot pray.[24]

Published since 1945, *Bratskii vestnik* has presented its message in a positive manner, rarely employing apologetics for its Biblical fundamentalism. The antireligious campaigns and crude smear tactics used against some of the presbyters, preachers, and laity remained unchallenged in print. To answer the charges could be construed to be religious propaganda, forbidden by Soviet law.

Various articles recorded in *Bratskii vestnik* attempted to reconcile scientific ideas and the ideals of communism with the Bible. They were repudiated by the Soviet press. The more subtle the religious article, the more dangerous it was considered to be. The Soviet readers were constantly reminded of the basic conflict between religion and communism. Scientific-atheistic propaganda maintained that science and religion were two mutually incompatible, exclusive concepts; two completely divergent approaches to the explanation of natural and social phenomena. Religion was labeled a deterrent to progress, a blindfold over the eyes, and a justifier of exploitation. Even the believers who worked well did not labor selflessly for society in the name of building communism, but were selfishly working to merit their own salvation, and recruiting others in the process. Such labor, pointed out the atheist, could not be creative, for it lacked faith in one's own strength and the strength of the collective.

The atheist workers did not assume that Soviet citizens, born and raised under communist doctrines were devoid of reflections about God and religion. During the forma-

---

[24] I. Motorin, speaking in the Russian Baptist Church, New York City, June 2, 1964. The definition of preachers and workers is not given. *Bv*, No. 1, 1958, p. 29 listed 5,400 ECB churches with 25,000 preachers. Most of the churches have one presbyter but several preachers.

tive period of life, human beings pondered the meaning of life and death, of happiness, of the causality of events, and these contemplations inevitably led to science and atheism or to religious inclinations, covert or manifest. Teachers were urged to put forth the maximum in initiative and inventiveness in order to make the propaganda of atheism not only versatile and persuasive, but also interesting and appealing. However, each class teacher accompanying his students to theaters and art exhibitions was likely to come into conflict with this problem, as were teachers of literature and history, who faced Scriptural reminders such as those found in Tolstoi's opening chapter of *Anna Karenina*, Solzhenitsyn's Baptist believer in *One Day In The Life of Ivan Denisovich*, Tretiakov's wall-size masterpiece of John the Baptist's introduction of Jesus, etc.

iii. Religious Literature

The atheist B. M. Arkhipov did not share the fears of the overly cautious methodologists who assumed that familiarity with the Bible might lead a person into the lap of the church. He conceded that such a danger did exist if the sectarians took advantage of passiveness in the school and subjectively acquainted the students with religious literature. However, Arkhipov negated this danger if such literature were to be critically analyzed from the posture of Marxist philosophy.[25]

Against a deluge of antireligious publications in the Soviet Union the trickle of AUCECB publications of Bibles, hymnals, and *Bratskii vestnik* was negligible. The magazine has guided its readers to serve their Soviet homeland loyally for it

[25] B. M. Arkhipov, "To Improve Atheistic Work," *Vecherniaia sredniaia shkola*, No. 5 (Moskva: 1962), pp. 66–70.

educated our ministers and members and churches in the response of love for homeland and its people. Its spiritual-patriotic articles summoned everyone to the practical, active service of one's country, to love her not in word, but in deed. . . .[26]

Although prophetical, eschatological articles and studies of Christ's coming reign have been few and far between, they actually were published in *Bratskii vestnik*, passed by censors and printed on Soviet printing presses. Evidence of increased preaching on the second advent of Christ and final judgment in certain areas was submitted by A. I. Klibanov's research of sectarians in Tambov province. Serving the Presidium of the USSR Academy of Sciences and the Coordinate Council for Atheism, Klibanov's researchers discovered that the sermons of the local Baptists were eschatological and they concluded that the material found in the official organ of the Evangelical Christians-Baptists differed fundamentally.[27] Doubtless greater caution was exercised on the printed page than in the pulpit. That the message of Christ's triumphant return to rule upon the earth was printed at all is surprising, for it clearly delineated an ideology, a power however distant in the future, that threatened the supremacy of Communism.

Concerning Scripture publications, the Russian Bible Society was established in Russia as early as 1814, and by decree was closed on April 12, 1826, following the reign of Tsar Alexander I. Almost one million portions of the Bible had been printed in twenty-six languages.[28] Upon

---

[26] Aleksandr Karev, "Report of the General Secretary—Abstract of the Last Four Years of Activity," *Bv*, No. 5, 1948, p. 34.

[27] L. N. Mitrokhin, "The Study of Sects in Tambov Province," *Voprosy filosofii*, No. 1 (Moskva: 1960), p. 145.

[28] S. R. Tomkins, "The Russian Bible Society," *American Slavic and Eastern European Review*, No. 7, (New York: Columbia U. Press), pp. 257–267.

the completed translation of the Bible into the Russian language in the 1860's, additional publications of the Bible were controlled by the Synod of the Russian Orthodox Church. As stated earlier, Pashkov and Prokhanov were successful in having large amounts of Russian Scriptures published and widely distributed.

For three decades, or since the successful printings of hymnals and Bibles by Ivan Prokhanov in 1926, the plea for additional Bibles was ignored by the Soviet Government. At a dinner on May 19, 1956, the American Bible Society honored five AUCECB ministers who were then visiting New York. The Russian delegation was offered the matrices of the New Testament in the Russian language. They were gratefully received and subsequently used in 1957 when 10,000 Bibles were printed for the AUCECB in the Soviet Union.[29]

In 1964, the atheists hailed a long awaited appearance of a volume which actually included the Bible story, in very small type, from the creation story to the tower of Babel. The text was followed by philological, historical, and archeological commentaries by the author, a Polish writer, who received a State prize.[30] It is possible that the immediate sell-out of 100,000 copies denoted that the majority of purchasers were believers delighted to own their first portion of the Bible. They likely ignored the commentary completely, except to refute some statements easily disproven.

iv. Civilian Labor and Citizenship Duties

Contrary to the evidences of animosity engendered by the independent evangelical leaders as they rebelled against various phases of Soviet activities, the AUCECB

---

[29] A Karev, "Sojourn of Delegates of AUCECB in the USA," *Bv,* Nos. 3–4, 1956, pp. 7, 83.

[30] Zenon Kosidovskii, "From Adam—What Is the Bible?," *Nauka i religiia,* No. 11 ,1964, p. 30.

executives consistently educated their members to prove themselves as model workers in Soviet society. Most of the presbyters were examples of productive laborers, spending a lifetime in honorable toil and industry, receiving no remuneration for their ministerial services.

An *Izvestiia* correspondent complained about managers who did not conduct an inquiry to discover why up to thirty young men at the Konotop Locomotive and Car Repair Plant were members of sects.[31] Far less concerned than the atheist agitators were the managers and foremen of plants and factories whose primary interest was confined to meeting the norm of production with dependable labor.

In Mead's study of the behavior of Soviet people it was noted that Party leadership of the workers' collectives in the factories actually contributed to the disorganization of factory administrations. It introduced distrust of the managerial staff which, in turn, encouraged conflicts and breaches of discipline by the labor force. However, these were counterbalanced by the mobilization of initiative and enthusiasm attained by the Party activists.[32]

Alcoholism and absenteeism, petty larceny and hooliganism, although satirized by *Krokodil,* the humor magazine published by Pravda, were matters of vital concern to Soviet community leaders. In sharp contrast, the puritanical teachings of the evangelicals forbade even social drinking and called for total abstinence. Several articles in *Bratskii vestnik* encouraged conscientious industriousness and diligence, promoted good health habits, pure wedded life, and the proper education of children.[33]

In order to project communist morality upon young Soviet citizens the Komsomol ideal could not risk a posi-

[31] I. Feofanov, "One Cannot Stand Aloof," *Izvestiia* (Moskva) March 15, 1959, p. 3.
[32] Margaret Mead, *op. cit.,* p. 122.
[33] A. V. Karev, "Record of Training in Our Churches," *Bv,* No. 3, 1946, p. 30.

tion of non-interference, aloofness or apathy when cognizant of violations. In the province of Odessa, a second secretary of the Komsomol, Comrade Slednev, known a long time for his unworthy behavior and immorality, had been receiving the support of the members.

"So what?" argued the members of the committee. "He carries out his duties at work, and his private and personal life is no concern of ours." Such arguments are anti-Marxist and alien to us. Comrade Slednev was dismissed from work. . . .[34]

Soviet writers reminded Komsomol and Party members of the absence of their concern for people found in difficult straits, warning them that they forfeited these unfortunates to the evangelicals who were ever alert to take advantage of all such opportunities. Garkavenko suggested that the presbyters were motivated by the desire for praise when they rendered philanthropic aid to those in need of clothing or the repair of a home.[35] He did not mention the fact that they circumvented legal boundaries in the performance of such deeds, but he rather chafed at the apparent gap between Communists and Christians in the pragmatic approach to surrounding needs.

Despite the fact that believers were found among the most exemplary laborers, whether in a kolkhoz, sovkhoz, hospital or factory, the *Sputnik ateista* repeated the hackneyed phrase that their religion numbed them into passive expectations of a happy life. "It hinders them from energetically and actively participating in the struggle for the building of a happy life on earth."[36] Conversely, the AUCECB reminded the atheists that their honored statement, "he or she who does not work shall neither eat,"

---

[34] "The Moral Look of the Young Soviet Person," *Komsomolskaia pravda* (Moskva) April 12, 1955, p. 1.
[35] Garavenko, *op. cit.*, pp. 37–39.
[36] Kovalev, *op. cit.*, p. 156.

found in Article 118 of the Soviet Constitution, was borrowed from the New Testament passage found in 2 Thessalonians 3:18. President Zhidkov declared:

Atheist propaganda does not bother us at all; as a matter of fact, it helps us to purify ourselves and get rid of our shortcomings. When one pamphlet accused us of obscurantism and reactionary tendencies, we used as our best argument our activities as loyal and energetic citizens; when anyone preaches to us about leading a "decent life," we suggest that he look at our community to find the best example of right living.[37]

Faced with the choice of completing a harvest or worshipping on Sunday, evangelicals were asked to perform their tasks faithfully and to pray inwardly, thus serving both people and God.

. . . last summer, the Harvest Holiday arrived . . . the koklhoz asked them to work a day or two more in order to finish the work. . . . The elder presbyter arrived, and setting the example by working himself, he encouraged the people to perform the task. There was great satisfaction while completing the work and a good witness was effected before the entire collective farm.[38]

Unwilling to accept the productive labors of industrious believers graciously, M. Vorobyev labeled the evangelical attitude toward labor a pious fraud, an about-face tactic calculated to regain the respect of fellow citizens. He judged the motive of the believer as basically selfish.[39]

---

[37] Grunwald, *op. cit.,* p. 169.

[38] I. I. Zhidkov, "The Relationship of Work to Sundays and Holidays," *Bv,* No. 2, 1946, pp. 19, 20.

[39] M. R. Vorobyev, "What One Needs to Know about the Sectarians 'New Tactics,'" *Gudok,* September 5, 1963, p. 4, cited in *Current Digest of the Soviet Press,* Vol. XV, No. 40 (NY: 1963), p. 31.

In defending the freedom of religion in the USSR, a Soviet embassy official, Spasov, unequivocally wrote:

No distinctions are drawn on the basis of religion, or between religious persons and atheists, in the factories and offices, on the collective farms, in the schools or in the army.[40]

More accurate was the oral statement of Grigolenko, aide of G. A. Zhukov, president of the Committee of the Council of Ministers pertaining to cultural relations, who said,

. . . It is impossible for us to give responsible positions to men whose philosophical convictions are diametrically opposed to ours. . . .[41]

It was obvious that the distinct ideological line of the Party excluded evangelical believers from various positions in the Soviet state, certainly in the political and pedagogical fields.

The position of the AUCECB regarding the citizenship duties of each member of the thousands of communities of the Evangelical Christians-Baptists was one of positive obedience to the State and the orderly fulfillment of its laws in the Soviet Union.

Give to Caesar that which is Caesar's (Mt. 22:21). As citizens of your country, fulfill all that lies within you to fulfill: pay your taxes, serve honorably and sincerely in all labors and duties. If any weapons are placed into your hands for the defense of your country, do not refuse them. . . .[42]

---

[40] Spasov, *op. cit.,* p. 31.
[41] Grunwald, *loc cit.,* p. 66.
[42] I. I. Zhidkov, "Thirtieth Anniversary of the Great October Revolution," *Bv,* No. 6, 1947, p. 4.

Never in print has the alternate choice been suggested, namely "We ought to obey God rather than men (Acts 5:29)." The AUCECB leaders were aware that the Soviet Bill of Rights granted class rights, the rights of a citizen as a member of the collective, and not individual rights. These rights were protected provided that they were not contrary to the policies of the Soviet State. The monolithic totalitarian nature of the Party made it clear that assent to official Soviet policy was a compromise of expediency. Each AUCECB executive, elder presbyter, and presbyter was faced with a choice between two negative factors. Those within the Union had chosen to work in cooperation with the Soviet Government in order to obtain the relative freedom of preaching and pastoring within the circumscribed boundaries set by the Soviet law. Otherwise, to become an independent, or non-Union member, refusing to compromise, involved functioning illegally, meeting clandestinely, and risking the imminence of arrest and the deprivation of freedom.

The offerings received by the registered church communities were taxed in conformity with the law.[43] Twice annually the entries of the AUCECB churches, already verified by their own auditing commission, were inspected by the representatives of the Soviet treasury department for taxable income.[44] Despite these strict controls, the antireligious press continued to accuse various presbyters of complete financial irresponsibility.

Not all antireligious accusations were Soviet fabrications or prevarications about dissensions and misdeeds in local Evangelical Christians-Baptists' communities. *Bratskii vestnik* admitted the necessity of the administration of disciplinary measures of wayward members, and excommunications have taken place. *Nauka i religiia* reported a scandal

---

[43] Kovalev, *loc cit.,* p. 389.
[44] "Auditing of Finances," *Bv,* No. 6, 1963, p. 24.

in the L'vov church in which the pastor was charged with misappropriating some church funds. Andreev, the elder presbyter, was summoned to resolve the situation.[45] At this approximate time, *Bratskii vestnik* reported a new address for this community of believers without, as usual, any explanation.[46]

v. The Closing of Churches

The closing of prayer houses and the discontinuation of the activities of religious societies occurred if the membership declined below the required minimum. Other reasons included the participation in activities contrary to Soviet State goals, the refusal to fulfill citizen's obligations—particularly the defense of the homeland—the refusal to vote during state and community elections, religious fanaticism, the excitement of national enmities, and any religious activities that inflicted harm to Soviet citizens or were contrary to their rights.[47]

Caution, however, was exercised in closing prayer houses. No village or regional Council of Deputies Workers was empowered to close a church. Only the Central Administration had the authority to disband religious associations. Avoidance of administrative pressure, reminiscent of the early days of collectivization and the purges of the thirties, was taken in order not to undermine the education of antireligious work among the populace. The Soviets came to the realization that to

> . . . close a church or to remove a religious society from registration does not mean that from that moment believers will become atheists. Often it is the opposite . . . not the weakening, but the strengthening of reli-

---

45 "Facts Expose," *Nauka i religiia*, No. 5, 1963, p. 33.
46 *Bv*, No. 2, 1962, p. 75.
47 Kovalev, *loc. cit.*, p. 390.

gious people. . . . Removal of a religious society from registration is often only a means of adding to the growth of the non-registered . . . we must not comfort ourselves with illusions.[48]

However, Soviet emotions did not remain calm and rational where failure with Soviet youth was concerned. In such situations coercion and brute force against bold believers have been used. Party members repeatedly forget the wise words of Lunacharski, a leading educator in the thirties, who declared that "Religion is like a nail; the harder you hit it into the wood, the deeper it goes."

Believers found the Constitutional Freedom in the Soviet Union to be conditional, granted upon the premise that the freedom of speech, press, assembly, and demonstration would strengthen the social system. This clearly implied that they were not to be used "in general" because the revolutionary legality, the Party programs and its State laws determined the criteria of right and wrong. Logically, anyone who strengthened religion could be considered anti-Party and therefore counterrevolutionary. In this manner, actions that were quite legal could be designed to appear counterrevolutionary.[49] This tactic was more often applied to the non-registered believers who had placed themselves in a vulnerable position as antisocial elements.

The antireligious laws were deceptive and could be carried out at the administrative level simply by changing their interpretation and application without any formal amendments of the Stalin Constitution.[50]

At times there were relaxations of the enforcement of antireligious laws, such as the allowance of regular choir rehearsals habitually found in most of the Evangelical Christians-Baptists churches. On the other hand, when

[48] "Answers to Questions," *Nauka i religiia*, No. 10, 1961, p. 92.
[49] Anderson, *People, Church and . . .*, loc. cit., pp. 153, 154, 226.
[50] Gecys, *op. cit.*, p. 128.

mass conversions necessitated large outdoor baptismal services shortly after the War, the presbyters were instructed by Zhidkov to limit the number of believers permitted to be present at a baptismal service to only a few assistants. The baptismals were performed hurriedly at pre-dawn hours, followed by a service in the house of prayer. Pressured AUCECB leaders found it expedient to urge the presbyters to find secluded locations and to prohibit large processions from accompanying the baptisms.[51] Zhidkov, uneasy because throngs of non-believers attended the open baptismal services, weakly suggested that it was harmful to a pious, prayerful spirit! Zhidkov concluded that "for the good of the work of the Lord, it is necessary to discontinue the practice of such a boisterous baptism."[52]

Atheist agitators made it embarrasing for the few Soviet citizens who rented part of their homes to believers for the use of prayer meetings. The railroad worker F. S. Mankevich received three times the allotted rental from sectarians, according to the report. A lecture at a Party meeting and tactful advice caused him to "understand" the "error" he committed. The burden of social disapproval was removed when the believers were no longer permitted to rent the quarters at any cost.[53]

The Leningrad congregation was the second largest church among the Evangelical Christians-Baptists, numbering 3,000 members. After the War, great expenditures were made by them in order to repair the destroyed edifice, install a heating system, and construct a baptistry. *Bolshoi okht* was a corner "very dear to Leningrad believers."[54] However, shortly after the death of its famed presbyter,

51 M. A. Orlov, "Water Baptism by Faith," *Bv*, No. 1, 1953, p. 40.
52 I. I. Zhidkov, "Water Baptism in the Year 1948," *Bv*, No. 1, 1953, p. 40.
53 *Nauka i religiia*, No. 6, 1961, p. 85.
54 "From the Life of the Leningrad Church," *Bv*, No. 1, 1948, p. 60.

M. A. Orlov, the congregation was obliged to leave its central location and occupy a former Orthodox church in the outskirts of the city. Except for recent photographs in *Bratskii vestnik,* no mention was made of the change, nor has the new address been listed in the publication.[55]

If the duly registered evangelical houses of worship faced such insecurity, one can imagine what the independent evangelicals constantly faced as they continued to gather for worship services. In a lengthy, dramatically detailed appeal to the United Nations General Secretary U Thant, dated June 5, 1967, the Council of Relatives of Prisoners (dissident Initiative members) requested assistance for the cessation of the repressions experienced by believers in the Soviet Union. It boldly challenged the very basis of the Law of 1929 which denied the fundamental rights to believers to freedom of conscience, thought, and peaceful assembly.

. . . after believers' refusal to accept these regulations, they are subjected to cruel persecution: tortures, massacres, fines beyond their ability to pay. . . .[56]

Prison sentences ranging from one to six years were meted out to 200 persons "condemned for the Word of God." Signed by five members on behalf of the Council of Relatives of Prisoners, the women described events which included oral and written slander of the believers, court processes conducted in violation of the juridical codex of the USSR, physical assault and arrests in the disruption of peaceful meetings, numerous searches conducted in the apartments of believers with confiscation of

---

[55] Orlov died in February of 1961. The following year a photo of the church in its new location appeared in *Bv,* Nos. 5–6, 1962, p.27. More photos were in *Bv,* No. 4, 1963, pp. 34, 52, and 72, again with no information about change of location.

[56] "Human Rights and Baptist Dissenters in Soviet Union," *RCDA,* Vol. VII, Nos. 3–4, 1968, p. 24.

Bibles and other religious literature, interrogation of children of believers by organs of the government with the aim of incriminating relatives and other believers, persecution of believers at work followed by dismissal, forcible commitment of healthy believers to psychiatric hospitals, inhuman treatment of an amputee from Tashkent, brutal beatings for refusal to sign the falsehood that anti-Soviet leaflets were read at religious meetings, death from tortures, kidnappings and the forcible placement of believers' children in a State children's home.[57]

From Box 520, Moscow, dated December 1967, I received a mimeographed Open Letter, sent to churchmen around the world, regarding the *Initsiativnaia gruppa,* charging them with the design of attempting to destroy the authority of the Union leaders in order to grasp the leadership into their own hands.

> People are not prosecuted in our country for their religious convictions, but to our deep regret, some brothers and sisters have been made answerable for non-observance of the laws on religion and for breach of the public order.[58]

Clearly, the wall of separation between the philosophy and action of the two evangelical camps is the Law of 1929, a decree that denied legal existence to all churches in the Soviet Union and allowed no activity other than the performance of worship to those alone who were duly registered.

vi. Espionage Charges

Soviet attempts have been made to suggest that believers were involved in espionage activities, using religion as a

---

[57] *Ibid.,* pp. 21–41.

[58] "OPEN LETTER of the All-Union Council of Evangelical Christians-Baptists of the USSR," Ilia G. Ivanov, Moscow, December 1967.

front. Kalugin, aiming at the Pentecostalists, wrote the following:

> . . . the Pentecostal center is in the USA. Huge amounts of literature are published there even in the Russian language. Powerful radio stations transmit special programs daily in Russian for the Pentecostals. All of this effort pursues one goal—the spread of calumny on the Soviet Union. In New York, a special journal of this sect is published called "Strannik," wherein the Pentecostal doctrine is propagandized, spreading slander on the Soviet Union and countries of the socialist camp.[59]

Attempting to cast a bad light upon Pentecostalists in the Soviet Union, many of whom remained outside the Union churches, Kalugin committed several errors in the above report. True, the Pentecostal denomination in which Ivan Voronaev held credentials was located in the United States, where it was known as the Assemblies of God. Under its missionary radio programs, Paul Demetrus has for years directed the work of producing up to thirty-four radio programs per week in the Russian and Ukrainian languages, released over powerful transmitters which reach the Soviet Union. The programs were non-political in format and presented a positive religious message in poetry, hymns, and sermonette. The quarterly magazine *Strannik* ("The Pilgrim") propagated Pentecostal doctrines, but the Russian publication was careful to avoid political involvements of any kind. Its editor for many years pastored the church founded by Voronaev in New York City. Demian Matysuk and some of his parishioners, far from slandering the Soviet Union, were disturbed even to hear negative reports given by Voronaev's sons who had returned to the States, afraid that the unfavorable statements somehow would be transmitted back to Soviet

---

[59] Kalugin, *op. cit.*, p. 19.

Russia and adversely affect the founder of the Russian Pentecostalists.

vii. Oral Roberts and Billy Graham

The Soviet political-literary magazine *Rovesnik* contained a derogatory article about American Pentecostalists, designed to castigate Russian tongues speakers by association. Evangelist Roberts, sponsored by Pentecostal pastors in large crusades across the United States and in many countries of the world, was accused of employing ideological diversionist tactics that concealed his "dirty work." One of his brochures published in the Russian language was viewed as serving to camouflage his political machinations. His "Happiness and Healing for You," an illustrated message, received the indictment of disseminating destruction rather than happiness, by attempting to isolate the believers from society.[60] The American Assemblies of God denomination also received a scornful tribute for its daily production of more than two tons of religious propaganda.[61]

In addition to an accusation of political involvement, the motive of monetary gain and the use of Madison Avenue techniques were directed against Billy Graham, the world's leading Baptist evangelist. Writing in *Nauka i religiia*, I. Senin quoted statistics from the *US News and World Report* on the vast expenditures of Graham's Madison Square Garden crusade which continued for months in New York City. Seven derogatory cartoons accompanied the article, one of which depicted Graham as a bald-headed, unshaven gangster counting money on an abacus. A total attendance of up to two million was reported and 80,000 persons made professions of faith. Senin concluded that

---

[60] *Rovesnik,* No. 8, (Moskva: 1963), p. 2.
[61] *Ibid.,* p. 3.

Graham "sanctimoniously fulfills the decree of his earthly master—the lord of the dollar."[62] Conversely, in the few references made to Billy Graham in *Bratskii vestnik,* only words of the highest esteem and praise have been used. The derisive reports published by the atheists served admirably to inform Russian believers regarding the phenomenal successes of world evangelists. The liberty with which Graham and Roberts were able to preach in many countries of the world was brought into sharp contrast to the absence of such religious freedom in the Soviet Union. The Moscow parishioners were well aware of the balcony visits of Graham in 1959 and Roberts in 1960, and they probably shared the embarrassed frustration of their presbyters who obviously were restrained from inviting the famous Americans to share the Moscow pulpit. However, other foreign clergymen who visited the USSR in times of less international strain have been permitted to greet the congregations of the Evangelical Christians-Baptists churches and some have even been permitted to preach. In 1963, while visiting the capital, Dr. R. O. Corvin and I were invited to the pulpit of Moscow's only Protestant church as representatives of Oral Roberts University. The political climate was most favorable, for that very week the Americans, British, and Russians successfully negotiated the nuclear test ban treaty.

American anti-Communist radio preachers Carl McIntire and Billy James Hargis have labeled the Russian churches as "fronts" to deceive foreign tourists, in order to cause them to believe that there is religious freedom in the Soviet Union. This problem will be analyzed in a succeeding chapter.

Despite the inconveniences, harassments, and the inability to enter important areas of leadership and power,

---

[62] "Twentieth Century Crusader," *Nauka i religiia,* No. 9, 1961, pp. 40–43.

members of the Evangelical Christians-Baptists churches have had opportunities to share their witness of faith in diverse areas and have gained the respect of many. The status of State recognition given to the members of registered churches may have added to the acceptability of these evangelicals by ordinary Soviet citizens despite the constant propaganda barrage against them.

Atheist agitators have constantly tried to improve their effectiveness among believers. Evening question and answer sessions, and evening discussions on atheism by prominent scientists and apostate ministers challenging believers, have been offered. Chemical experiments were employed widely because of their striking effect on believers in weakening their faith in miracles. Free showings of popular science films were presented in the squares and streets, drawing large attentive audiences. Although the effectiveness of atheist films was lauded, evidence revealed that an inadequate budgetary allotment was the cause for an insufficient quantity of film copies. Duplicates of short antireligious films averaged 800 to 850 copies, far too few for the huge network of film establishments spread over the entire Soviet Union.[63]

viii. Intensifying Atheist Education

In February of 1964, the Central Committee of the Communist Party published a decree envisioning an intensification of the atheist education of the citizenry. The new decree included the establishment of a new Institute of Scientific Atheism which would control all the atheistic indoctrinational activities of the institutions of higher education and the institutions connected with the various Ministries of Culture. All students were to be examined on a course in "The Fundamentals of Scientific Atheism."

---

[63] "The Way to the Intellect and Emotions," *Nauka i religiia*, No. 3, 1963, p. 5.

Teachers and professors in high schools and universities, as well as writers, journalists, and advanced students, were obliged to actively participate in the antireligious program. Competitions were to be held in order to select the best works on atheist subjects in the fields of literature, drama, films and painting. All political and scientific journals were to inaugurate new columns for antireligious propaganda. In order to forestall the illegal activities of religious leaders, church groups, and individual believers, measures were planned to protect children and adolescents from the influence of church activists and from parental efforts to induce their children to join them in religious observances.[64]

L. F. Ilichev, a secretary of the Central Committee of the Communist Party, explained the move as a countermeasure to undo the harm brought on by Stalin's New Religious Policy.[65]

The need for effective action was readily confessed, for in the period from 1955 to 1962, of the 10,000 dissertations on philosophy, history, jurisprudence, pedagogy and aesthetics defended, only fifty were devoted to the problems of scientific atheism. During the same period of time, only four out of 4,500 master's dissertations in history were on atheistic topics![66]

---

[64] A. Avtorkhanov, "New Assault on Religion," *Problems of the Peoples of the USSR* (Munich: Buchdruckerei und Verlag, Spring 1964), pp. 12, 13.

[65] *Ibid.*, pp. 13, 14.

[66] "The Theory of Scientific Atheism Should Be Raised To Modern Standards," *Voprosy filosofii,* No. 5 (Moscow: 1964), p. 11.

PART V

THE INVOLVEMENT OF THE RUSSIAN
EVANGELICALS IN THE BAPTIST
WORLD ALLIANCE, THE WORLD
COUNCIL OF CHURCHES, AND THE
CHRISTIAN PEACE CONFERENCE

16

The Baptist World Alliance

i. The Stockholm Baptist Congress Peace Resolution

We have observed the relationship of the registered evangelical believers to the Soviet Government within the borders of the Soviet Union. Now let us consider the involvement of the AUCECB around the world as it actively participated in the affairs of three international Christian organizations.

The seeds for a global Baptist fellowship were already planted by the late seventeenth century when Thomas Grantham, General Baptist in England, voiced the desire for such a gathering. In 1790 John Rippon, a British preacher and editor of *The Baptist Annual Register,* wrote an editorial suggesting a world organization of Baptists. However, not until 1904 when John Newton Prestridge, editor of *The Baptist Argus,* trumpeted the call for such a creation did assent and cooperation result in the first world gathering of Baptists in Exeter Hall, London, July 11-18, 1905.[1]

The Baptist World Alliance, which now has a constituency of almost thirty million members from 122 countries, became a reality on July 17, 1905. Twenty-three nations were represented in London, including the "serious-looking delegates from Russia, most of whom have known

---

[1] Norman Wade Cox (ed.) *Encyclopedia of Southern Baptists,* Vol. I (Nashville: Broadman Press, 1958), pp. 127, 128.

prison and exile for their faith."[2] During the historic congress, President Alexander Maclaren led all the delegates in repeating the Apostles' Creed as an assertion that the Baptists stood in the "continuity of the historic Church."[3]

The Alliance was formed at the joint initiative of the British and American Baptists, and for the first forty-three years of its existence London was its world headquarters. The Alliance is a voluntary association which provides world fellowship for Baptists and wields no ecclesiastical authority. Its constitution did not permit fund-raising, lest it become a rival to the Baptist Unions and Missionary Societies. Basically, the Alliance served to meet the following needs:

1. To complete Baptist polity, supplying that necessary complement of the local independence and autonomy which has always been strongly emphasized.

2. To demonstrate Baptist unity and emphasize the freedom of a genuine brotherhood based not on legal authority or hierarchal claims but on inward spiritual experience.

3. To strengthen young and small communities, encourage the oppressed, and defend religious liberty.[4]

Listed with the Russian delegates was the Estonian, Baron Waldemar Uixkiull, who pastored the local Baptist church near his castle in the Baltic province. Baron Uixkiull was a member of the committee responsible for framing the constitution of the Baptist World Alliance. Other notable pioneer Baptists from Russia were D. I.

---

[2] R. J. W. Bevan, *The Churches and Christian Unity* (London: Oxford University Press, 1963), p. 5.

[3] *Ibid.*, p. 6.

[4] F. Townley Lord, *Baptist World Fellowship* (Nashville: Broadman Press, 1955), v.

Mazaiev, V. G. Pavlov, and V. V. Ivanov. Pavlov addressed some 3,000 delegates in English, one of the many languages under his command. Present for the convocation was Lord Radstock who must have rejoiced to renew the friendship of the representatives of 23,000 Russian Baptists.

At the second Baptist World Congress, which was held in Philadelphia, June 19-25, 1911, two dominant personalities were among the Russian delegates: Ivan S. Prokhanov and Wilhelm A. Fetler. Prokhanov, the president of the Evangelical Christians, was always considered by the Alliance to be a member of the Baptist family, so similar was the doctrinal position of the two unions before the 1944 merger. Thus did Prokhanov become one of the ten vice-presidents of the Alliance, while Fetler served on the Peace Committee and in the Young People's organization. Four others from Russia held executive posts in the Alliance. Now representing 50,000 Baptists in Tsarist Russia, six women joined the twenty-four delegates in a stirring song before the congress.

Dr. Russell H. Conwell urged all delegates to

... always speak kindly of Russia, for our words that are uttered here will be read by the Little Father in his home, by the short-hand reports that I know are to be taken and sent from this place ... when he reads your kind expressions for Russia and for the Russian people, ... these brethren will go back to their homes received as messengers of good. ...[5]

In contrast to subsequent congresses attended by delegates from the Soviet Union the candid reports of their persecution, arrests, and exile experienced because of their faith were never to be repeated. The AUCECB delegates,

---

[5] Philip L. Jones (ed.), *The Baptist World Alliance, Second Congress* (Philadelphia: Harper & Brother Company, 1911), p. 3.

far from seeking financial aid from brethren abroad, always reported financial adequacy, whereas in 1911 Fetler spoke of the American Baptists as big brothers and fathers in his request for financial assistance, saying, "to whom can the little boy go but to the father?"[6]

Pavlov so effectively challenged the congress with Russia's dire need for a college to educate evangelical preachers that F. B. Meyers raised $66,000 in pledges for this purpose during one morning's session.[7] Plans were formulated to request the Tsar's consent to establish such a college on Russian soil, aided by additional finances which were to be raised by the Northern and Southern Baptist Conventions in the United States.[8]

I. S. Prokhanov also addressed the Second Congress revealing that the first evangelical church in St. Petersburg to be legalized had received this status on November 26, 1908. This was followed by other churches being granted the right to hold public meetings, receive offerings, construct meeting halls, own property, and to found schools and philanthropic institutions. He added

> Of course we cannot say that our religious liberty is perfect . . . standards of liberty we are enjoying now give great possibility for the work.[9]

Prokhanov's associate minister and successor, Iakov Zhidkov, who assumed the presidency of the AUCECB in 1944, never yielded to such candidness, but consistently expressed gratitude for religious liberty granted under the Soviet regime.

The plans to convene a third world congress in 1916 were interrupted by the first World War. It was finally

---

[6] *Ibid.*, p. 25.
[7] *Ibid.*, p. 242.
[8] *Ibid.*, pp. 264, 265.
[9] *Ibid.*, pp. 439, 440.

held in 1923, in Stockholm, and only at the last moment did the Soviet Government sanction the attendance of forty Russian delegates. No objections were recorded by them when J. C. Carlile of England declared that Baptists

> . . . have neither part nor lot in principle nor in sympathy with the red revolution. We are the advocates of peace between the nations and classes. . . .[10]

At a later congress, the seventh, no such embarrassment to the delegates from the Soviet Union was risked, for the Russian Evangelical-Baptists, aware of a speech to be presented against Communism, refused or were not permitted to attend.

At the Stockholm Congress addresses were delivered by P. Pavlov and I. Prokhanov, the latter again being elected to a vice-presidency of the Baptist World Alliance. Pavlov served with a committee that drafted a resolution on international peace. Intense horror for war was expressed, but the doctrine of non-resistance was not collectively adopted. However, loyalty to the principle of conscientious objection was respected. In relation to international affairs, the Baptists recorded their profound conviction against war and favored cooperation among the nations of the world to promote peace.[11] The AUCECB has often referred to the early Baptist Congresses and their promotion of world peace as a pattern they consistently follow, not for political reasons, but in the best of Baptist traditions.

In 1928 almost 5,000 delegates met at the fourth Baptist World Congress, which convened in Toronto, Canada. Among them were twenty-eight representatives from the Soviet Union, bursting with optimism. P. V. Ivanov-Klishnikov, secretary of the Russian Baptist Union, declared that the evangelization of his country was

---

[10] W. T. Whitley (ed.), *The Third Baptist World Congress* (London: Kingsgate Press, 1923), p. 64.

[11] *Ibid.*, p. 228.

. . . of world importance in the propagating and spreading the cause of God on earth. Russia is not Europe, but she is also not Asia; she is the medium between two worlds. And the light that burns within her, will kindle and keep aflame the West and the East.[12]

Ignorant of the dark years of persecution immediately ahead he told of the splendid opportunities for evangelistic expansion and submitted a request for financial aid to enable the Russians to construct new prayer halls and to expand the scope of itinerant evangelism.

This Congress adopted a detailed definition of the Alliance which contained the promise that it would in no way interfere with the independence of its member churches nor assume the administrative functions of existing organizations.[13] The results of the Baptist World Alliance efforts were

. . . principally intangible but richly valuable. It has brought to small minority groups, giving their testimony in the fact of overwhelming odds, the consciousness that 300 years ago all Baptists were worse off than they are. . . . To Baptists more privileged, the Alliance furnishes the knowledge of needs and opportunities.[14]

In 1933 the Baptist World Alliance sent a letter to President Roosevelt relative to United States' recognition of the Soviet Union. It was a plea to obtain some definite modification of the antireligious laws in order to permit the freedom of conscience, worship, and preaching as a human right to be practiced in Soviet Russia.[15]

The fifth congress was held in Berlin, August 4-10,

---

[12] *Ibid.*, p. 78.
[13] *Ibid.*, p. 312.
[14] Cox, *loc cit.*, Vol. I, p. 132.
[15] J. H. Rushbrooke (ed.), *Fifth Baptist World Congress* (London: Baptist World Alliance, 1934), pp. 25, 26.

1934, beginning the day after German President Paul von Hindenburg's death. Three days later Adolf Hitler declared himself the Fuehrer. At one of the sessions the German delegate F. Fullbrandt lauded Hitler as a "problem solver," and in his address on the religious deterioration in the Soviet Union, he said:

> . . . no one has more passionately and effectively opposed this flood of unbelief than Adolf Hitler with his Brown Shirts. . . .[16]

Without a single representative from the Soviet Union present at the congress, appeals were made to Baptists the world around to pray on their behalf. The congress adopted a resolution which struck at the religious repression in Russia. It also passed a resolution against war and actually urged its members to induce their governments to declare themselves ready to surrender whatever national sovereignty was necessary in order to establish international authority sufficient for the maintenance of world peace on the basis of equity and righteousness. The congress welcomed the launching of an international conference of Christian churches to avert war and to extend the peace.[17] Although such a conference was not established by the Baptists, it was brought into existence in 1958 by the Ecumenical Council of Churches of Czechoslovakia and was called the Christian Peace Conference.

ii. Baptist Grievance Against Soviet Antireligious Tactics

In 1939, just before the Soviet Union's New Religious Policy was introduced, the sixth and largest Baptist World Congress to date met in Atlanta, Georgia. The Alliance

---

16 *Ibid.*, p. 154.
17 *Ibid.*, p. 14.

expressed its grievance against Soviet tactics concerning religious freedom in these words:

> The members of this Congress deeply deplore the fact that the Government of the U.S.S.R. has maintained through many years, and still maintains, an attitude and policy of hostility to religion.
> . . . truly cordial and intimate relations are made impossible by the existence of repression and persecution.[18]

I. V. Neprash, formerly a pastor in Leningrad, defined two varieties of Communism—one for export and the other as actually practiced: "while the most altruistic words are used in theory the most egotistic aims are pursued in practice."[19] He went on to state that all influential Baptists, both men and women, were either in prison or in exile. Of course, no Russian representatives were present at the congress.

In 1943, in the midst of the world holocaust and the allied effort against the "problem solver" Hitler, England's Rushbrooke, the Alliance president, was so optimistic about the plans for the following World Congress that he said, "dare we hope it might assemble in Moscow?"[20] Rushbrooke died on February 1, 1947, just months before the Seventh Congress convened, not in Moscow, but in Copenhagen. The Russian delegates, absent from the Congresses of 1934 and 1939, sent word of their refusal to attend the convocation. The AUCECB presidium explained that its decision to be absent had been provoked by the inclusion in the agenda of a speech against Communism which was labeled a hindrance to the work of

---

18 J. H. Rushbrooke (ed.), *Sixth Baptist World Congress* (Atlanta: Baptist World Alliance, 1939), p. 15.

19 *Ibid.*, pp. 214, 215.

20 J. H. Rushbrooke, *Baptists in the U.S.S.R.* (Nashville: Broadman Press, 1943), p. 16.

world evangelization. The Russian Baptists declared that Communism was not

> . . . a hindrance to the work of evangelism, but fully maintain that its socio-economic principles are not contradictory to the teaching of our Lord Jesus Christ.
>
> We Evangelical Christians-Baptists of the USSR could not be present at the Congress indifferently listening to speeches against our beloved homeland, which has done so much for all freedom-loving mankind in the last World War.[21]

Indeed, the loyal delegates from the Soviet Union would have been uncomfortable at the pointed remarks of the Britisher Ernest Brown when he addressed the Congress on the subject of the Baptist Contribution to World Peace, stating that they were

> . . . passionately opposed to the coerced system, for it is atheistic in its essence and tyranny is its political face. We Baptists are not democrats who are willing to gain economic progress at the cost of religious, civil, and political liberty.[22]

iii. Copenhagen Charter of Freedom—Too Free for the USSR

The Baptists at Copenhagen outlined a Charter of Freedom, one which included the freedom to control the education of its denomination's ministers, the freedom to give religious instruction to its youth, and the liberty to conduct relief work and missionary activities both at home and abroad, all of which struck at the basis of the Soviet

---

[21] "To the Leaders of the Seventh Baptist World Congress," *Bv,* No. 4, 1947, p. 7.

[22] Walter O. Lewis (ed.), *Seventh Baptist World Congress* (London: The Carey Kingsgate Press, 1948), p. 66.

Law of 1929. The AUCECB members averted many embarrassing questions by remaining behind Stalin's iron curtain. It is significant that Kalugin, a Soviet antireligious writer, commended the loyal position of the AUCECB in taking its stand against the agenda of the Copenhagen Congress. He applauded the non-participation of the Russian evangelicals, agreeing with them that the "discussion was not a religious, but a political problem."[23] By the time the Ninth Congress convened in 1955 the Russian evangelicals were to exhibit a dramatic about-face, avidly supporting political discussions on the "International Responsibilities of Baptists" especially in the work of strengthening world peace, facing the "Race Problem," looking to the "United Nations," etc., but never have they been able to espouse the Charter of Freedom, for this is diametrically opposed to the Soviet Union's antireligious posture.

Once again—at the Eighth Baptist World Congress, which convened in Cleveland, Ohio, in July of 1950—the political situation prevented the Russian evangelicals from attending. During the years 1950-1952, publication of *Bratskii vestnik* ceased as the cold winds generated by Stalin blew upon the evangelicals.[24] Korean war clouds were hovering menacingly as President Harry S. Truman's message was read to the Baptist delegates, including the statement that

. . . there has come upon the world today, through the machinations of atheistic communism, a suppression of freedom of conscience over wide areas. . . .[25]

In the second postwar Congress of 1950 Latvian A. Klaupiks reported that

[23] Kalugin, *op. cit.,* p. 9.
[24] Interview with I. I. Motorin, Moscow minister, July 7, 1965.
[25] Arnold T. Ohrn (ed.), *Eighth Baptist World Congress* (Philadelphia: The Judson Press, 1950), p. 49.

... late in 1944 the steam roller of the Soviet Dictatorship began to roll again . . . thousands tried to cross the Baltic Sea in small, open fishing boats.[26]

Miss Tabea Korjus of Estonia also described the mass evacuation of more than 20,000 to Sweden, mostly in small boats.

All radios were collected. . . . In our capital city only one Baptist church was allowed to be used for worship for "older people that cannot be changed." . . . It was a time when people had to be "radishes," red on the outside and white inside.[27]

She further stated that during the first Soviet occupation in 1941, some 10,000 citizens had been arrested and deported to slave labor camps in Russia. She maintained that deportations had continued periodically, even as late as March of 1950.[28]

The Baptist Alliance President C. O. Johnson attempted to temper the various charges against the Communists by declaring that

Against this cloud of Communist conspiracy it is ours to shine. . . . But do not forget all our lands are dark— in the United States commercialism and materialism threaten the light. . . .[29]

It is important to note that addresses at the Baptist World Congresses represented the views of individual speakers and not any body of Baptists. The Alliance exercised no censorship; its executives were respected for their choice of speakers on the program, but no individual or

---

26 *Ibid.*, pp. 101, 102.
27 *Ibid.*, pp. 103, 104.
28 *Ibid.*
29 *Ibid.*, p. 65.

group was bound by any pronouncement of the Alliance. Although the executive committee was well represented by Baptists of various conventions, even the Congressional resolutions were not authoritative expressions of the world Baptists. They simply represented an overwhelming consensus of Baptist opinion indicative of the trends of thought among Baptists around the world, yet binding on no single Baptist Union or Convention.[30]

Additional damaging charges against the Soviet Union were made at the 1950 Congress, including the blunt statement that "No man or woman could come from the other side of the 'iron curtain.' "[31] The mid-century call to religious freedom challenged the Communist rulers to

> . . . cease their policy of discrimination against religion and to refrain from intimidating Christian churches and their leaders by arrests and threats of arrest, . . .[32]

W. O. Lewis, speaking on the importance of Europe in the world picture shared this devastating analysis of the Soviet rule:

> . . . there is a certain amount of toleration but no real freedom. At present the Russian state seeks to use the churches for its own purpose. Many ministers of religion have been "liquidated." When ministers of religion are imprisoned or banished, the Soviet Government never admits this is because they are preachers. Some trumped-up charge is made against them. . . .[33]

The Kremlin's desired image of religious freedom in the Soviet Union suffered greatly before the open platform of the Baptist World Congresses. The inadequacy and in-

---

[30] *Ibid.,* vi.
[31] *Ibid.,* p. 343.
[32] *Ibid.,* p. 338.
[33] *Ibid.,* pp. 109, 110.

herent weakness of the Soviet position was often projected in painfully sharp focus. That the Soviet Government was sensitive to the opinion of such world congresses was indicated by its obvious attempts to change its image before leading world evangelicals. *Izvestiia* published a notice of the arrival of three executives of the Baptist World Alliance for a three-week visit to the Soviet Union, including the above-mentioned W. O. Lewis.[34] A full-page photograph of the Alliance visitors was published in *Bratskii vestnik*.[35] F. Townley Lord, the first Alliance president to visit the Soviet Union, brought greetings from the world's twenty million Baptists to the AUCECB officials in the Moscow church office and Lord presented a statue of the famed Baptist preacher, Charles Hadden Spurgeon, to the Russians.

This historic meeting did not take place until the year after Stalin's death and the cessation of hostilities effected by the Korean truce. The dust of the Soviet churchmen's invective upon the United States had somewhat settled. The Alliance executives were escorted by Zhidkov, Levindanto, and Mitskevich to Voronezh, Stalingrad, Rostov-on-Don, Taganrog, and Kharkov. In each of the churches they addressed overflowing, responsive congregations, and the salutory effect of these visits was evidenced in the statement of General Secretary Dr. E. A. Payne: ". . . many causes exist separating us. But our visit to you in some measure swept away these causes."[36] Much greater progress was suggested by *Tass* in its remark that F. Townley Lord had observed that the people in the Soviet Union fully and clearly expressed their desire for peace.[37] But the crowning

[34] I. I. Zhidkov, "Visit of the Baptist World Alliance Delegates to the USSR," *Bv*, Nos. 3–4, 1954, pp. 84–100.

[35] *Ibid.*, p. 87.

[36] *Ibid.*, p. 104.

[37] "Workers of the Baptist World Alliance: About Their Trip Across the Soviet Country," *Izvestiia*, Moscow, July 2, 1954, p. 4; *Bv*, Nos. 3–4, 1954, p. 110.

comments were published in *Izvestiia* in an interview
with President Lord, who was quoted as stating:

> Getting acquainted with the life of the Baptist church
> in the Soviet land, we found that the Baptists here have
> full freedom of doctrine and equal rights among other
> churches.[38]

Further efforts to change the Soviet Union's world image
was in evidence during the post-Stalin years. The Baptists'
Russian Seminary Fund, which had increased from $66,000
in 1911 to over $98,000 by 1951,[39] had been untouched due
to the Soviet regime's refusal to permit the erection or
purchase of a building for a seminary on Russian soil. In
1956 the fund was probably tapped when Mikhail I.
Zhidkov, son of the AUCECB president, and the assistant
pastor of Leningrad, Anatolii N. Kiriukhantsev, attended
Spurgeon College, while Il'ia M. Orlov and Matvei V.
Mel'nik studied at Bristol Baptist College, both in England.[40] Eleven long years passed before three additional
Russians in their thirties were to school in England.[41]

The step-up of exchange visits following the death of
Stalin was in sharp contrast to the single visit permitted
to M. I. Golaiev and A. L. Andreev when they met fellow-
believers in Scandinavia in 1946. In 1947, the American
Baptist and politician Harold Stassen was in Moscow and
spoke to the evangelicals, followed by a visit of English
Quakers in 1951. The trickle increased in 1953 and began
to flow by 1955. In mid-1957, the *Bratskii vestnik* publication adopted a new series of regular exhortations and

---

[38] *Ibid.*

[39] F. Townley Lord, *Baptist World Fellowship* (Nashville: Broadman Press, 1955), p. 155.

[40] I. Orlov, "On Study in England," *Bv*, No. 4, 1957, pp. 70, 71.

[41] *Bv*, No. 1, 1968, p. 64. The three men were L. F. Tkachenko,
V. L. Fedichkin, and D. V. Krasnenkov, sent to Spurgeon College,
London on September 7, 1967.

articles championing world peace, urging all believers to become engaged actively and consistently in efforts toward this goal.

Before the 1954 arrival of the Baptist World Alliance executives, Aleksandr Karev, AUCECB General Secretary, wrote to W. O. Lewis, the Alliance General Secretary, taking issue with his charge that the Soviet Government had initiated the convocation of all the religious representatives in the Soviet Union to a peace conference at Zagorsk.

> Why do you think that believers in God within our country, sincerely longing for peace, did not themselves have the ability to initiate the good work for such a sacred Christian task as a Conference of Christian churches and the representatives of other religions in the defense of peace. . . . We, conversely, are surprised that many Christians from the West are so inert about the affairs of the defense of peace and go under the thumb of their governments in the approval of an arms race and the preparation of a new world war. If all the Christians of the West would call such a conference . . . then the arms race would have ceased long ago and the colossal cost . . . would be used for works of love and mercy, culture and progress.[42]

Karev maintained that there was no ground for Lewis to criticize the Soviet Government in any case, if by its action the fervent longing of the people for peace was realized. He again explained that the absence of the Russian delegates at the Seventh Baptist World Congress was due to the malevolent attitude toward his country on the part of the West. Karev opened the door for confrontations that would rather lead to the strengthening of friendship and mutual understanding among nations.

---

[42] "Letters of the AUCECB Abroad," *Bv*, No. 1, 1953, pp. 65, 66.

The AUCECB warmly welcomed the Stockholm Appeal which sought millions of signatures on behalf of peace, and the Evangelical Christians-Baptists signed it as one.[43] They reminded the Baptist Alliance to renew its protest against war, as stated in the World Congresses of 1911 and 1923, especially during the Korean conflict.

In June 1950, they [the Americans] burst a fire of war conflagration in Korea. The armed powers of the USA started their devastating campaign against North Korea. American planes dropped bombs . . . on fields where peasants peacefully worked; on little countrysides where innocent children played; on factories where food products are made; on schools and hospitals—in a word, they subjected Korea to total bombing.[44]

In a protest to the Council of Safety, condemnation was heaped upon the Americans, who "once sent their missionaries to Korea" but were now engaged in the "inhuman destruction of the peaceful people of Korea. . . ."[45]

The AUCECB supported the demand of its government for the immediate cessation of war activities in Korea. It challenged the Baptist World Alliance to take a decisive stand for peace and to unanimously condemn atomic arms. Zhidkov sought for American and British Baptists to summon mankind to the sacred struggle for peace.

We know there are Baptists, and especially in the United States of America and England who support the war and approve their aggressive actions. We, the Baptists of the Soviet Union, hold that these Baptists defame Christianity, and are unworthy to be called Baptists. . . .[46]

---

[43] "Participation of the EC-Bs of the USSR in the Work of the Defense of Peace," *Bv*, No. 1, 1953, pp. 4, 5.
[44] *Ibid.*
[45] *Ibid.*
[46] *Ibid.*, p. 6.

17

War and Peace

i. The Zagorsk Religious Peace Conference

From May 9-12, 1952, seventy-four delegates from twenty-seven religious associations in the Soviet Union representing eighteen nationalities, answered the invitation of the Patriarch Aleksis to gather at the famed Troitse-Sergievo monastery at Zagorsk for the purpose of uniting their voices in the defense of peace. *Bratskii vestnik* reported six of its representatives at the gathering,[1] whereas the Conference report listed only five.[2] It is possible that Ivanov, who also attended, was not an official delegate, as were Zhidkov, Karev, Andreev, Levindanto, and Chechnev.

At this unprecedented conference Zhidkov was named a member of the Presiding Council and chaired the third day's session, while Karev served on the Secretariat and Editorial Committee for Drafting Resolutions. Patriarch Aleksis expressed his gratitude for so unanimous a response to his invitation. The suspicions of the World Baptist executive, W. O. Lewis, that the Soviet Government had initiated the conference seemed plausible because of such a response, especially when the diversity of faiths included the Orthodox, Catholic, Protestant, Moslem,

---

[1] *Ibid.*, p. 7.
[2] *Conference in Defense of Peace of All Churches and Religious Associations in the U.S.S.R.* (Moscow: Moscow Patriarchate, 1952), p. 14.

Molokan, Old Believers, Buddhist, and Jewish Communities.

Vitriolic, denunciatory remarks were hurled against the United States at the Peace Conference. Aleksis charged the American enemy with the use of bacteriological weapons, an action which called for the curbing of crimes against love and truth.[3] Mufti Kurbanov of the Moslem Council stated:

> The American imperialists, with Truman at their head, are doing their black diabolic work of establishing military, aggressive blocs directed against our Homeland. . . .[4]

The Molokan, A. Remizov, was convinced that the American "imperialists" were a threat to the destruction of mankind, warning that "these maniacs hope to force a life of slavery on us Soviet folk too."[5] Rabbi Itsko Shechtman of Kiev denounced the U.S. for "conducting a cruel and bloody intervention in Korea," and resorting to "the horrible biological weapon. . . ."[6]

The demand for the cessation of the Korean War was repeated to the United Nations by the Patriarch and the Holy Synod with the claim that

> When the American cannibals resorted to bacteriological war against the Korean and Chinese people, our Church issued an angry protest which was published in the press on March 21, 1952.[7]

Zhidkov and the AUCECB were complimented for their struggle on behalf of peace, for their protest sent to the Security Council of the United Nations against the bomb-

[3] *Ibid.*, pp. 29–32.
[4] *Ibid.*, p. 224.
[5] *Ibid.*, pp. 241, 242.
[6] *Ibid.*, p. 255.
[7] *Ibid.*, pp. 68, 69.

ing of the civilian population of Korea, for Zhidkov's radio appeal to Baptists all over the world, and for his ardent protest against "bacteriological warfare in Korea."[8]

The Stockholm Appeal received almost 500 million signatures favoring its manifesto for the absolute prohibition of atomic weapons. It further proposed that the first nation to use nuclear weapons be proclaimed a war criminal.[9] In the face of such massive response, President Truman, the only person to order the dropping of atomic bombs upon an enemy nation, found it impossible to permit General MacArthur the use of atomic weapons in Korea.

In marked contrast, the Zagorsk Conference had nothing but laudatory acclaim for Stalin, some of which brought the religious delegates to their feet in a prolonged ovation.

> . . . his . . . heart, which absorbs the pain of all who are in distress is filled with restrained but implacable anger against tormentors and with great love for mankind. . . . Glory to the great Stalin![10]

In this manner did the AUCECB completely identify with its government as peacemakers, favoring peaceful coexistence and the cooperation and competition between the two social and economic systems. The western "imperialists" were exposed as morally bankrupt, unable to tolerate their own moral inferiority.[11]

ii. Charges of Bacteriological Warfare

Were the voices of these religionists but the willing, obsequious tools of Soviet anti-Western propaganda, or were they sincerely convinced of the need for concerted

---

[8] *Ibid.*, pp. 77, 78.
[9] *Ibid.*, pp. 44, 45.
[10] *Ibid.*, p. 86.
[11] *Ibid.*, pp. 34–38.

action? Communist parties throughout the world marked the climax of organized propaganda campaigns in the Stalin era by the effort to convince people everywhere that the United States was using bacteriological weapons in the Korean War. In John C. Clews's study, he revealed a propaganda case history of the 1951-1953 campaign by the Communists to brand the U.S. contingent of the United Nations forces in Korea as war criminals who deliberately resorted to the use of bacterial weapons against the armed forces and the civilian population of North Korea and Northeast China. It started in 1951, developed in 1952, and continued past the armistice in the U.N. debates of 1953.

> The accusations acquired tremendous force and credibility because it seemed impossible that so many responsible people should deliberately lie as part of a concerted plan.[12]

In March, April, and May of 1952, Soviet delegate Malik repeatedly raised the question of the use of bacteriological weapons by the United States in Korea and China before the United Nations' Disarmament Commission. On May 11, 1952, *Tass* published a letter directed to President Truman and Soviet delegate Malik from the American Association of Scientific Workers condemning bacteriological warfare. During this period, Peking and Moscow sent out the first of a large mass of "documentation" to Communist organizations throughout the world. It was at this time that the Zagorsk Peace Conference convened. Unknown to the delegates were the official denials of the allegations of bacteriological warfare by American Secretary of State Acheson and his request that the International Red Cross investigate the charges. On March 13, 1952,

---

[12] John C. Clews, *Communist Propaganda Techniques* (New York: Frederick A. Praeger, 1964), p. 180.

the Red Cross agreed to participate, but both the Red Cross and the World Health Organization were refused the role. They were called special agents of the United Nations who would whitewash the Americans of guilt by means of a false report.[13]

In a Harvard study, it was learned that many Soviet citizens believed the press and other official media without major reservations. The greatest success was attained in shaping the Soviet citizens' distorted image of the outside world, especially as it related to the foreign policy of "capitalistic" countries.[14]

There were also some influential Americans who believed the stories told to the Russian public. Harry F. Ward, professor-emeritus of Christian Ethics at Union Theological Seminary in New York City, gave this analysis of the Korean War:

> In Korea we burned to death with jellied gasolene innocent peasants with their wives and children, their livestock and crops, their homes. In Hiroshima and Nagasaki we blasted with atomic fire tens of thousands of men, and women and children who had never lifted a hand against us, disfigured thousands more, and poisoned the blood stream and genetic capacities of other thousands. Now our government is preparing to do this on a one hundred times larger scale. The fact that we do not rebel against this inhumanity means that, under this indifference, the spirit of barbarism lies within us.[15]

The germ warfare accusations received worldwide publicity which brought on a wave of anti-American fervor

---

[13] *Ibid.*, pp. 194–207.

[14] Alex Inkeles and Raymond A. Bauer, *The Soviet Citizen* (Cambridge: Harvard University Press, 1959), p. 178.

[15] Harry F. Ward, *The Story of American-Soviet Relations, 1917–1959* (New York: National Council of American-Soviet Friendship, 1959), p. 79.

and created controversy among scientists in many countries, with well-known figures taking each side.

On July 27, 1953, the Korean Armistice agreement was signed at Panmunjon. The full background story of how the Communists extorted confessions from the American prisoners was told in the United Nations Political Committee by the American delegation in October of 1953. Early in November, the General Assembly decided to refer it to the Disarmament Committee, where it remained. The bacterial weapon question ceased to be a live issue in the United Nations. After 1954, the Korean bacterial weapons charges were dropped by the Communists, but general accusations against the West were to continue. Jin Chull Soh's thesis, drawing on new documentation from Chinese, Japanese and North Korean sources, revealed that the North Korean attack was a carefully planned incident in Sino-Soviet expansion.[16] However, in the mood and atmosphere of the time, the AUCECB was enveloped by unilateral, vituperative reports directed against the United States. As loyal citizens of the USSR, and as evangelicals obedient to the Biblical injunction to be subject to the higher powers, participation in the Zagorsk Peace Conference seemed to be wholehearted and without pretext.

In the post-Stalin era AUCECB representatives have echoed the voice of the Soviet peace proposals both at home and abroad in the name of the Prince of Peace. Their influence among the world Baptist leaders of over one hundred nations in propagating the peace proposals could only have received approbation from the Soviet Government.

---

[16] Jin Chull Soh, "Some Causes of the Korean War of 1950: A Case Study of Soviet Foreign Policy in Korea (1945–1950), with Emphasis on Sino-Soviet Collaboration" (unpublished Ph.D. dissertation, University of Oklahoma, 1963).

iii. Carl McIntire's Spy Charges and the Penkovskiy Papers

In his "Scrapbook No. 10," entitled *The Russian Baptists* Carl McIntire compiled and edited a booklet of seventy-two pages with the express aim of exposing the AUCECB and its leaders as propagandists and agents of the Communists. He chided the Baptist World Alliance for not receiving them

. . . as propagandists or spokesmen for the Communists in this cold war battle, but simply as "good Baptists!"[17]

McIntire, on inconclusive evidence, stated as fact that

Two veteran agents and spies of the Kremlin in the Baptist field are Jakov Zhidkov and Alexander Karev. . . . The Baptist World Alliance has been an easy prey . . . particularly in this field of the Baptists that the Russians have been using the church, especially since the close of World War II.[18]

Apparently guilt by association was employed. McIntire made reference to the Soviet defector Peter Deriabin who reported that Metropolitan Nikolai of the Orthodox Church was an agent of the Soviet secret police.

The *Penkovskiy Papers*, the writings of Colonel Oleg V. Penkovskiy, a Soviet military intelligence officer (GRU), which were translated by Deriabin cast light upon the terms and conditions under which Soviet citizens were permitted to travel abroad.

[17] Carl McIntire, "Analysis of Zhidkov's Address," *The Russian Baptists* (Collingswood: 20th Century Reformation Hour, n.d.), p. 31.

[18] Carl McIntire, "Communist Infiltration and Use of Baptist World Alliance," *The Russian Baptists* (Collingswood: 20th Century Reformation Hour, n.d.), p. 24.

If a delegation is small, let us say, two or three people, and it is difficult to insert a GRU officer into it, a co-optee is sent. If there is not one available, they will make one in one day.[19]

Penkovskiy, sentenced to death by the Soviet Government on espionage charges, stated that no delegation ever traveled abroad without some form of KGB involvement and careful preparation. The departure of each delegation required a separate decree from the Central Committee of the Communist Party.

Co-opted specialists are very useful. . . . Each Soviet specialist who goes abroad has to submit a detailed report of his trip, and if this report contains nothing valuable, he is reprimanded, criticized, and as a rule, is never sent abroad again.[20]

The statements above indicated that in the midst of the evangelicals who traveled abroad one was a drafted informant. This was not, however, to be equated with a card-carrying Party member employed by the KGB or the GRU. After having made two trips to the Soviet Union, I recently was called by the Federal Bureau of Investigation while in New York City and asked to meet an agent at the New York Public Library. Casually standing outside the building, the agent, after proper identification, received answers to his questions in a twenty-minute meeting. I had served as a modified "co-optee," a role which seemed to be very strange for one accustomed to the easy-going freedom of an American democracy. Conversely, in a monolithic Communist society, anyone fortunate enough to visit the outside world accepted his government's orders as a matter-of-fact routine. Coupled with Scriptural sup-

---

[19] Oleg Penkovskiy, *The Penkovskiy Papers* (Garden City: Doubleday & Company, 1965), p. 183.
[20] *Ibid.*, pp. 179, 180.

port (subjection to higher powers) and a strong sentiment for world peace, a pastor from the Soviet Union would be highly insulted if accused of being a Communist and espionage agent. Karev, so accused by McIntire, crossed my path while in the United States in 1960. For a person supposedly a Soviet agent, his plea for more Bibles in the form of a stirring challenge, was difficult to explain.

Many Christians visit our country from the West. Why doesn't each one bring a Russian Bible with him and leave it with us. You have failed us![21]

The words did not fade away, but motivated me to discover a method to supply free Russian New Testaments to more than 1500 American tourists preparing to visit the Soviet Union during the following two years. It is doubtful that the "co-optee" reported his plea to the Soviet officials.

iv. Religious Liberty

General Secretary Arnold T. Ohrn addressed the Ninth Baptist World Congress in London in 1955 on the problem of religious liberty in this manner:

All liberty is relative. When nations considered unfree by other peoples declare "We are free," they may be partly justified by the fact that they now enjoy liberties which they formerly did not have. When churches which once were persecuted, now possess some degree of freedom of worship, they are naturally grateful because heavy chains have been removed and think little of the lighter ones still remaining. But our gratitude for piecemeal betterment in the situation of our brethren must

---

[21] Interview with Aleksandr Karev, November 10, 1960.

not mean that we shall cease to work and pray for complete liberty of soul and conscience. . . .[22]

At the roll call, AUCECB President Zhidkov boasted that the nine Soviet Baptist delegates tripled the Russian delegation present at the First Baptist World Congress. He did not, however, remind the Congress that twenty-four Russians had attended the second session in 1911, forty were at the third convocation in 1923, and twenty-eight delegates enjoyed the Fourth Congress in 1928, the last in which Soviet Evangelical Baptists were to be seen for over two decades. Before the enactment of the restrictive law of April 8, 1929, opportunities for evangelism in the Soviet Union surpassed those enjoyed during the early years of the New Religious Policy.

Despite the enforced absence of Soviet delegates from the four preceding Baptist World Congresses Zhidkov spoke of freedom at the Golden Jubilee Congress in this manner:

All our churches enjoy full freedom for preaching the gospel, and nurturing and educating new members. This liberty, this freedom, is guaranteed by the basic laws of our country, and in conducting services we do not encounter any obstacles.[23]

Moscow delegate Claudia Tyrtova, however, candidly admitted the limitations of the Russian evangelicals in relation to its young people when she stated:

The functions which Christian youth organizations perform in the West are carried out by the youth organizations created by the State, . . . sports, travel, cultural and educational activities and everything that is neces-

---

[22] Arnold T. Ohrn (ed.), *Golden Jubilee Congress* (London: The Carey Kingsgate Press, 1955), p. 99.
[23] *Ibid.*, p. 261.

sary for physical and intellectual development. But it is our churches that give our Baptist youth spiritual education.[24]

As the Baptists of the world gained added insights into the problems of the Russian believers at the Congresses, even so the readers of *Bratskii vestnik* enjoyed a window on the West, sharing items of interest such as the meeting of their representatives with evangelist Billy Graham; they learned of the massive crowd of 40,000 that attentively listened to Graham's closing sermon in Arsenal Stadium; the visit to Bristol College, where Prokhanov once studied; a visit to the British Bible Society display which exhibited the note of gratitude for Russian Bibles signed by Pashkov and Korf; the knowledge that the one city of Birmingham alone contained fifty-seven active Baptist churches, etc. Comments of this nature served to remind the Russian believers that they were part of a great world movement. They also revealed the glaring contrasts in the Soviet Union such as the obvious shortage of prayer houses, limited to one Evangelical meeting place per city or town (except rare cities such as Kiev, which has three, and Alma-Ata, which has two). The dearth of Bibles convinced no Russian believers that religious freedom in the Soviet Union matched that of the West. Although causal relationship cannot be proven, the fact that an AUCECB executive could boast of the Soviet publication of 10,000 Russian canonical Bibles at the following World Congress in Rio de Janeiro suggested the occasional sensitive feeling of the Soviet Government to world opinion.

At the Tenth Baptist World Congress which convened in 1960, Zhidkov was again elected one of the vice-presidents of the Alliance and delivered a devotional sermon on "The Lord of Peace" in which he stated:

---

[24] *Ibid.,* p. 306.

. . . shall we have more enmity and disaster, which finally might annihilate all mankind. In reality, wars are the most awful sin against mankind.

My family and I lost three sons and seven other relatives during the last war, and I cannot but long for peace.[25]

Zhidkov praised Khrushchev's declaration which was submitted to the United Nations in September of 1959, urging universal and complete disarmament. He viewed the proposal as "a Christian solution of the problem of disarmament. . . ."[26]

At this Congress the Baptists passed a resolution which urged all nations to dispense with the testing and the production of nuclear arms,

. . . and cooperatively to agree on satisfactory methods of inspection designed to ensure that all nations shall exercise good faith in this matter. . . .[27]

In its pronouncements on world peace the Congress meeting in Brazil stated that war undermined all Christian values and that the current arms race had subjected the world "to an increasingly exhaustive burden of taxation and fear" which was bound to lead to war. In addition to prayer the Congress called for open channels of communication and a practical program of international disarmament.[28] Again, Dr. Billy Graham climaxed the session by addressing a massive audience of 185,000 in Rio de Janeiro.

At the 1965 Congress held in Miami, Florida, General Secretary Josef Nordenhaug pictured the importance of the sixty-year relationship of the Baptist World Alliance to the Russian believers when he stated:

---

[25] Arnold T. Ohrn, *Tenth Baptist World Congress* (Nashville: Broadman Press, 1960), p. 200.

[26] *Ibid.*, p. 202.

[27] *Ibid.*, p. 301.

[28] *Ibid.*, pp. 302, 303.

One important function of the Alliance in regard to religious liberty and human rights is to gather facts and make them known to the Baptist constituency around the world. Our intercession for those who must bear their Christian witness under severe restrictions gives comfort and courage to fellow believers in such lands. . . .

Another function is to maintain contact with governments and embassies and seek to make known our ideals of religious liberty and to plead for the lifting of restrictions. The impact of public opinion is great, and the publication of protests against discrimination and persecution plays a vital role when it is designed to encourage positive solutions.[29]

---

[29] Josef Nordenhaug, *The Truth That Makes Men Free: Official Report of the Eleventh Congress* (Nashville: Broadman Press, 1966), p. 470.

18

The World Council of Churches

i. The Amsterdam Basis for Fellowship

The Russian Baptists have enjoyed a close relationship with the Baptist World Alliance since its establishment in 1905. Only in recent post-Stalin years has the AUCECB launched out into deeper waters of international religious affiliations to join the Christian Peace Conference (CPC) in 1958 and the World Council of Churches (WCC) in 1962.

Although the Edinburgh Missionary Conference of 1910 was the antecedent of the World Council of Churches, the decisive steps to establish the WCC were not taken until 1937, only to be delayed for eleven years due to the outbreak of war. At the Amsterdam Assembly in 1948 the formal Basis for fellowship in the WCC was briefly stated as follows:

> The World Council of Churches is a fellowship of churches which accept our Lord Jesus Christ as God and Saviour.[1]

Held to be inadequate, the Third Assembly which convened in New Delhi, India, in 1961 adopted an expansion of the Basis which read:

> The World Council of Churches is a fellowship of churches which confess the Lord Jesus Christ as God

---

[1] David P. Gaines, *The World Council of Churches* (Peterborough: Richard R. Smith Co., 1966), p. 883.

and Saviour according to the Scriptures and therefore seek to fulfill together their common calling to the glory of the one God, Father, Son and Holy Spirit.[2]

The World Council imposed no political conditions upon its members and identified itself with no political ideologies, but "reserved the right to criticize any and all."[3] Representatives of all denominations within the membership of the WCC were eligible for election to office. From its inception, the WCC had membership denominations in Communist countries, "whose survival depended on the acknowledgment of authority of state and obedience to its decrees."[4] The WCC was unwilling to deny membership to such churches and understanding their need of Christian fellowship even courted their affiliation, hoping that they in time would regain their freedom. It is not surprising, therefore, that after a convocation of Orthodox churches in Moscow in July of 1948, G. G. Karpov, the Soviet chairman of the Council for the Affairs of the Russian Orthodox Church (CAROC), opposed such efforts from abroad. He suggested that the World Council's political aims and methods produced an influence "inimical to true religion and international peace."[5] The Russians were not to be seen in Holland.

John Foster Dulles, then adviser of the Federal Council of Christian Churches, spoke in Amsterdam on "Christian Responsibilities in Our Divided World," indicating that the Soviet Communist party did not believe in peaceful evolution, but only by means of violence and coercion could it be able to secure its goals.[6]

The Soviet embassy official G. Spasov struck back saying:

---

[2] *Ibid.,* p. 1011.
[3] *Ibid.,* p. 1060.
[4] *Ibid.,* p. 804.
[5] *Ibid.,* p. 793.
[6] *Ibid.,* p. 253.

. . . the so-called World Council of Churches, which directs the work mainly of the Protestant churches, has been formed. One of the leaders of this council is the known warmonger, John Foster Dulles. . . . Wall Street has brought into action every pressure, mobilizing also the ecclesiastical servants of imperialism. . . .[7]

M. Shein, writing in *Nauka i zhizn* ("Science and Life"), censured the ecumenical movement for supporting "Truman's piratical policy in Korea."[8] *Nauka i religiia* (Science and Religion) informed its readers that the World Council of Churches had issued a declaration condemning communism in the Amsterdam Assembly of 1948, and had maintained the same position in the Evanston Assembly of 1954. The Soviet antireligious magazine saw the WCC as an enemy serving

. . . the black-banner of anti-communism, the reactionary religionists are now united with all the enemies of social progress; the financial oligarchy, militarism, fascism, colonialism, and the landowning classes of the world.[9]

The WCC had opposed the Communist-supported Stockholm Appeal for disarmament and peace because of its ineffective international inspection and control procedures, both immediate and continuous, and regarded the appeal as a "strategy of propaganda rather than a genuine peace proposal."[10]

On the Korean situation, the Central Committee of the WCC (meeting in Toronto, Canada, in 1950) in a direct statement against the Communist powers charged that

[7] G. Spasov, "Church Servants of Imperialism," *Literaturnaia gazeta,* March 18, 1950, p. 4.

[8] M. Shein, "American Imperialism and Church Organizations," *Nauka i zhizn,* December 1950, p. 44.

[9] *Nauka i religiia,* No. 10, 1961, pp. 28–33.

[10] Gaines, *op. cit.,* p. 380.

. . . an act of aggression has been committed . . . a calculated, co-ordinated attack prepared and launched
with secrecy. . . .[11]

The blame was squarely placed on the North Korean
troops.

Another avowed opponent of the World Council of
Churches was the International Council of Christian
Churches, promoted by Carl McIntire and founded a few
days before the WCC, in the very same city of Amsterdam,
Holland, as a protest group whose chief activity seemed
to be the harassment of the sessions held by the World
Council.

Carl McIntire began his protest crusades in 1934 when
he was part of a dissident group outspoken against the
liberalism of the Presbyterian Church USA. In 1936, the
Synod of the Presbyterian Church USA found McIntire
guilty of the violation of his ordination vows and he was
formally deposed from the ministry. McIntire then established the Bible Presbyterian Church, an ultra-funda-
mental denomination. Later in 1941 he founded the American Council of Christian Churches, which has drawn to
itself fundamental denominations which firmly repudiate
ecumenicity.[12]

Members of the World Council of Churches viewed the
International Council of Christian Churches as a source
of much misunderstanding and mischief. The WCC staff
member Norman Goodall found it impossible to follow
the activities and read the publications of McIntire without concluding that they constituted nothing more honorable than the "smear campaign" which Dr. John A.
Mackay had called them. McIntire made allegations that
the leaders of the World Council were, at one and the

---

[11] *Ibid.,* p. 758.
[12] Norman Goodall, *The Ecumenical Movement* (London: Oxford University Press, 1961), pp. 150, 151.

same time, " 'modernists,' 'Communists' and 'Romanizers.' "[13]

The World Council of Churches has drawn most of its criticism for its attitude toward politics and for its doctrinal position. The religious critics portrayed it as paving the way for the advantage of Communism, while the Communists described it as subjecting the world to Western imperialism. There were those who maintained that the WCC was basically a modernist movement whereas others attacked the Council for its refusal to compromise and for its Christo-centric basis.[14]

ii. Baptists and the World Council of Churches

As early as 1939 the Baptist World Congress, in reference to the formation of the WCC, reported:

> We should look with appreciation on all movements promoting true ecumenicity and catholicity, prepared to share in these movements as far as our supreme loyalty permits and encourages. . . .[15]

At the Baptist World Congress of 1947, enthusiasm to join the WCC was expressed, motivated by the desire to stimulate the World Council to evangelical zeal. A motion was made to join the WCC but it was found to be out of order on the basis that the Baptist World Alliance in no way interfered with the independence of the churches, or assumed the administrative functions of existing organizations. Furthermore, the motion would have conflicted with the Constitution of the WCC, which did not admit international bodies as members.[16]

---

13 *Ibid.*
14 Gaines, *op. cit.,* p. 331.
15 Rushbrooke, *Sixth BWC, loc. cit.,* p. 134.
16 Lewis, *op. cit.,* pp. 58, 59.

At the Baptist Jubilee Congress of 1955, General Secretary A. T. Ohrn indicated that "about one-third of our Baptist people have found it possible to affiliate with the World Council of Churches."[17] Joining the WCC were the Baptist Unions of Great Britain and Ireland, New Zealand, Denmark, Holland, the American Baptist Convention, and the Conference of Seventh Day Baptists.[18] Although the American Baptist Convention voted to bring the denomination into the WCC, many dissenters from its ranks viewed the step as

> aligning the churches with "theological modernism and sociological radicalism" in a relationship compromising "distinctive convictions of Baptists."[19]

The Southern Baptist Convention refused to affiliate with the WCC, but four pastors from this Convention were admitted as accredited visitors as a result of personal application to the Amsterdam Assembly.

W. R. Estep explained the Southern Baptist Convention's attitude of aloofness as one based upon the premise that a local New Testament church was the highest tribunal of Christendom. Its autonomy was subordinated to no one but Christ as interpreted by the express democratic action of its members.

> As a federation of independent democracies, the organic church union of Baptist churches with other denominations is deemed impossible.[20]

According to a resolution adopted by the first Assembly

---

[17] Ohrn, *Golden Jubilee* . . . , *loc. cit.,* p. 100.

[18] Gaines, loc cit., p. 354. (American BC was formerly named Northern BC; the Conference of SDB is also in the US).

[19] *Ibid.,* p. 353.

[20] William R. Estep, *Church Union and Southern Baptists* (Fort Worth: Baptist Book Store, 1955), pp. 99, 100.

at Amsterdam the limitations of the authority of the WCC were clearly defined:

> The Council desires to serve the churches, which are its constituent members, as an instrument whereby they may bear witness together to their common allegiance to Jesus Christ, and co-operate in matters requiring united action. But the Council is far from desiring to usurp any of the functions which already belong to its constituent churches, or control them, or to legislate for them, and indeed is prevented by its constitution from doing so.[21]

According to the agreement reached in the Toronto Declaration of 1950, no church by virtue of its membership in the WCC was under an obligation to suppress, truncate, or alter its full confession of truth by which it maintained its raison d'etre and ministry as a church.[22]

With such safeguards it was not doctrinally compromising for the Russian evangelicals to join the WCC. President I. I. Zhidkov and A. N. Stoian, the AUCECB Director of Foreign Affairs, were among the participants at the meeting of the WCC Central Committee in Paris, August 6-12, 1962. At that time the AUCECB, along with the Armenian, Georgian, and Evangelical-Lutheran churches of the USSR, were welcomed into the WCC fellowship. Official membership was effected following a mandatory waiting period of six months. Zhidkov declared that the entry of the AUCECB into the WCC would bring a great blessing to the Russian evangelicals and also fulfill the great work of the Kingdom of God.[23] K. V. Somov believed that the benefits of membership afforded fine evangelistic opportunities.

---

[21] Gaines, *loc. cit.,* p. 374.

[22] *Ibid.,* p. 858.

[23] "The Conference of the Central Committee of the WCC in Paris," *Bv,* Nos, 5-6, 1962, p. 20.

We entered into membership of the World Council of Churches in order that, by our evangelical point of view, we could render illumination on many questions in the Council.[24]

With no sense of embarrassment, Somov proposed that the "intense fire of the love to Christ," displayed by the Russian believers, could, at the WCC conferences and in personal encounters, "ignite those servants who have very little or none of this fire in their hearts with the same fire."[25] This argument may have quieted the Russian laity who preferred to have the AUCECB executives visit their oblasts rather than expend their time in travels abroad. The dissident "Initsiativniki," however, condemned the Union's association with the WCC and wrote these words to the churches:

Brothers and sisters, keep yourself pure of the sin of apostasy of the All-Union Council of Evangelical Christians-Baptists and their pastors, who cooperate with the World Council of Churches, that unites all religious trends, that is Babylon of our days—the mother of harlots and abominations of the earth.[26]

Opinions as to the reason for the entry of the fifty-million-member Russian Orthodox Church into the World Council of Churches varied considerably. They included the political motivation of the Soviet Government to secure a listening post deep in the free world, counteraction of WCC agitation which espoused democratic freedom, and a blow from within by the Russian Orthodox Church to

---

[24] K. V. Somov, "One Flock and One Pastor," *Bv*, No. 5, 1964, p. 33.

[25] *Ibid.*

[26] OPEN LETTER of the AUCECB of the USSR, dated December, 1967, mimeographed in English, signed by the new president Ilia G. Ivanov.

divide or destroy the WCC followed by the establishment of an Eastern counterpart under its own domination. The general opinion seemed to favor the Russians' need for fellowship and their sincere desire to promote Christian unity and world peace.[27]

If the Russian Orthodox Church had any designs for promoting an Eastern counterpart of the World Council, the opportunity was available within the international body of the Christian Peace Conference which was established in 1958, in Prague, Czechoslovakia.

---

[27] Gaines, *loc. cit.*, p. 1033.

19

The Prague Christian Peace
Conferences

i. The World Council of Churches and the
Christian Peace Conference

As the key figure and President of the Christian Peace
Conference (CPC), Josef Hromadka maintained that this
religious body and the WCC did not stand in each other's
way. On the contrary, he was confident that they could
supplement and mutually aid each other.[1]

In 1961, Hromadka rejoiced to note that the number
of representatives from Western churches in the Christian
Peace Conferences had grown each year and he optimistically looked forward to the time when representatives of all
churches of the world would view the Conferences as their
own. However, the WCC declined to cooperate with the
"Soviet-inspired Prague Peace Conferences." The Russian
Orthodox Church had assisted in the promotion of CPC
and failed to understand the reason for the aloofness of
the WCC. Certain World Council officers who had attended them unofficially criticized the "non-cooperative
attitude." The WCC and the West had been denounced
during the Prague Conference in 1961. Bishop K. H. Ting
of China ignored the topic assigned to him and "de-

---

[1] "All Christian Congress of Peace in Prague, June 13–18, 1961,"
Bv., No. 4, 1961, p. 5.

livered an invective against the United States and its churches. . . ."[2]

In an apparent effort to improve the understanding of the functions of the two international religious bodies and their relationship to each other, representatives of both bodies held discussions in Geneva, Switzerland, on March 27, 1962. It became clear, according to the Prague inter-denominational weekly, *Kostnicke Jiskry*, that the Christian Peace Conference was not a competitive ecumenical movement but consisted of aroused Christians who desired a common Christian responsibility for peace in the world.[3]

ii. Russian Charter Members

The AUCECB became a charter member of the Christian Peace Conference and its Moscow executives have attended and actively participated in all the CPC sessions. An international movement of theologians, religious workers, and ordinary believers, the goals of the CPC were

. . to awaken Christianity to the realization of both its blame in both World Wars and the necessity of its involvement in the work of strengthening friendship, peace and peaceful coexistence among nations. . . .[4]

It appeared that the Soviet Government not only endorsed the involvement of the Russian ecclesiastical unions in the Prague peace conferences, but endorsed its promotion in other countries. At a committee meeting of the Baptist World Alliance in Oslo, Norway, in August of

---

2 Gaines, *loc. cit.*, p. 1035.

3 "Discussion Between Representatives of the Christian Peace Conference and the World Council of Churches," *Kostnicke Jiskry*, April 26, 1962 cited in *RCDA*, Vol. I, No. 8, 1962, p. 1.

4 "Contacts of the AUCECB with Foreign Christian Organizations and Their Workers," *Bv*, No. 6, 1963, p. 19.

1962, A. I. Mitskevich urged the Baptists to cast their lot with the Christian Peace Conference, attesting that the conference representatives from both East and West were free to express their views with complete freedom.[5] A Lutheran present at the Prague Conference registered a different impression as he observed little opportunity for real dialogue due to the highly structured nature of the meeting. From fifty countries, 675 persons attended the First All-Christian Peace Assembly held in Prague in 1961, including 285 delegates from Western countries. The Western delegates, somewhat disappointed in the sessions, believed that there would be

> . . . a minimal participation by Western churches in these meetings because of their obviously political nature. On the other hand it is to be hoped that individual Christians will attend and thus communicate with those who are cut off from the mainstream of Christianity.[6]

Carl McIntire, requesting information from the US Department of State concerning the Christian Peace Conference, prior to its convocation in June of 1961, received a reply from Temple Wanamaker, Director of the Office of Public Services, stating that

> . . . earlier conferences have reflected sympathy with current Soviet Bloc propaganda and foreign policy objectives and ignored the position of the United States and other non-Communist countries. It is the Department of State's understanding that a few Americans who attended previous meetings, have found little opportunity for fruitful exchanges with other church groups,

---

[5] "Council of the Plenary Committee of the Baptist World Alliance in Oslo," *Bv*, Nos. 5–6, 1962, p. 22.

[6] Darril Hudson, "Prague in Retrospect," *Lutheran World* No. 9, (Geneva: Lutheran World Federation, 1962), pp. 154–160.

and generally were unable to make a satisfactory presentation of the American viewpoint.[7]

The dominant figure in the Christian Peace Conference since its inception has been Josef Hromadka, who, with the Ecumenical Churches of Czechoslovakia, planned the first conference which was called in 1958. With headquarters in Prague, members of the CPC consisted of churches, church unions, and individual Christians who agreed with the principles and the goals of the movement.

Flying to the initial Christian Peace Conference in a Soviet TU-104, Zhidkov and Karev found a warm and friendly atmosphere among the forty-five delegates present. Lively discussion centered around the presentation of four papers delivered by theologians. The conclusion was supported unanimously—the Christian Church was urged to firmly raise its voice against atomic weapons, the use of which was "a clear sin against God and mankind." A resolution was passed to write letters to all Christian churches of the world, to the rulers of the Soviet Union, the United States, and Great Britain, advocating that all international disputes be resolved in peaceful ways.[8]

iii. Josef Hromadka—Key Figure

Since the establishment of the Christian Peace Conference in 1958 Josef Hromadka has served as its president. A professor, and at various times Dean of the Comenius Protestant Theological Faculty at Prague, Hromadka also taught at Princeton Theological Seminary from 1939 to 1947. He chose to return to his homeland that year, and

---

7 "—The State Department Did Not Recommend Attendance," Scrapbook Number Seven, (Collingswood: 20th Century Reformation, n.d.), p. 2.

8 I. Zhidkov, "Christian Peace Conference in Prague," *Bv*, Nos. 5–6, 1958, pp. 7, 8.

when the new Czechoslovakian communist regime seized
the reins of government in the coup d'etat of February
1948, Hromadka cast his lot with the new rulers. Concerning this decision Matthew Spinka wrote:

> . . . his ambition to be the "conscience" of the regime,
> would not let him take refuge in neutrality. Henceforth,
> Hromadka was inevitably drawn deeper into coopera-
> tion with the government . . . a government astute
> enough to realize a man of his reputation and talents
> could be immensely useful to it. His services have indeed
> been invaluable to the regime, for he has been accepted
> as its spokesman among Protestants the world over.[9]

Spinka admitted that Hromadka's desire to modify and
to "Christianize" the policies of the regime was genuine,
but viewed the CPC President's assumption that he could
change Communist theory or practice as naïve.

In the world forum provided by the World Council of
Churches in Amsterdam, Hromadka received the applause
of the world churchmen as a result of his speech which
included this challenge:

> What can we offer toward the overcoming of the con-
> fusion and chaos of our day? Where is our Lord? What
> can we offer against "atheism" which we denounce so
> frequently? Liberalism without conviction? Freedom
> without faith? Tolerance without our own commit-
> ment? Political rights without social foundation? Nos-
> talgia after the old, bygone order of political and eco-
> nomic privilege? Economic well-being without soul?
> Liberty but for what, for what goal?[10]

The Czech churchman has not only been a member of

---

[9] Matthew Spinka, *Church in Communist Society* (Hartford: The
Hartford Seminary Press, 1954), p. 33.
[10] *Ibid.*, p. 35.

the World Council of Churches, but he has also served as a member of its key Central and Executive Committees since its founding in 1948. At the meeting of the Central Committee in August of 1957, Hromadka narrowly escaped the loss of these posts when he was charged by fellow delegates as "an outspoken apologist for Communism."[11] More than half of the seventy-five members present abstained from voting, but Hromadka managed to receive a majority of the thirty-five votes cast.

The much-traveled General Secretary of the AUCECB, Aleksandr Karev (sixteen foreign trips from 1947 to 1963), credited his presence at these conferences with foreign religious leaders with having served, to some extent, the attainment of the "great and blessed goal of bringing the East and the West closer, and decreasing international tension in the defense of peace."[12]

In a Working Committee of the Christian Peace Conference which convened in Moscow on September 12-19, 1962, the United States was charged with the violation of international law regarding the blockade of Cuba. The CPC requested a change in policy toward Cuba that would lessen the dangerous tension. Hromadka defended the Soviet position in an article printed in *Kostnicke Jiskry*, in which he wrote:

> Old leading nations cannot face the reality that the Soviet Union with her allies must be one of the pillars of a new world organization. . . . The Cuban crisis illuminated the division of the world and exposed the brutal reality that mankind is divided politically and according to social classes: that we are in the middle of a world class struggle.
>
> I believe that the way Chairman of the Council of Ministers Khrushchev proceeded and particularly his

---

[11] "The All Christian Congress of Peace in Prague, June 13–18, 1961," *Bv*, No. 4, 1961, p. 5.

[12] A. V. Karev, "The Path of My Life," *Bv*, No. 1, 1955, p. 63.

letters to the American President ... will remain unique documents of statemanship, prudence and responsibility.[13]

A controversial figure in the ecumenical world, Hromadka had the ability to make the WCC members of both East and West feel uncomfortable. At Amsterdam he challenged the Christian churches to reject the ideologies of both Communism and laissez-faire capitalism. That these two extremes were the only alternatives was a wrong assumption, suggested Hromadka. He urged Christians to seek new, creative solutions which would never allow the economic justice of Communism or the free enterprise of capitalism to destroy the other.[14]

Warning against the dangers of religious self-deception, Hromadka addressed the World Council delegates at Evanston, Illinois, declaring that the most

> ... imperceptible temptation the Church lives in lies in the avowed desire to use God for human ends, to profit from what we call religion, to attain a false security, to convert the faith and cult into safeguards of human earthly treasures and possessions. . . .[15]

At the same time, Hromadka attempted to justify the suppression of the Hungarian revolution of 1956 by the Soviet Union, claming that the leaders of the uprising were reactionaries and fascists who necessarily were removed in order to save Hungary "from terrible bloodshed and disintegration. . . ."[16]

In 1964, telegrams were sent to Premier Khrushchev, President Johnson, and Prime Minister Douglas-Home by

---

[13] J. L. Hromadka, "Is the Crisis Over?," *Kostnicke Jiskry,* Prague, November 8, 1962, cited in *RCDA,* Vol. I, No. 22, 1962, pp. 1–3.
[14] *loc. cit.,* p. 296.
[15] *Ibid.,* p. 769.
[16] *Ibid.,* p. 792.

the Second All-Christian Peace Assembly in Prague, applauding the Moscow test ban agreement which had "paved the way for new steps toward a peaceful future. . . ."[17]

Nikita Khrushchev "gladly" replied, congratulating the Christian Peace Conference on its desire to contribute toward strengthening peace. He assured them of the Soviet Union's devotion to the cause of peace, the principles of coexistence between countries of different social systems, and their striving to "bring about general and complete disarmament under strict international control." Khrushchev wished the CPC delegates success in their endeavors for peace.[18]

Bratskii vestnik regularly includes an outline of the table of contents published in the organ of the Christian Peace Conference. Peace theses are now routine and prominently displayed in the opening pages of each issue. In addition, Box 520, Moscow, occasionally sends letters to its foreign readers of *Bratskii vestnik* advocating involvement in the activities that would deter a Third World War.

In 1963, R. O. Corvin and I visited twenty-three countries of Europe and the Middle East in order to invite Protestant ministers to an International Seminar held in Tulsa's Oral Roberts University. We invited three AUCECB members to attend as Russian representatives and as our guests. Alexander Stoian angrily refused the offer, reminding us of the rude reception he and other Russian clergymen had received from Carl McIntire's followers during their recent visit to two American cities. Stoian pressed instead for increased American participation in the Prague Christian Peace Conference.

---

17 "All Christian Peace Assembly's Message to World Leaders," CTK International Service in English, Prague, June 29, 1964 cited in *RCDA*, Vol. III, No. 17, 1964, p. 115.

18 "Khrushchev's Message to All-Christian Peace Assembly," CTK International Service in English, Prague, July 2, 1964 cited in *RCDA*, Vol. III, No. 17, 1964, p. 116.

At the 1965 camp conference of the Russian Evangelical Baptists held in Ashford, Connecticut, I again met President Zhidkov's son, Mikhail, and asked whether the AUCECB membership in the Baptist World Alliance, the Christian Peace Conference, and the World Council of Churches was, in effect, promoting the Soviet Union as a champion of peace. Mikhail Zhidkov, increasing in prominence in international religious conferences, quickly remonstrated, declaring that the evangelical believers of the Soviet Union, together with their government, were passionate peace promoters because of the twenty million Russians who perished in the last terrible war.[19]

In 1959, I was able to converse with literally hundreds of Soviet citizens as well as with church leaders, both Orthodox and Evangelical, and I was convinced that the Russian people fervently desired peace. It was this passionate drive for peace, unfeigned, that supplied the rationale and justification for AUCECB's full support of its government in every phase of peace propaganda. The AUCECB organ *Bratskii vestnik* has given increased coverage and prominence to the Soviet Union's peace appeals, especially since 1960, with a constant and consistent voice to both believers at home and to all Christians abroad. The Soviet Government's endorsement of the churches' peace role was evidenced by the cooperation and privileges extended to them in their relationships to international religious bodies, both on Soviet soil and abroad.

The duplicity employed by the Soviet rulers' treatment of its domestic religious bodies and its foreign ecumenical guests was apparent. In February of 1964, the Plenary Committee of the World Council of Churches converged upon the city of Odessa to discuss, along with other items

---

[19] Interview with Mikhail Iakovich Zhidkov, July 5, 1965. He is now the President of the European Baptist Federation.

on the agenda, the freedom of religion.[20] At the very same time this religious conference was being held upon Soviet soil the Central Committee of the Communist Party published a decree "aimed at intensifying the atheistic education of the citizenry."[21]

[20] "Resolutions of the World Council of Churches Adopted by the Plenary Committee of the WCC in Odessa," *Bv,* No. 3, 1964, pp. 9–13.

[21] A. Avtorkhanov, "New Assaults on Religion," *Problems of the Peoples of the USSR,* No. 1 (Munich: 1964), p. 12.

PART VI

CONCLUSION

20

Russia's Religious Future— Revolution or Evolution?

i. Past Errors

A season of joyous jubilee attended the celebration of the Russian evangelicals as they completed one hundred years of effective ministry on August 20, 1967. It was a century of harassment and persecution equally shared under the Orthodox-autocratic reign and the Soviet-atheistic regime. The evangelicals learned to live and even thrive under repression, discovering that the purging process purifies the faithful believers.

The interpretation of the past and the implications for the future of the Russian evangelicals cannot be divorced from the warp and woof of Soviet totalitarian society and the antireligious psychosis of the Communist Party.

The confiscation of the productive communes administered by believers was the result of the Soviet dekulakization drives ordered by Stalin. He did indeed achieve a "Dizziness from success" but it was too late to prevent his man-made famine and the subsequent death of millions. Other millions were exiled to add to the tragic waste of human resources. Formerly a leading exporter of grain, would the Russians now be purchasing wheat from abroad had they heeded the People's Commissariat of Agriculture and Soviet voices such as Vladimir Bonch-Bruevich who favored the continuation and expansion of Christian communes?

Somehow the believers survived the terrible Thirties and readily acquiesced to the Soviet Government's centralization of the Evangelical sectarians. The mergers prompted by the Soviets accomplished a religious feat unparalleled anywhere else in the world—the union of Baptists and Pentecostalists engaged in common endeavor in the Kingdom of God! Can we justify the existence of fortynine Baptist and Pentecostal denominations in the United States?

Ecumenical success does not come easily. It is evident that the Russian Pentecostalists joined the AUCECB not only to obtain governmental acceptance and registration benefits otherwise impossible for the glossolalists, but also to infiltrate the union churches with Pentecostal doctrines despite the August Agreement. Two-thirds of the Pentecostal believers entered the union and the growth of the three denominations working together was phenomenal. Each year over the span of a decade an average of 18,000 new members were added to the united churches.

Were the evangelicals who refused all offers to join the AUCECB making the right decision? Were they correct in judging AUCECB subservience to the Soviet Government as an evil step dishonoring to God? Was their bias against the inclusion of the Pentecostalists justified? Would the granting of the dissident Initsiativniki's request for a separate union solve for them the problems now facing the AUCECB? These are questions yet to be answered.

It is not difficult to understand the logic involved in the Soviet's refusal to permit the Initsiativniki to organize a second union since the doctrinal beliefs of both groups were identical. Would union independence enable them to ignore or violate the Law of 1929? Probably less so than the present union members who take the liberty of conducting regular choir practices and enjoy young people's birthday parties which afford evangelical opportunities. Changes of the Soviet laws regarding religion may not occur for decades, unless the new college-trained generation of young people, disgusted with the doctrinaire position of the Party directed against all believers, assume key positions of leadership.

ii. Poland's Greater Religious Freedom

We live in a changing world and Soviet Russia is part of this world. The unexpected changes which followed the brief but valiant democratization attempt in Czechoslovakia included a dialogue designed to correct past mistakes in church-state relations. Then came the Soviet Union's invasion of the little nation to, as former President Johnson stated, "stamp out a resurgence of ordinary human freedom." Communism will continue to lose its hold on human spirits even as it forces its will upon human bodies. The blood bath of Budapest and the perfidy in Czechoslovakia cannot stay the advance, however slow, of freedom.

Changes may be seen in Communist Poland, a satellite in which the evangelicals enjoy a greater degree of religious liberty than the Russians. During my 1959 visit to a number of cities and villages of Poland I preached seventeen times in complete freedom in the union churches of the United Evangelical Church. This union is comprised of five Protestant denominations—the Church of Christ, Evangelical Christians, Plymouth Brethren, and two Pentecostal groups. The majority of its 10,000 members are Pentecostal. I know several foreign missionaries who have ministered the Word of God freely in Poland for a period of six weeks on a preacher's visa.

Stanislav Krakiewicz, the president of the Polish union, approached Communist officials concerning the possibilities of producing religious programs in Warsaw for the international broadcasters at Trans World Radio, whose giant transmitters are located in Monte Carlo, Monaco. His faith was rewarded three months later, when permission was granted. Since Christmas of 1965 Warsaw-produced programs have been beamed back to Poland twice a week.[1] Polish listeners write to the church headquarters in Warsaw for evangelical publications and Scripture portions! Converted communists? Hardly. Due to the fact that more than 90 per cent of Poland's inhabitants are Roman Catholics the Gomulka regime probably sought to weaken the cohesive strength of this preponderant majority by assisting the evangelicals in the winning of converts.

In January of 1968 the new AUCECB president, I. G. Ivanov, visited the believers in Warsaw and urged the 6,000 member Baptist Union and the United Evangelical Church to merge on the basis of Christ's prayer "That they may all be one."[2]

The AUCECB has proven its loyalty to the Soviet Union, its members are good citizens, and its officials have represented their country in a most favorable light before the religious leaders of many nations. However, despite the evangelicals' cooperation and the weight of world opinion directed against Soviet antireligious persecution the Communists have not eased their tenacious hold in circumscribing religious activities. Furthermore, regardless of the frequency of the Party's announcement of allegiance to the educational methodology of scientific atheistic propaganda, they have yet to reject their brutal action against the evangelicals if those means promised substantial gains in its persistent struggle to destroy the faith of the believers.

---

[1] "Target Poland," Trans World Radio, Chatham, N.J., undated pamphlet.

[2] "Visit to an AUCECB Delegation to Warsaw," *Bv*, No. 3, 1968. pp. 15, 16.

iii. The Second One Hundred Years

As the Russian evangelicals embark upon the second century of their voyage in a sea of hostility, the AUCECB members face crucial tests from without and from within. Loyal to their church and at the same time loyal citizens of the USSR, the AUCECB leaders patiently persist in believing that God is sovereign and that Christ is able to calm the most troubled waters and usher in true peace. Complete faith is placed in the promise of Christ that when God's time to open the doors of gospel opportunity in Russia arrives, no mortal being will be able to shut them.[3] When that happens they will be in a position to reap the greatest spiritual harvest ever experienced in Russia's evangelical history. They wait in quiet confidence.

The dangers, however, are apparent. AUCECB is in a compromising position which places them at the disposal of the Soviet regime as a useful pawn in the Party's chess-like deliberations for world supremacy. On the other hand, the dissident non-registered evangelicals may adopt the martyr's role by pressing their insistent demands for an actual separation of church and state as documented in Soviet law.

Unfortunately, after all the years of pitting atheism against the believers in the USSR the Communist Party has refused to heed the wisdom of the Soviet educator Lunacharski who declared that "religion is like a nail, the harder it is driven into the wood, the deeper it goes." There will ever be intense believers in Russia so long as persecution prevails. Nicolas Berdyaev, a Marxist converted to Orthodoxy, did not believe in the existence of pure atheists but maintained that the Russian revolu-

---

[3] Moscow ministers such as I. I. Motorin and M. Zhidkov have quoted Revelations 3:7 several times in my presence.

tionary obsession with atheism is a form of "religiousness turned inside out."

Attempting to evaluate decades of antireligious work in the Soviet Union, Veschikov tried to convince his fellow Party members in 1962 that

> . . . no state ever succeeded in preventing people by force from either renouncing religion or accepting another faith. On the contrary, such pressure has always incited fanaticism. The Communist Party denounces these methods of fighting religious vestiges. The decisive element in the success of its propaganda is the creation of conditions which will enable the believers to accept the principle of atheism.[4]

He concluded his analysis with an affirmation of faith in the final victory of Communism over religion, saying that his country stood

> . . . in the anteroom of Communism. The time is not too far away when all of the conditions will be established in order to secure the complete disappearance of religion.
>
> This is our task in these days and it cannot be postponed. A considerable amount of work has already been done, but much remains yet to be done.[5]

The goal has been clearly and frequently stated. All attempts to suggest that religion and the Marxist-Leninist ideology are compatible have been denounced by the Soviet atheists. Despite the incessant indoctrination, or because of it, the credibility gap engendered by Soviet censorship in the USSR is discerned by its citizens and the most unexpected reversals do happen. In her autobiog-

[4] A. Veschikov, "Milestones of a Great Journey," *Nauka i religiia*, No. 11, 1962.

[5] *Ibid.*

raphy Stalin's daughter Svetlana, trained to be an atheist from childhood, shared her discovery of faith in God. How unlikely a prospect for conversion! No doubt this facet of her life has reached many Russians through short-wave radio broadcasts and tourists. The citadel of the secret recess of Soviet minds cannot be fully possessed by the ubiquitous secret police.

Whether the loyal subservience of the AUCECB to the Soviet Union, based upon the Scriptural injunction that Christians be "subject to the higher powers," will minimize the atheists' deep prejudice against religion in the Communist world view remains to be seen. The Soviet regime will not likely tolerate dissident sectarians such as the Initiative Group, considered socialist "enemies" who may become cores of opposition to the Soviet way of life.

As world capitalism and communism become less dissimilar because of the increased socialist tendencies of many Western governments the choice between the "religion" of Communism and the claims of Christianity will yet face multiplied millions the world over. For a quarter of a century the leaders at Box 520, Moscow, have projected Christ's ideal for His own—"that they all may be one." Each Russian who is called by His name as an ambassador of Christ must be a dynamic example of Christ's love, proving himself to be relevant to the basic needs of human beings. Russian Communists, although atheists, may respond sooner than church-oriented non-possessors of the love of God, if they could behold Christians loving one another, loving the unlovely, and translating Christ's promise of hope to a sick world.

Bibliography

ANDERSON, PAUL B. *People, Church and State in Modern Russia.* New York: The Macmillan Company, 1944.

———. *Russia's Religious Future.* London: Lutterworth Press, c. 1935.

Antireligious Activities in the Soviet Union and in Eastern Europe. Washington: U.S. Government Printing Office, 1965.

BACH, MARCUS. *God and the Soviets.* New York: Thomas Y. Crowell Company, 1958.

BARGHOORN, FREDERICK C. *The Soviet Cultural Offensive: The Role of Cultural Diplomacy in Soviet Foreign Policy.* Princeton: Princeton University Press, 1960.

BARRON, J. B. and WADDAMS, H. M. *Communism and the Churches: A Documentation.* New York: Morehouse-Gorham Company, 1950.

BENNETT, JOHN C. *Christianity and Communism Today.* New York: Association Press, 1960.

BERDYAEV, NICOLAS. *The Russian Idea.* Boston: Beacon Press, 1962.

BEVAN, R. J. W. *The Churches and Christian Unity.* London: Oxford University Press, 1963.

BLUMIT, OSWALD A. and SMITH, OSWALD J. *Sentenced to Siberia.* Washington: Mayflower Publishers, 1947.

BOLSHAKOFF, SERGE. *Russian Nonconformity: The Story of "Unofficial" Religion in Russia.* Philadelphia: The Westminster Press, 1950.

BRAUN, LEOPOLD L. S. *Religion in Russia from Lenin to Khrushchev, an Uncensored Account.* Paterson: St. Anthony Guild Press, 1959.

BROADBENT, E. H. *The Pilgrim Church.* London: Pickering & Inglis., 1931.

BROWN, JOHN. *The Stundists: The Story of a Great Religious Revolt.* New York: Methodist Episcopal Church, 1893.

BRUMBACK, CARL. *What Meaneth This?* Springfield: The Gospel Publishing House, 1947.

BRZEZINSKI, ZBIGNIEW K. *The Permanent Purge: Politics in Soviet Totalitarianism.* Cambridge: Harvard University Press, 1956.

CASEY, ROBERT PIERCE. *Religion in Russia.* New York: Harper & Brothers, 1946.

CLEWS, JOHN C. *Communist Propaganda Techniques.* New York: Frederick A. Praeger, 1964.

COCKBURN, J. HUTCHISON. *Religious Freedom in Eastern Europe.* Richmond: John Knox Press, 1953.

Conference in Defence of Peace of All Churches and Religious Associations in the U.S.S.R. Moscow: Moscow Patriarchate, 1952.

CONQUEST, ROBERT. *Common Sense About Russia.* New York: The Macmillan Company, 1960.

CONYBEARE, FREDERICK C. *Russian Dissenters.* Cambridge: Harvard University Press, 1921.

COX, NORMAN WADE (ed.). *Encyclopedia of Southern Baptists.* 2 vols. Nashville: Broadman Press, 1958.

CURTISS, JOHN S. *Church and State in Russia: The Last Years of the Empire (1900-1917).* New York: Columbia University Press, 1940.

CURTISS, JOHN SHELTON. *The Russian Church and the Soviet State 1917-1950.* Boston: Little, Brown & Co., 1953.

DALLIN, DAVID J. *The Changing World of Soviet Russia.* New Haven: Yale University Press, 1956.

DARK, SIDNEY and ESSEX, R. S. *The War Against God.* New York: The Abingdon Press, 1938.

DeKOSTER, LESTER. *Communism and Christian Faith.* Grand Rapids: Eerdmans, 1962.

DMYTRYSHYN, BASIL. *USSR: A Concise History.* New York: Charles Scribner's Sons, 1965.

DOSSICK, JESSE J. *Doctoral Research on Russia and the Soviet Union.* New York: New York University Press, 1960.

ESTEP, WILLIAM R. *Church Union and Southern Baptists.* Fort Worth: Baptist Book Store, 1955.

EVANS, STANLEY. *Religion in the U.S.S.R.* London: Crafton Press Ltd., n.d.

————. *Soviet Churches and the War.* London: Farleigh Press Ltd., 1944.

FINOT, JEAN. *Modern Saints and Seers.* London: William Rider and Son, Ltd., 1920.

FISHER, RALPH TALCOTT JR. *Pattern for Soviet Youth: A Study of the Congresses of the Komsomol, 1918–1954.* New York: Columbia University Press, 1959.

Fundamentals of Soviet Criminal Legislation, the Judicial System and Criminal Court Procedure: Official Texts and Commentaries. Moscow: Foreign Languages Publishing House, 1960.

FLETCHER, WILLIAM C. and STROVER, ANTHONY J. (eds.). *Religion and the Search for New Ideals in the USSR.* New York: Frederick A. Praeger, 1967.

FLETCHER, WILLIAM C. *A Study in Survival: The Church in Russia 1927–1943.* New York: The Macmillan Company, 1965.

GAINES, DAVID P. *The World Council of Churches: A Study of Its Background and History.* Peterborough, N.H.: Richard R. Smith Co., 1966.

GEE, DONALD. *Upon All Flesh: A Pentecostal World Tour.* 2d ed. revised. Springfield, Mo.: The Gospel Publishing House, 1947.

GOODALL, NORMAN. *The Ecumenical Movement: What It Is and What It Does.* London: Oxford University Press, 1961.

GRUNWALD, CONSTANTIN DE. *The Churches and the Soviet Union.* New York: The Macmillan Company, 1962.

GSOVSKI, VLADIMIR (ed.). *Church and State Behind the Iron Curtain.* New York: Frederick A. Praeger, 1955.

GUTSCHE, WALDEMAR. *Westliche Quellen des russischen Stundismus.* Kassel, 1957.

HAYS, BROOKS and STEELY, JOHN E. *The Baptist Way of Life.* Englewood Cliffs: Prentice-Hall, Inc., 1963.

HEARD, ALBERT F. *The Russian Church and Russian Dissent.* New York: Harper & Brothers, 1887.

HECKER, JULIUS F. *Religion and Communism: A Study of Re-*

ligion and Atheism in Soviet Russia. London: Chapman & Hall Ltd., 1933.

———. *Religion Under the Soviets.* New York: Vanguard Press, 1927.

HIEBERT, P. C. *Feeding the Hungry: Russia Famine 1919–1925.* Scottdale, Pa.: Mennonite Central Committee, 1929.

HROMADKA, JOSEPH L. *Doom and Resurrection.* Richmond: Madrus House, 1945.

HUBBARD, LEONARD E. *The Economics of Soviet Agriculture.* London: Macmillan and Co., 1939.

HUNT, R. N. CAREW. *The Theory and Practice of Communism.* 2d ed. revised. New York: The Macmillan Company, 1951.

INKELES, ALEX and BAUER, RAYMOND A. *The Soviet Citizen: Daily Life in a Totalitarian Society.* Cambridge: Harvard University Press, 1959.

INKELES, ALEX and GEIGER, KENT (eds.). *Soviet Society.* Boston: Houghton Mifflin Company, 1961.

IWANOW, BORIS (ed.). *Religion in the USSR.* Munich: Institute For the Study of the USSR, 1960.

JASNY, NAUM. *The Socialized Agriculture of the USSR: Plans and Performances.* Stanford: Stanford University Press, 1949.

JOHNSON, HEWLETT. *Christians and Communism.* London: Putnam and Co. Ltd., 1956.

———. *The Soviet Power.* New York: Modern Age Books, 1940.

———. *Soviet Russia Since the War.* New York: Boni & Gaer, 1947.

JONES, PHILIP L. (ed.). *The Baptist World Alliance: Second Congress.* Philadelphia: Harper & Brother Company, 1911.

KARPINSKY, V. A. *What Are Collective Farms?* London: Lindsay Drummond Ltd., 1944.

KASSOF, ALLEN. *The Soviet Youth Program.* Cambridge: Harvard University Press, 1965.

KAUFFMAN, DANIEL (ed.). *Mennonite Cyclopedic Dictionary.* Scottdale, Pa.: Mennonite Publishing House, 1937.

KAUFMAN, EDMUND GEORGE. *The Development of the Missionary Interest and Philanthropic Interest Among the Mennonites of North America.* Berne, Indiana: The Mennonite Book Concern, 1931.

KELSEY, MORTON T. *Tongue Speaking: An Experiment in Spiritual Experience.* New York: Doubleday & Company, 1964.

KENDRICK, KLAUDE. *The Promise Fulfilled: A History of the Modern Pentecostal Movement.* Springfield, Mo.: Gospel Publishing House, 1961.

KLINE, GEORGE L. (ed.). *Soviet Education.* New York: Columbia University Press, 1957.

KOLARZ, WALTER. *How Russia is Ruled.* London: The Batchworth Press, 1953.

————. *Religion in the Soviet Union.* New York: St. Martin's Press, 1961.

KRAHN, CORNELIUS (ed.). *From the Steppes to the Prairies (1874–1949).* Newton, Kansas: Mennonite Publication Office, 1949.

KULSKI, W. W. *The Soviet Regime: Communism in Practice.* 3rd ed. revised. New York: Syracuse University Press, 1959.

LATIMER, ROBERT SLOAN. *Dr. Baedeker and His Apostolic Work in Russia.* London: Morgan & Scott, 1907.

————. *With Christ in Russia.* London: Hodder and Stoughton, 1910.

LENIN, VLADIMIR IL'ICH. *Selected Works.* New York: International Publishers, 1935.

LEWIS, WALTER O. (ed.). *Seventh Baptist World Congress.* London: The Carey Kingsgate Press, Ltd., 1948.

LORD, F. TOWNLEY. *Baptist World Fellowship: A Short History of the Baptist World Alliance.* Nashville: Broadman Press, 1955.

MAGIDOFF, ROBERT. *The Kremlin vs. the People.* New York: Doubleday & Company, 1953.

MAYNARD, JOHN. *Russia in Flux.* New York: The Macmillan Company, 1948.

McINTIRE, CARL. *Servants of Apostasy.* Collingswood, N.J.: Christian Beacon Press, 1955.

MEAD, MARGARET. *Soviet Attitudes Toward Authority: An Interdisciplinary Approach to Problems of Soviet Character.* New York: McGraw-Hill Book Company, 1951.

MELISH, WILLIAM HOWARD. *Religion Today in the U.S.S.R.*

New York: The National Council of American-Soviet Friendship, 1945.

The Mennonite Encyclopedia: A Comprehensive Reference Work on the Anabaptist-Mennonite Movement. 4 vols. Hillsboro, Kansas: Mennonite Brethren Publishing House, 1955–1959.

MILIUKOV, PAUL. *Outlines of Russian Culture—Part I: Religion and the Church.* Perpetua edition. New York: A. S. Barnes and Company, 1960.

————. *Russia and Its Crisis.* Chicago: University of Chicago Press, 1905.

MULLINS, E. Y. *The Christian Religion In Its Doctrinal Expression.* 16th reprint. Valley Forge: The Judson Press, 1964.

NEWTON, LOUIE D. *An American Churchman in the Soviet Union.* New York: American Russian Inst., 1946.

NOBLE, JOHN. *I Found God in Soviet Russia.* New York: St. Martin's Press, 1959.

NORDENHAUG, JOSEF (ed.). *The Truth That Makes Men Free: Official Report of the Eleventh Congress.* Nashville: Broadman Press, 1966.

OHRN, ARNOLD T. (ed.). *Eighth Baptist World Congress.* Philadephia: The Judson Press, 1950.

———— (ed.). *Golden Jubilee Congress.* London: The Carey Kingsgate Press, Limited, 1955.

———— (ed.). *Tenth Baptist World Congress.* Nashville: Broadman Press, 1960.

PEARLMAN, MYER. *Knowing the Doctrines of the Bible.* Springfield, Mo.: The Gospel Publishing House, 1937.

PENKOVSKIY, OLEG. *The Penkovskiy Papers.* Translated by Peter Deriabin. Garden City: Doubleday & Company, 1965.

POLLOCK, J. C. *The Faith of the Russian Evangelicals.* New York: McGraw-Hill Book Company, 1964.

PROKHANOFF, I. S. *In the Cauldron of Russia.* New York: John Felsberg, Inc., 1933.

Meeting the Russians: American Quakers Visit the Soviet Union. Philadelphia: American Friends Service Committee, 1956.

RIGGS, RALPH M. *We Believe: A Comprehensive Statement of*

Christian Faith. Springfield, Mo.: Gospel Publishing House, 1954.

ROTHSTEIN, ANDREW (ed.). *History of the Communist Party of the Soviet Union.* Moscow: Foreign Languages Publishing House, 1960.

RUSHBROOKE, J. H. (ed.). *Baptists in the U.S.S.R.* Nashville: Broadman Press, 1943.

———— (ed.). *Fifth Baptist World Congress.* London: Baptist World Alliance, 1934.

———— (ed.). *Sixth Baptist World Congress.* Atlanta: Baptist World Alliance, 1939.

SHAKESPEARE, J. H. (ed.). *Baptist World Congress.* London: Baptist Union Publication Department, 1905.

SHERRILL, JOHN L. *They Speak With Other Tongues.* New York: McGraw-Hill Book Company, 1964.

SIMMONS, ERNEST J. (ed.).*USSR: A Concise Handbook.* Ithaca: Cornell University Press, 1945.

SMITH, C. HENRY. *The Story of the Mennonites.* 4th ed. Newton, Kansas: Mennonite Publication Office, 1957.

SPASOV, G. *Freedom of Religion in the USSR.* Washington: The Soviet Embassy, 1951.

SPINKA, MATTHEW. *Church in Communist Society.* Hartford: The Hartford Seminary Press, 1954.

————. *The Church in Soviet Russia.* New York: Oxford University Press, 1956.

STALIN, JOSEPH. *Leninism.* 2 vols. Moscow: Co-operative Publishing Society of Foreign Workers in the USSR, 1934.

SZCZESNIAK, BOLESLAW (ed.). *The Russian Revolution and Religion: A Collection of Documents Concerning the Suppression of Religion by the Communists, 1917–1925.* Notre Dame: University of Notre Dame Press, 1959.

TIMASHEFF, NICHOLAS S. *The Great Retreat: The Growth and Decline of Communism in Russia.* New York: E. P. Dutton & Co., 1946.

TIMASHEFF, N. S. *Religion in Soviet Russia, 1917–1942.* New York: Sheed & Ward, 1942.

TORBET, ROBERT G. *A History of the Baptists.* Philadelphia: The Judson Press, 1950.

TREADGOLD, DONALD W. *20th Century Russia.* Chicago: Rand McNally & Company, 1964.

TURAJEV, V. (ed.) .*USSR: Questions and Answers.* Moscow: Novosti Press Agency Publishing House, n.d.

WARD, HARRY F. *The Story of American-Soviet Relations, 1917–1959.* New York: National Council of American-Soviet Friendship, 1959.

WEST, CHARLES C. *Communism and the Theologians.* New York: The Macmillan Company, 1958.

WHITLEY, W. T. (ed.). *Fourth Baptist World Congress.* Toronto: Stewart Printing Service, 1928.

——— (ed.). *Third Baptist World Congress.* London: Kingsgate Press, 1923.

WILLIAMS, ERNEST S. *Systematic Theology.* 3 vols. Springfield, Mo.: Gospel Publishing House, 1953.

WOLFE, BERTRAM D. *Communist Totalitarianism.* 2nd ed. revised. Boston: Beacon Press, 1961.

YAROSLAVSKI, E. *Religion in the U.S.S.R.* London: Modern Books Ltd., 1932.

Unpublished Dissertations

ALBERT, I. J. "A Study of the Eastern Orthodox Church in the Ecumenical Movement." Unpublished Ph.D. dissertation, Harvard University, 1964.

BLANE, ANDREW QUARLES. "The Relations Between the Russian Protestant Sects and the State, 1900–1921." Unpublished Ph.D. dissertation, Duke University, 1964.

DENNO, THEODORE FREED. "The Communist Millenium: The Soviet View." Unpublished Ph.D. dissertation, University of Maryland, 1962.

FLETCHER, WILLIAM CATHERWOOD. "The Russian Orthodox Church in the USSR, 1927–1943: A Study in Survival." Unpublished Ph.D. dissertation, University of Southern California, 1964.

FOSTER, GEORGE A. "The Attitude of Russian Communism to Religion." Unpublished B.D. dissertation, Duke University, 1933.

FULE, ZOLTAN JOSEPH. "The Goal and Means of the Communist Society: A Christian Ethical Analysis." Unpublished Th.D. dissertation, Union Theological Seminary, 1961.

GECYS, CASIMIR C. "The Soviet Bill of Rights." Unpublished Ph.D. dissertation, Department of Political Philosophy, Fordham University, 1952.

HOLLENWEGER, WALTER J. "Handbook of the Pentecostal Movement." Unpublished Th.D. dissertation, University of Zurich, 1965.

KLEINER, EUGENE M. "Anti-Religious Propaganda in the U.S.S.R. Between 1950 and 1957." Unpublished M.A. dissertation, Russian Institute, Columbia University, 1959.

KRAMER, RICHARD. "Practical Morality Taught to Soviet Children As Illustrated in Four Official Soviet Periodicals 1937–1951." Unpublished Ph.D. dissertation, Columbia University, 1953.

RUEKBERG, BENJAMIN G. "Soviet Doctrines Regarding the Struggle for Peace and Soviet Objectives vis à vis Non-Communist States in Promulgating Its Struggle for Peace Doctrines (1955–1961)." Unpublished Ph.D. dissertation, Syracuse University, 1964.

SOH, JIN CHULL. "Some Causes of the Korean War of 1950: A Case Study of Soviet Foreign Policy in Korea (1945–1950), With Emphasis on Sino-Soviet Collaboration." Unpublished Ph.D. dissertation, University of Oklahoma, 1963.

STROYEN, WILLIAM B. "Some Effects of the Russian Communistic Revolution Upon the Patriarchate of the Russian Orthodox Church in the Soviet Union: 1943–1963." Unpublished Ph.D. dissertation, Syracuse University, 1964.

SUDHALTER, DAVID LOUIS. "The Political and Psychological Indoctrination of School Children in the U.S.S.R." Unpublished Ph.D. dissertation, Boston University, 1962.

WINDEMILLAR, DUANE A. "The Psycho-Dynamics of Change in Religious Conversion in Communist Brainwashing." Unpublished Ph.D. dissertation, Boston University, 1960.

Books: Russian

ABRIKOSOV, K. N. (ed.). *Angliiskaia khrestomatiia po sel'-*

skomu khoziaistvu (English Reader on Agriculture) . Leningrad: Tsentrizdat, 1930.

Bolshaia sovetskaia entsiklopediia (The Large Soviet Encyclopedia) . Moskva: 1948.

BONCH'-BRUEVICH, VLADIMIR. *Iz mira sektantov* (From the World of Sectarians) . Moskva: Gosudarstvennoe izdatel'stvo, 1922.

―――. *Presledovanie baptistov evangelicheskoi sekti* (Persecution of the Evangelistic Sect of Baptists) . Hants, England: Tchertkoff, 1902.

BONDAR, S. D. *Sekta mennonitov v Rossii* (The Mennonite Sect in Russia) . Petrograd: Tipografiia V. D. Smirnov, 1916.

DOLOTOV, A. *Tserkov' i sektantstvo v Sibiri* (The Church and Sectarianism in Siberia) . Novosibirsk: Sibkraiizdat, 1930.

ENISHERLOV, M., LUKACHEV, A. and MITIN, M. (ed.) . *Voinstvuiushchee bezbozhie v SSSR za 15 let 1917–1932* (Militant Atheism For the Fifteen Years 1917–1932) . Moskva: Gosudarstvennoe antireligioznoe izdatel'stvo, 1932.

Ezhegodnik knigi SSSR (Annual Books of the USSR) . Moskva: Izdatel'stvo vsesoiuznoi knizhnoi palaty, 1944–1964.

GARKAVENKO, FEDOR I. *Chto takoe religioznoe sektantstvo* (What Religious Sectarianism Is) . Moskva. Nauchnopopuliarnaia biblioteka, 1961.

GRAMMATIKOV, V. (ed.) . *Bezbozhniki za rabotoi* (The Godless At Work) . Leningrad: Leninzdat, 1938.

IAROSLAVSKII, E. *Bibliia dlia veruiushchikh i neveruiushchikh* (The Bible for Believers and Unbelievers) . Moskva: Gosudarstvennoe iz-vo, 1958.

―――. *Kommunisty i religiia* (Communists and Religion) . Moskva: Moskovskii rabochii, 1931.

IARTSEV, A. *Sekta evangel'skikh khristian* (Evangelical Christians' sect) . Moskva: Bezbozhnik, 1928.

Ispovedanie very khristian-baptistov (The Confession of Faith of the Christians-Baptists) . Moskva: N. V. Odintsov, 1928.

KALUGIN, VALERII MAKSIMOVICH. *Sovremennoe religioznoe sektantstvo, ego raznovidnosti i ideologiia* (Contemporary Religious Sectarianism, Its Various Forms and Ideologies) . Moskva: Gosudarstvennoe iz-vo, 1962.

KANDIDOV, BORIS P. *Tserkov' i shpionazh* (The Church and Espionage). Moskva: Gosudarstvennoe antireligioznoe izdatel'stvo, 1937.

KOGEN, S. (ed.). *Antireligioznyi sbornik* (Antireligious Collection). Moskva: Moskovskii rabochii, 1940.

Kommunisticheskaia partiia i sovetskoe pravitel'stvo o religii i tserkvi (The Communist Party and the Soviet Government on Religion and the Church). Moskva: Politicheskaia literatura, 1961.

Komsomol i antireligioznaia propaganda, sbornik statei i ocherkov (The Communist Youth League and Antireligious Propaganda: A Collection of Articles and Outlines). Moskva: Molodaia gvardiia, 1937.

Konferentsia vsekh tserkvei i religionznykh ob'edinenii v SSSR (The All-Church and Religious Union Conference in the USSR). Moskva: Moskovskaia patriarkhiia, 1952.

KOVALEV, S. I. (ed.). *Sputnik ateista* (The Atheist's Companion). Moskva: Gos. izd-vo polit. lit-ry, 1959.

Kratkii nauchno-ateisticheskii slovar' (The Concise Scientific-Atheist Dictionary). Moskva: Iz-vo nauka, 1964.

KRYVELEV, I. *Kniga o biblii* (A Book About the Bible). Moskva: Nauchno-populiarnye ocherki, 1958.

KURANTOV, ALEKSANDR PAVLOVICH (ed.). *Znanie i vera v boga* (Knowledge and Faith in God). Moskva: Izdatel'stvo "Znanie," 1960.

LENIN, VLADIMIR IL'ICH. *Religiia, tserkov' i partiia* (Religion, Church and Party). Moskva: Gos. izd-vo, 1929.

LESKOV, N. S. *Velikosvetskii raskol'* (Dissent in High Society). Moskva: 1877.

LIVSHITS, G. M. *Religiia i tserkov' v proshlom i nastoiashchem* (Religion and the Church in the Past and Present). Minsk: Izdatel'stvo ministerstva vysshego srednogo spetsial'nogo i professional'nogo obrazovaniia BSSR, 1961.

MAIAT, E. V. and UZKOV, N. N. *"Brat'ia" i "sestry" vo Khriste* ("Brothers" and "Sisters" in Christ). Moskva: Izd: "Sovetskaia Rossiia," 1960.

MARTIROSOV, G. A. *Religioznoe sektantstvo* (Religious Sectarianism). Minsk: Belgosuniversiteta, 1961.

MEZENTSEV, V. A. (ed.) . *My porvali s religiei (Rasskazy byv-shikh veruiushchikh)* (We Broke With Religion: Accounts of Former Believers) . Moskva: Voennoe izdatel'stvo minis-terstva oborony SSSR, 1963.

Novyi entsiklopedicheskii slovar' (New Encyclopedic Dictionary) . Sv. Peterburg: Brokgayz-Efron, c. 1911.

OBOLENSK, P. *Kriticheskii razbor' veroispovedaniia russkikh' sektantov'-ratsionalistov': dukhobortsev', molokan' i shtun-distov'* (A Critical Estimate of the Religion of the Russian Sectarians-Rationalists: Dukhobors, Molokans and Stundists) . Kazan: Imperatorskago universiteta, 1903.

Pravda o religii v Rossii (The Truth About Religion In Russia) . Moskva: Moskovskaia patriarkhiia, 1942.

Programma po antireligioznomu samoobrazovaniiu partiino-politicheskikh rabotnikov i propagandistov krasnoi armii (The Program for Antireligious Self-education of Party-Political Workers and Propagandists of the Red Army) . Moskva: Gosudarstvennoe voennoe izdatel'stvo narkomata oborony soiuza SSR, 1940.

PUTINTSEV, F. M. *Politicheskaia rol' i taktika sekt* (The Political Role and Tactic of the Sects) . Moskva: Gosudarstvennoe antireligioznoe izdatel'stvo, 1935.

————. *Politicheskaia rol' sektantstva* (The Political Role of Sectarianism). Moskva: Bezbozhnik, 1928.

REINMARUS, A. and FRIEZEN, G. *Mennonity* (The Mennonites) . Moskva: Akts-izd-o-vo "Bezbozhnik," 1930.

ROZHDESTVENSK, ARSENII. *Iuzhnorusskii shtundizm'* (South-Russian Stundism) . Sv. Peterburg: Departmenta udelov', 1889.

————. *Sektantskii professor'-gomiletiki* (Sectarian Professor-Homiletics) . Khar'kov: 1912.

SHAMARO, ALEKSANDR A. *Neprimirimost'* (Irreconcilability) . Moskva: Izdatel'stvo "Znanie," 1960.

SHEINMAN, M. *Bor'ba religiei i bezbozhnoe dvizheni v kapi-talisticheskikh stranakh* (The Struggle With Religion and the Godless Movement in Capitalistic Countries) . Moskva: Izdatel'stvo "Bezbozhnik," 1931.

SHEINMAN, M. M. *Religiia v period imperializma* (Religion in the Period of Imperialism). Moskva: Izdatel'stvo "Znanie," 1955.

TIKHOMIROV, V. *Baptizm i ego politicheskaia rol'* (Baptism and Its Political Role). Moskva: Gosudarstvennoe izdatel'stvo, 1929.

TUCHKOV, E. A. *Sektantstvo i ego ideologiia* (Sectarianism and Its Ideology). Moskva: Izdatel'stvo "Znanie," 1955.

UZKOV, I. N. *Chto takoe religioznoe sektantstvo* (What Religious Sectarianism Is). Moskva: Izdatel'stvo "Znanie," 1956.

————. *Vsesoiuznoe obshchestvo po resprostraneniu politicheskikh i nauchnikh znanii* (The All-Union Society For the Dissemination of Political and Scientific Knowledge). Moskva: Izdatel'stvo "Znanie," 1956.

Voprosi istorii religii i ateizma (Questions of the History of Religion and Atheism). Moskva: Akademi nauk SSSR, 1950.

VVEDENSKI, ALEKSANDR IVANOVICH. *Sektanty o sektantakh'* (Sectarians On the Sectarians). Odessa: Eparkhial'nago doma, 1915.

ZHABKO-POTAPOVICH, L. *Khristove svitlo v ukraini* (The Light of Christ in the Ukraine). Winnipeg: The Gospel Press, 1952.

ZIURIUKIN, V. E. *Mennonity* (Mennonites). Pokrovsk: "Unzere Virtshaft," 1923.

Periodicals

Abundant Life (Tulsa), 1960.
Baptist World (Washington).
Bulletin (Lausanne, Switzerland), 1960.
Bulletin of the Institute for the Study of the USSR (Munich, Germany).
Communist Affairs (Los Angeles).
Current Digest of the Soviet Press (New York), 1949–1964.
Ecumenical Press Service (Geneva, Switzerland).
Foreign Policy Association Information Service (New York), 1930.

Freedom Facts Against Communism (Washington).
Lutheran World (Geneva), 1962.
Pentecost (London), 1947–1966.
Pentecostal Evangel (Springfield, Mo.).
Problems of Communism (Washington).
Problems of the Peoples of the USSR (Munich, Germany).
Religion in Communist Dominated Areas (New York), 1961–1966.
Slavic Review (New York).
Slavonic and East European Review (London, England), 1944.
Soviet Society: Soviet Periodical Abstracts (White Plains, N. Y.).
U. S. Joint Publications Research Service (Washington).

Periodicals and Newspapers: Russian

Baptist (Moskva), 1925–1928.
Bezbozhnik The Godless. (Moskva), 1939.
Bratskii vestnik The Fraternal Messenger. (Moskva), 1945–1968.
Evangelist (Odessa), 1928.
Istoriia SSR History of the USSR. (Moskva).
Izvestiia News. (Moskva).
Kievskaia starina Kievan Antiquity. (Kiev), 1884.
Komsomol'skaia pravda Young Communist Truth (Moskva).
Literaturnaia gazeta Literary Gazette (Moskva).
Molodoi kommunist Young Communist. (Moskva).
Nauka i religiia Science and Religion. (Moskva), 1959–1966.
Nauka i zhizn Science and Life. (Moskva).
Pravda Truth. (Moskva).
Rovesnik Contemporary. (Moskva), 1963.
Uchitel'skaia gazeta Teacher's Gazette. (Moskva).
Vecherniaia srednaia shkola Evening High School. (Moskva).
Vestnik Evropy Messenger of Europe. (Sv. Peterburg), 1910.
Voprosi filosofii Questions of Philosophy. (Moskva).
Voprosi istorii Questions of History. (Moskva).
Zhurnal moskovskoi patriarkhi Journal of the Moscow Patriarchate. (Moskva).

Appendix

Statistics of local church membership rolls were published frequently in *Bratskii vestnik* between 1946 and 1958. Listed below are the highest figures given, numbering from 400 to 4818 members.

CITY	MEMBERS	YEAR LISTED IN BV
Moscow	4818	1964
Leningrad	3000	1958
Tallin	2000	1953
Kharkov	2000	1955
Riga	2000	1956
Tashkent	1320	1955
Kiev[1]	1200	1956
Frunze	1000	1946
Rostov	1000	1956
Voronezh	1000	1955
Novosibirsk	1000	1953
Tbilisi	830	1947
Krasnodar	800	1956
Dzaudzhikau	800	1947
Zaporozh	751	1955
Odessa	730	1955
Baku	700	1956
Alma-Ata[2]	700	1955
Dnepropetrov	580	1956
Maikop	560	1947
Donbass	519	1956

[1] Kiev has two other churches; no given membership.

[2] Alma-Ata has one other ECB church, membership unlisted. These are the only two cities listed in *Bv* as having more than one ECB church.

Nikolaev	504	1957
Piatigorsk	500	1946
Ventspil	500	1955
Simferopol'	494	1957
Groznyi	464	1947
Melitopol	419	1955
Barnaul	409	1954
L'vov	406	1954
Ridala	400	1948
Orel	400	1954

Index